ON FIELDS OF FURY

D0966568

Other Books by Richard Wheeler

The Bloody Battle for Suribachi

In Pirate Waters

Voices of 1776

Voices of the Civil War

We Knew Stonewall Jackson

We Knew William Tecumseh Sherman

The Siege of Vicksburg

Sherman's March

Iwo

A Special Valor

Sword Over Richmond

Witness to Gettysburg

Witness to Appomattox

ON FIELDS OF FURY

From the Wilderness to the Crater:
An Eyewitness History

RICHARD WHEELER

HarperCollins*Publishers*

ON FIELDS OF FURY. Copyright © 1991 by Richard Wheeler. All rights reserved. Printed in the United States of America. No part of this book may
be used or reproduced in any manner whatsoever without written permission except in the case of brief quotations embodied in critical articles and
reviews. For information address HarperCollins Publishers, 10 East 53rd
Street, New York, N.Y. 10022.

FIRST EDITION

Library of Congress Cataloging-in-Publication Data
Wheeler, Richard.
    On fields of fury : from the wilderness to the crater, an
eyewitness history / Richard Wheeler. — 1st ed.
        p. cm.
    Includes index.
    ISBN 0-06-016582-0
    1. Virginia—History—Civil War, 1861–1865—Campaigns.
2. Virginia—History—Civil War, 1861–1865—Personal narratives.
3. United States—History—Civil War, 1861–1865—Campaigns.
4. United States—History—Civil War, 1861–1865—Personal
narratives.   I. Title.
E476.52.W47   1991
973.7'37—dc20   90-40385

91 92 93 94 95 CC/MPC 10 9 8 7 6 5 4 3 2 1

Contents

Preface   xi

1. After Three Years   1

2. Life in the Union Camps   6

3. Lee and His Command   21

4. Grant Comes East   38

5. A Lion at Bay   56

6. Pontoons across the Rapidan   65

7. Lee Accepts the Challenge   78

8. The Contest Begins   87

9. Events on the Turnpike Front   93

10. Encounter on the Plank Road   107

11. A New Storm at Daybreak   120

12. Red Stains in Every Thicket   133

13. On to Spotsylvania   146

14. Sabers at Yellow Tavern   156

CENTRAL ARKANS... ....ARY SYSTEM
LITTLE ROCK PUBLIC LIBRARY
700 LOUISIANA STREET
LITTLE ROCK, ARKANSAS 72201

15. Stuart Makes His Exit   170

16. Prelude on a New Field   179

17. Hancock Breaks Through   195

18. The Bloody Angle   206

19. Stalemate on the North Anna   220

20. First Clash at Cold Harbor   238

21. The Deadly Climax   252

22. Toward a New Campaign   263

23. The Battle of the Crater   272

Quotation Sources   287

Supplementary References   291

Index   295

LITTLE ROCK, ARKANSAS 72201

Illustrations

Union winter huts	*7*
General Post Office, Army of the Potomac	*9*
On picket between the lines	*17*
Robert E. Lee	*22*
John B. Gordon	*24*
Mrs. Robert E. Lee	*27*
The great Confederate snowball fight	*32*
Confederate theatricals	*34*
Ulysses S. Grant	*39*
Pen and ink sketch of Abraham Lincoln	*41*
Mary Todd Lincoln, the President's wife	*43*
Winfield S. Hancock	*50*
Philip H. Sheridan	*52*
Jefferson Davis	*57*
James Longstreet	*61*
Richard S. Ewell	*62*
Union supply wagons	*67*
George G. Meade	*70*
Julia Dent Grant, the general's wife	*71*
Federals crossing the Rapidan on pontoons	*75*
A Confederate straggler	*81*
Grant's headquarters at Germanna Ford	*84*
Fighting in the Wilderness	*95*
Federals trying to save their wounded from the flames	*103*

Confederates awaiting orders during Wilderness
   fighting   110
Federals throwing up breastworks at Wilderness
   front   113
Second day in the Wilderness, viewed from the
   Union side   123
Frontline troops urging Lee to go to the rear   126
James S. Wadsworth, mortally wounded May 6   130
Lee interrogating Federals captured in the
   Wilderness   135
Confederate hospital in a Wilderness clearing   139
Lee's men assaulting Hancock's burning
   breastworks   140
Section of Federal breastworks as it looked on
   the morning of May 7   148
George A. Custer   160
The cavalry fight at Yellow Tavern   167
Jeb Stuart   177
Confederate breastworks at Spotsylvania   187
A Union field hospital: Fifth Corps,
   Spotsylvania   189
Hand to hand at the Bloody Angle   210
Grant in the field   213
Union Coehorn mortars   216
Waiting for breakfast. A Yankee invasion of a
   Virginia home   224
Union artillerists fording the Mattapony   225
Northern soldier and Virginia woman   227
Runaway slaves entering Union lines   229
Confederate entrenchments on the North Anna
   River   232
Federals laying a corduroy road   241
A break in a Union march   244
The first day at Cold Harbor   250
An incident of the skirmishing on June 2   256
Outbreak of the fighting on June 3   258
Union positions at Petersburg   270

Maps

Bounds of the Confederacy   2

The regions of the Rapidan   5

The waterways of the Chesapeake   48

Routes of Lee and Grant   76

Plan of the Battle of the Wilderness   89

Sheridan's Richmond Raid   158

*Relative positions of the opposing forces at
    Spotsylvania, May 8–21*   180

Hancock's flank movement   184

The Salient at Spotsylvania   199

Plan of the Battle of the North Anna   234

*Country traversed by Lee in his march from the
    North Anna*   239

Plan of the Battle of Cold Harbor   254

Defenses of Richmond and Petersburg   268

Petersburg lines showing location of mine   273

The mine in cross section   275

Section of mine under Confederate works   278

Preface

On Fields of Fury continues my series of Civil War histories presented as largely as possible in the words of participants, with the emphasis on the human side of events. The accounts have been linked together so as to form a chronological narrative. Although the book is intended for the general reader rather than the Civil War scholar, it is offered as a veracious study. The technical statements have been checked against the official records, and the personal episodes have been analyzed for credibility. Although most of the book's ellipses indicate the employment of condensation, some were used to eliminate details that appeared to be faulty. It was occasionally necessary to include clarifications enclosed in brackets. Some of the quotes were extracted from the Civil War's better-known eyewitness records, but many others represent material that never achieved more than transient notice. Numbers of the illustrations, all of which were taken from *Battles and Leaders of the Civil War* and other publications of the postwar decades, are adaptations of sketches or photographs made while the campaign was in progress.

ON FIELDS OF FURY

1

After Three Years

By the beginning of 1864 the Civil War was approaching the end of its third year. The preceding July had seen the Federals gain the great victories of Gettysburg and Vicksburg, which gave them the upper hand. But the Confederates had known too many victories of their own to accept this condition as final. To be sure, their faith in their cause had been shaken. Moreover, their ranks were thinning and their supplies were dwindling. But they were persisting as though everything were going well.

The North's inability to make faster progress against the South, despite a great superiority in manpower and other resources, involved more than the quality of the resistance. The Northern effort had been poorly managed. As explained by William Swinton, a correspondent for the *New York Times* who became one of the war's chief historians: "When hostilities began . . . the theater was so vast, the circumstances were so novel, and the country so green in war, that the conduct of military operations was of necessity almost wholly experimental. The North undertook to subdue rebellion throughout a country . . . stretching from the Potomac to the Rio Grande—a country in which [nearly] the whole population was in arms and animated by the bitterest hostility. . . .

"The North, strong in the faith of the Union . . . formed armies. It sent them forth to battle. Of course, the conduct of the war was crude. There were three or four different armies in Virginia, three or four between the Alleghenies and the Mississippi. . . . These armies were placed frequently on faulty or indecisive lines. And there was no unity in their action.

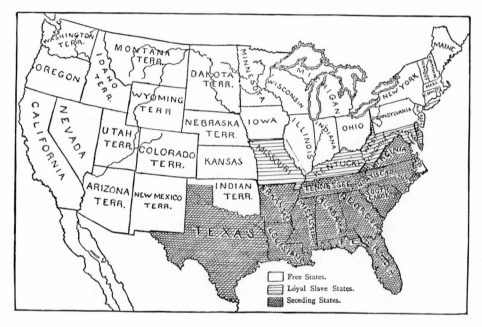

Bounds of the Confederacy

"Nevertheless these armies went to work. . . . And . . . they . . . produced results somewhat notable in their way. . . .

"In considering the operations in Virginia, there are two facts that should be borne in mind. . . . The Army of the Potomac had there not only to combat the main army of the South, but . . . in addition to [this] offensive charge, was the custodian of the National Capital—a duty that governed all strategic combinations in Virginia. Having thus at once to make head against the most formidable, the best disciplined, and the most ably commanded army of the Confederacy, and to guard Washington . . . it is not wonderful that the Army of the Potomac had not yet been able to attain its goal—the capture of Richmond. . . .

"While victory so long shunned in Virginia the Union standards, she crowned them through the West with constant laurels. . . . Even where, at the West, energy and address were replaced by carelessness and blundering, there, too, the star of success shone fixed in the ascendant. . . . Confederate offensive campaigns met, when at the very summit of success, unexpected and improbable checks. . . . Confederate defensive campaigns were suddenly turned to disasters. . . .

"The profit of these western successes was not confined to that region, but more than once roused the Union from the almost fatal melancholy into which the ruinous havoc repeated upon its eastern armies was plunging it. . . .

"The three years of war . . . had reduced the belligerent force of the Confederacy to two armies—the one . . . in Georgia, the other . . . in Virginia. And in reducing the area of the rebellion it practically limited the functions of the Union force to the destruction of these two armies. . . . If much yet remained to be done, there was at least a clear unity in the objectives to be attained. . . .

"[But] for three years the war had been without a head. . . . Operations were directed sometimes by the President, with or without the approval of his military counsellors, sometimes by one or another of his military counsellors, without the approval of the President, and sometimes by the general in the field without the approval of anyone. . . . Between the armies in the two zones, there had hitherto been [a] lack of combination of effort. . . . And in truth the wonder was not that the war was not already brought to a close: rather the wonder was that so much should have been accomplished."

In response to a belated realization that the appointment of a supreme commander was necessary, the House of Representatives took an important step on February 1, 1864, passing a measure reinstating the rank of lieutenant general, which had been allowed to lapse with the death of George Washington. The Senate passed the measure on February 24, and President Abraham Lincoln approved it five days later.

The man the solons had in mind for elevation to the new post was Major General Ulysses S. Grant, then serving in the West, where he had begun work as an obscure colonel of volunteers and had made himself into the chief architect of the region's Union successes.

This initiative by the national government was destined to have its greatest effect on affairs in Virginia, where the opposing armies had been wintering and waiting, the Rapidan River between them, with George G. Meade, of Gettysburg fame, commanding the Army of the Potomac, and the Army of Northern Virginia commanded by the redoubtable Robert E. Lee.

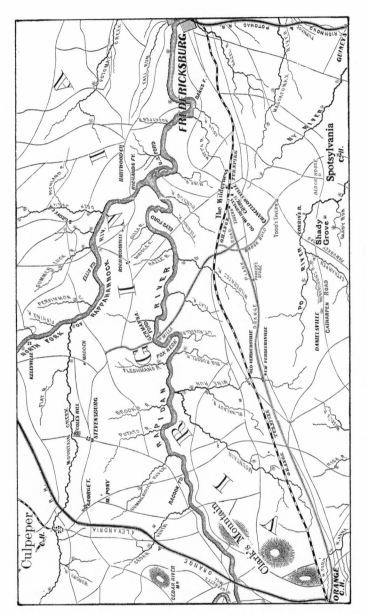

The regions of the Rapidan

2

Life in the Union Camps

The Union camps were scattered through the country about Culpeper Court House, and the winter the men spent here, with combat almost unknown, became an interlude that many of them would always recall with a certain pleasure. To begin with, their cabins and tents were not only weatherproof but also appealingly snug.

"Our winter hut," says a private from Massachusetts named Warren Lee Goss, "was very comfortable. It was built of logs, the chinks filled with mud, while the roof was made from split pieces lapped one over the other. A capacious chimney, built of sticks and mud, formed a picturesque turret at the end of the hut. Its interior was in keeping with its unpretentious exterior. On each side, at right angles with a spacious fireplace and a door, were two bunks, one above the other, each wide enough for two men to sleep in. The floor was of earth beaten down hard and smooth. A rude shelf was fixed above the wide fireplace. On this were pipes, matches, tobacco pouches, and other conveniences.

"A small rough table, the top made from crackerboxes, with a rubber blanket for its cover, and with knotty oaks crossed for its legs, occupied the center of the hut. Our burnished muskets, brasses, and bayonets were hung around the interior on pegs, with picturesque effect. The knapsacks were at the head of each bunk for pillows, while leaves, and in some instances grass and straw, covered by the blankets, formed the beds. Eight men occupied this habitation, and were proud of their quarters. A small aperture over the door, and another at the end near the chimney, over which were stretched pieces of white cotton cloth, admitted light and air."

Union winter huts

"Our whole army," adds a Michigan soldier, Color Sergeant D. G. Crotty (speaking in the present tense), "has comfortable winter quarters. . . . We have our churches, theaters, debating schools, plenty to eat and drink, and clothing to keep us warm. Everything passes off very quietly along the lines, and all seems to be working well. Once in a while our cavalry wake up the enemy on the outposts [between the armies], but nothing more than a skirmish takes place."

According to George T. Stevens, a surgeon with the 77th Regiment New York Volunteers: "This was the most cheerful winter we had passed in camp. One agreeable feature . . . was the great number of ladies, wives of officers, who spent the winter with their husbands. On every fine day great numbers of ladies might be seen riding about the camps and over the desolate fields, and their presence added greatly to the brilliancy of the frequent reviews. Great taste was displayed by many officers in fitting up their tents and quarters for the reception of their wives. The tents were usually enclosed by high walls of evergreens, woven with much skill, and fine arches and exquisite designs beautified the entrances to these happy retreats."

A captain of the 11th Regiment Massachusetts Volunteers, Henry N. Blake, says that "balls and similar festivities relieved the monotony of many winter quarters. Large details that sometimes comprised a thousand men were ordered to report at certain headquarters for the purpose of constructing suitable halls of logs. . . . The enlisted men, who rarely enjoyed the benefit of these structures which they erected, originated dances of a similar character. By searching the cabins and houses of the natives [i.e., the Virginians of the surrounding areas] and borrowing apparel, and a liberal use of pieces of shelter tent and the hoops of barrels, one half of the soldiers were arrayed as women, and filled the places of the seemingly indispensable partners of the gentler sex. The resemblance in the features of some of these persons was so perfect that a stranger would be unable to distinguish between the assumed and the genuine characters."

Private Theodore Gerrish, of the 20th Maine Volunteers, claims that the camps saw no diversion that was more appreciated than the practical joke, which was widely applied. Gerrish himself was a party to some of these pranks. "Many recruits came to us during that time, and of course they were proper subjects for practical jokes. One fellow from the backwoods of Maine reached the regiment late in the afternoon. He soon revealed to a number of the boys that his only fear in becoming a soldier was that he would not be able to stand on a picket post. [This

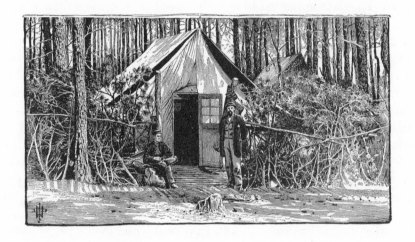

General Post Office, Army of the Potomac

was really only simple guard duty out in front of the lines, but the recruit believed he would have to balance himself on a post in order to increase his field of vision.] He felt that it would require a great deal of practice to do this in a skillful manner, and since he had decided to enlist he had not had a moment's time to practice it.

"Of course the boys had a great deal of sympathy for him, and kindly promised to assist him, for which he was very thankful. They informed him how difficult a thing it was for them when they first began. They accompanied him to the lower end of the street, where a post some four feet in height and six inches in diameter was set upright in the ground, the upper end being sharpened nearly to a point. With a little assistance the recruit succeeded in reaching its sharpened top, and in the evening twilight for nearly two long hours he managed to maintain his position [with his feet, of course, on the point's sloping sides], and received the compliments of his comrades. He then went to his tent, proud of the fact that he had mastered so difficult a problem in so brief a time. . . .

"These jokes were not confined to [the victimization of comrades], but the men in the ranks took great delight in practicing them upon the officers whom they did not like, when it could be done innocently. At one time a regiment in camp was living upon very poor rations [an exceptional situation, since this was a period when food was generally both palatable and abundant]. The bread [for example] was moldy, hard, and unfit to eat. . . . There was a chaplain in the regiment who was supposed to look after the interests of the men . . . but the boys thought that this one paid too much attention to the officers and too little to them, as he never came to their tents or spoke with them when he met them. He was a remarkably sleek and well-fed looking individual.

"One day he, together with some officers of another regiment, passed through a company street just as the men were eating dinner. The chaplain had his hands behind him and wore a self-satisfied look. A wag by the name of Dick sat on the ground by his tent door, trying to eat the musty hard-tack. Assuming almost an idiotic look as the chaplain approached, he inquired very innocently, 'Chaplain, will you be kind enough to tell me what the two capital letters, B. C., stand for when they are printed together upon anything?'

" 'O, yes,' blandly answered the chaplain, raising his voice so loud that it would attract the attention of all the men in the street, 'it means before the birth of our Savior, previous to the beginning of the Christian era.' He proceeded to give quite a profound theological exposition of the matter, and then inquired, 'But, my man, why did you ask so unusual a question?'

" 'O, nothin',' answered the innocent Dick, 'only we have seen it stamped on these sheets of hard-tack, and were curious to know why it was there.' At this point the listeners all exploded with laughter, while the chaplain saw that he was sold, and walked rapidly away."

As interjected by Warren Goss, the private from Massachusetts: "For some reason the chaplains of the army, speaking generally, were not a great success. Their intercourse with whiskey-drinking, profane superiors soon contaminated their piety, and little acts, such as selling postage stamps given them by the Sanitary Commission [a civilian volunteer service organization] at a large advance on the regular price, and similar speculations, brought many of them into contempt among the rank and file. . . . There were many exceptions to this rule of worthlessness, and many noble men 'filled the bill,' as the boys termed it. I remember at one time overhearing a general officer introduce a new chaplain to some brother officers as 'a damned good fellow for a chaplain.' "

Returning to Private Gerrish: "The practical jokes and fun were not confined to the camp, but were often indulged in on the picket line. . . . Four of us were stationed for three days on the picket line where a [Virginia] physician resided, and we took possession of his stable, spread our blankets upon the straw, and thus had very comfortable quarters. We were instructed to protect the property from any raid our soldiers might make upon it. The physician was a man some sixty years old, and . . . was proud, pompous, and a genuine 'Secesh' [Secessionist].

"Once in a while he would come out to the stable and chat with us. He did not attempt to conceal his sympathy with the South, and would talk about the superiority of the Southern troops, and of the certain success of the Confederacy. We replied very respectfully to his insults, but decided that, if it was possible, we would play some joke upon him before we were relieved, that would give him reason to remember us.

"In calling upon his patients in his professional work, he drove a spirited horse harnessed to an old-fashioned gig. The gig was a clumsy affair, with two huge wheels and a seat long enough to hold three persons.

"One night about twelve o'clock I was awakened by Dick, who slept by my side, punching his fist into my ribs and saying, '. . . Let's get up and harness the old doctor's horse into the gig and ride into camp!' By this time all were awake. 'Lord, won't the old fellow storm when he finds it out!' chuckled Mac, and we began to make arrangements for the ride. Three of us would go, and the fourth would remain on guard. We must leave before daylight, or the old man would be awake.

"The old carriage was taken from the stable, and the wheels with noiseless revolutions rolled through the door-yard. The horse was led around by a back passage so that his steps upon the yard would not awaken his owner. The old harness, patched and tied together in many places, was taken from the peg where it was hanging; an old whip . . . was taken from a beam where we had observed it the day previous, and we began to prepare for the forward movement.

"It had been so long a time since we had harnessed a horse that our movements were slow and awkward, but after a time our perseverance was rewarded. The horse was harnessed and all was ready. Three of us mounted to the seat, the reins were pulled taut, the whip cracked along the side of the nag, and away we went. There was something in the situation that imparted an inspiration of joyous excitement. The horse was a rapid roadster, the roads were quite smooth, and we made remarkable time.

"We decided that it would be best for us to reach the regiment about the time of morning roll call, as we would make quite a display riding into camp before the whole regiment. So we rode up and down the roads, talking and laughing . . . until we heard the regimental bugle blow for roll call. Just as they were breaking ranks, they were surprised by seeing us drive down across the parade ground at a three-minute gait, behind a smoking steed.

"In a moment they took in the whole situation, and, with wild cheers, three hundred men made a rush for us. It was now a 'race for life.' The old horse displayed speed that we never dreamed he possessed. Back and forth between the charging lines we dashed. The huge wheels seemed to smoke as we rushed to and fro over the parade ground. We turned square corners, made angles, and described circles. The whip cracked and cut across the shoulders of the assailants when they were within reach. We cheered; the carriage creaked and groaned, while the horse dashed madly on.

"Our line of communications was cut. We were flanked, surrounded, overpowered, but would not yield. We were turning a square corner to escape the enemy when a score of them caught the wheel of our carriage, and in a moment after we were sprawling upon the ground, and the horse dashing down at a break-neck rate over the rocky hillside toward home, while the air was filled with pieces of the carriage and harness.

"The boys gathered us up, and voted on the spot that it was one of the most remarkable defenses ever made in the history of war. But how to meet the doctor was the question that confronted us. Not that we feared the wrath that he would pour upon us, but he perhaps would report the matter at headquarters, and the officers might misunderstand the nature of the harmless amusement in which we had participated, and punish the innocent offenders.

"Fortune favored us. In our company was a sergeant whose name was Joe, brave, witty, generous, and always ready for any emergency. We reported the situation to him, and informed him of the disloyal sentiments of the doctor. He studied a moment and then exclaimed, 'By Jove, I can fix him!' His arrangements were rapidly made. Wearing his sergeant's chevrons and side arms, and having tucked a revolver in his belt and a huge package of papers in his breast pocket, and having secured the services of three of the boys, who were to accompany him with their rifles, we all glided quietly from camp without attracting attention.

"We three who had ridden in with the doctor's team went in advance along the road that led to his residence, Joe and his command proceeding some forty rods in our rear. We had passed over two-thirds of the distance to the doctor's house when we saw him coming with long rapid strides. He recognized us, and of course began to give vent to his rage. 'You unprincipled Yankee scoundrels, horse thieves—if I live to get to your headquarters, [see] if I don't punish you for this outrage! I, an honored citizen of the State of Virginia, to be thus robbed and outraged by you Northern vandals!' In vain we endeavored to reason with him, and offered to pay him for all the damage done. This only added fuel to the flames of his wrath.

"At this moment [the] sergeant and [his] file of soldiers with fixed bayonets arrived upon the scene. The physician, noticing that he was an officer of some grade, poured forth his tale of indignation to him. When he stopped for want of breath to proceed further, Joe, with a gravity that could not be surpassed, asked, 'Is this Dr. ———?' 'Yes, sir, that is my name,' replied the other. 'Then, sir,' said the sergeant, placing his hand upon the physician's shoulder, 'you are my prisoner.' 'For what?' demanded the astonished Virginian.

"Joe, with the importance of a commanding general, made answer: 'First, for treasonable utterances made against the United States Government. Second, for riding several times to the enemy's lines and giving them important information in regard to the Union army. Third, entertaining rebel officers or spies at your house, and secreting them from the Union soldiers.'

"For a moment the old fellow was dumbfounded. Joe, with solemn gravity, had rattled off charge after charge in such a manner that it sounded almost like a death warrant. The doctor then protested his innocence. Joe touched the bundle of papers in his pocket, and informed him that he had all the proof he needed. The doctor then admitted that he had often spoken in favor of secession; that once, and but a few weeks before, he had ridden nearly to the rebel camp to visit a patient, but claimed that no rebel officers had been at his house since our army had advanced the previous November. The tables were turned, and he began to beg. He would do anything in the world if the officer would only let the matter drop.

"For a long time Joe was immovable. 'An unconditional surrender' was his only terms. But at last a compromise was effected. The doctor was to return home; he was never to come inside the Union lines again while we were encamped there; and if any [Union] officers went to his house or came in contact with him, he was never to mention the matter of the horse. With many [other] words of counsel as to his future conduct, Joe ordered him to be released, and he hastened to his home. We followed him [back to our picket post], while Joe and his guard returned to camp.

"The doctor never mentioned his harness and carriage that had been destroyed. The horse was uninjured, and from that time the professional visits were made on horseback.

"We were relieved on the following day and returned to camp, and . . . the tents of Company H rang with shouts of laughter as we made known the adventure of Sergeant Joe."

Private Gerrish goes on to tell of a time when he himself was made the victim of a prank: "Milk, of course, was a luxury in the army, and many were the expeditions made from the picket line . . . to secure the coveted article. Having learned one day from a contraband [a former slave under Union protection] . . . that there was a plantation about three miles out where several cows were kept, two of us arranged to go out and secure some milk. The only possible danger was that we might fall in with some of the rebel cavalry who were occasionally scouting in that vicinity; but we decided, if we went out before daylight, that even this danger would be removed; and so, the next morning about four o'clock, two of us sallied forth.

"I was armed with a camp kettle that would contain twenty quarts. My companion carried his rifle. The distance was greater than we anticipated, and when we reached the plantation day was dawning. We soon ascertained that the cows were in a yard near the house. The program was for me to enter the yard and milk the cows, while Sam was to stand guard and give the alarm in case of danger. The cows were wild, and some little time was consumed in skirmishing around the yard before I could begin to milk.

"My position was such that my back was toward the house and very near the fence that enclosed the yard. I was meeting with great success, and several quarts of the precious fluid already repaid me for my industry. I was thinking of the rebel cavalry, when, in the dim, gray light of morning, a huge form towered upon the fence above me and sprang with terrific force to my side; and at the same moment a loud, unearthly yell saluted my ears. I thought Mosby [Colonel John S., the famed Confederate cavalry commander] and his whole gang of cutthroats were upon us.

"I sprang to my feet, upset the pail, rushed through the herd of astonished cattle, climbed the fence, and dashed toward the picket line. After I had run an eighth of a mile, I thought of Sam. I looked around, expecting to see a squad of the enemy following me, but to my surprise saw Sam coming, roaring with laughter and motioning for me to return. I returned and demanded the cause of my alarm. Poor Sam could only roll on the ground and ejaculate between his bursts of laughter, 'It is so good, so good!'

"After a time I learned that while I was milking, a colored lady of gigantic proportions had come out of the house with a milk pail and proceeded to the yard. Sam, from his outlook, saw her, but she did not know of our presence. Sam saw that she intended to climb the fence near where I was milking, and decided that it would be a grand chance to settle some old scores with me; and so, when she descended from her elevated position he had given me the benefit of the yell. It had operated in a double capacity, for the Negress had rushed to the house in a fright while I was running away.

"We returned to the yard and secured some milk. Sam promised me most solemnly that the boys in camp should never hear of it, but before the close of that day it was known to every man in the regiment."

It must not be supposed that life in the camps was an endless lark.

As delineated by Private Frank Wilkeson, a New Yorker who served with the artillery: "When the weather was fit the soldiers were drilled, and drilled, and drilled again. . . . In front of the ground on which the battery I belonged to was camped, was a large plain. On it several [infantry] regiments, in heavy marching order, were drilled every pleasant day. Instead of practicing the men in the simple flank and line movements used in battle, or at targets, or in estimating distances, they were marched to and fro and made to perform displayful evolutions. . . .

"In the artillery service the drill was still more absurd. Teams were hitched to the guns almost daily, and they were whirled over comparatively dry ground in a highly bewildering [and] exceedingly useless manner. Every enlisted man in the army knew that we were to fight in a rugged, wooded country where the clearings were surrounded by heavy forests, and where deep shrub and timber-clad ravines hazed the air, and where practice and practice and still more practice in *estimating distances* was required, if we were to fire accurately and effectively.

"Did the artillery officers zealously practice us in estimating distance? Never, to my knowledge. They taught us . . . [maneuvers] of as much practical use to us as if we had been assiduously drilled to walk on stilts or to play on the banjo. . . .

"How tired I got of camp, and drill, and guard duty! And how tired I got of the rain and mud!

"A large portion of the battery men were religious. Almost nightly these men held a prayer-meeting. Next to us, on the right, a battery manned by Irishmen was parked, and almost nightly *they* indulged in a fist fight. Once in a while they evinced a desire to fight with us, and at long intervals some of the unregenerate men of our battery gratified them and got whipped.

"Still farther to the right a battery of the Fourth United States Artillery was parked. The men of that [regular army] command were either Irish or Irish-Americans, and they were keen to gratify the desire of volunteer Irish, or any other volunteers, to indulge in personal combat.

"To our left a full regiment of Germans, heavy artillerymen, were camped. Between [these volunteers] and the regular army artillerymen a bloody feud existed. Many and many a German was savagely beaten by the Irishmen. This regiment of Germans interested me greatly. In their camp I first saw lager beer. I bought a glass of it, but finding it a weak, sloppy drink, I left the almost full glass on the counter. . . . This

On picket between the lines

regiment of Germans made more noise in their camp than two brigades of Americans would or could have done. . . .

"The discipline throughout the Army of the Potomac during the winter of 1863–64 was necessarily severe. The ranks of the original volunteers, the men who sprang to arms at the tap of the Northern war drum, had been shot to pieces. Entire platoons had disappeared. Regiments that had entered the great camps of instruction formed around Washington in 1861–62, a thousand men strong, had melted before the heat of Confederate battle fire till they numbered three hundred, two hundred, and as low as one hundred and fifty men.

"During the winter of 1863–64 these regiments were being filled with bounty-jumpers [criminal types who accepted special compensation for signing up, then deserted, sometimes repeating the process several times—men who could be retained only through constant watchfulness, and who were difficult to train]. . . . These men had to be severely disciplined, and that entailed punishment. . . .

"There was no necessity for punishing the volunteers. They were men of high intelligence. They could be reasoned with. They could and did see the necessity of soldier-like and decent behavior in their camps. They cheerfully obeyed orders because they realized the necessity of obedience. But with large bounties came a different class of recruits, the bounty-jumpers. These men had to be heartlessly moulded into soldiers. . . .

"The punishments inflicted . . . were various, and some of them were horribly brutal and needlessly severe; but they apparently served their purpose. . . . One punishment much affected in the light artillery was called 'tying on the spare wheel.' Springing upward and rearward from the center rail of every caisson [ammunition carriage] was a fifth axle, and on it was a spare wheel. A soldier who had been insubordinate was taken to the spare wheel and forced to step upon it. His legs were drawn apart until they spanned three spokes. His arms were stretched until there were three or four spokes between his hands. Then feet and hands were firmly bound to . . . the wheel.

"If the soldier was to be punished moderately he was left, bound in an upright position, on the wheel for five or six hours. If the punishment was to be severe, the ponderous wheel was given a quarter-turn after the soldier had been lashed to it, which changed the position of the man . . . from an upright to a horizontal one. Then the prisoner had to exert all his strength to keep his weight from pulling heavily and cuttingly on the cords that bound his upper arm and leg to the wheel.

"I have frequently seen men faint while undergoing this punishment, and I have known men to endure it for hours without a murmur, but with white faces and set jaws and blazing eyes. To cry out, to beg for mercy, to protest, ensured additional discomfort in the shape of a gag, a rough stick, being tied into the suffering man's mouth. 'Tying on the spare wheel' was the usual punishment in the artillery service for rather serious offenses; and no man wanted to be tied up but once. . . .

"Daily many men were tied up by the thumbs, and that was far from pleasant. The impudent bounty-jumper who had stood on his toes under a tree for a couple of hours to keep his weight off of his thumbs, which were tied to a limb over his head, was exceedingly apt to heed the words of his officers when next they spoke to him. The bounty-jumper lacked the moral qualities which could be appealed to in an honest endeavor to create a soldier out of a ruffian; but his capacity to suffer physically was unimpaired, and that had to be played upon."

The ultimate punishment was reserved for deserters who were captured and brought back to camp. In the words of Color Sergeant Crotty: "The monotony of camp life is to be broken by the shooting of a deserter. . . . Military discipline must have its course. The soldier who deserts his command . . . deserves all the punishment due him, which is shooting to death by musketry. . . . The ceremony is a sad one, and ought to be a warning to all soldiers to stand up like men and endure the hardships alike, with his comrades by his side.

"The day of execution has come. The bugle sounds the call to fall in, and the whole division forms. . . . Oh, what must be the poor culprit's thoughts when he hears *that call,* for it is the signal for him that his last hour on this earth has come.

"The division is formed in a square, the head of which is left open, where the grave of the unhappy man is dug and waiting to receive its tenant. One regiment faces another, leaving space between for the procession to pass by. We hear in the distance the slow and mournful strains of the band as it leads the procession, playing the dead march. The mournful cortege comes slowly along—band first, then a posse of soldiers, then the coffin, borne on the shoulders of four men, and the doomed man behind it. By his side walks the man of God, preparing him for his last moments. After them in the rear is the squad of twelve men with their loaded muskets. . . .

"At last the solemn procession halts at the grave. The coffin is laid by its side. The squad of men take twelve or fifteen paces to the rear, turn about, and face the man to be shot. The Provost Marshal of the division moves forward and reads in distinct words the charges to the man and the sentence of the Court Martial, after which he steps back. . . . The chaplain kneels with the culprit and sends forth a prayer to the throne of grace for the unhappy man. At this time the stoutest heart melts into sympathy, and many a handkerchief is seen to go to wipe the scalding tears that fall thick and fast. . . .

"After the good chaplain has done his duty, the doomed man is blindfolded and stands erect, waiting for the awful moment to come for him to be sent before his Maker. The marshal gives the order to fire by signs with his sword. One, two, three, and [as a crash resounds] the unhappy man is before the Great Commander of us all, to give an account of all his doings in life.

"The guns of the squad are inspected to see that every man has fired his piece. The muskets [have been] loaded by other parties, and out of the twelve is one blank cartridge. Each man thinks, probably, that he had the gun containing the blank. The division marches by the corpse, which lays where it fell. Each take a last look at the unhappy deserter, and then march back to camp."

The bounty-jumpers were not alone in their aversion to soldiering. This frame of mind was also evident among many of the conscripts, or draftees. As a class, however, these latter men made the adjustment and became good soldiers. If there were a few deserters among those who could not adjust, there were also men who gained their freedom through gentler tactics.

As recalled by Private Goss: "One incident occurs to me of a conscript who was apparently demented on the subject of fishing. With a pin hook and cotton line and a pole, he would sit or stand, with a blank look of simplicity on his face, before a mud-puddle in the road or by the camp, in rain or sun, the butt of many a joke and jeer. He was examined by a board of surgeons and pronounced insane. His discharge was finally ordered, and so little was he esteemed capable of taking care of himself that a comrade was put in charge of him to see him safe on his way to the cars. As his comrade got him safely on the train, he said, 'Now, Jim, go home to your mother.' A new light filled the blank in Jim's eyes as he made reply, 'That's what I've been fishing for!' He had humbugged not only the whole camp but an able board of surgeons."

3

Lee and His Command

The camps south of the Rapidan were less extensive than those to the north. Whereas the Army of the Potomac numbered well over 100,000 men, the Army of Northern Virginia could boast no more than 70,000. Morale in the lesser army was sustained by its bond with Robert E. Lee. The general had led these lean and poorly accoutered men to international fame as great soldiers, and, in spite of current uncertainties about Southern prospects, the bond was as strong as ever.

Lee was in his mid-fifties, and the war had tired him, but he was still an impressive figure. A British observer with the Confederate army, Colonel Arthur Fremantle, described him thus: "General Lee is, almost without exception, the handsomest man of his age I ever saw. He is tall, broad-shouldered, very well made, well set up, a thorough soldier in appearance; and his manners are most courteous and full of dignity. He is a perfect gentleman in every respect. I imagine no man has so few enemies, or is so universally esteemed. . . .

"He has none of the small vices, such as smoking, drinking, chewing, or swearing; and his bitterest enemy never accused him of any of the greater ones. He generally wears a well-worn, long, gray jacket, a high, black felt hat, and blue trousers, tucked into his Wellington boots. I never saw him carry arms, and the only marks of his military rank are the three stars on his collar. He rides a handsome horse, which is extremely well groomed. He himself is very neat in his dress and person."

Lee kept a personal watch on the Federals across the river. In the words of one of his brigade commanders, the hard-fighting but gentlemanly and articulate general from the deep South, John B. Gordon:

21

Robert E. Lee

"My camp and quarters were near Clark's Mountain, from the top of which General Lee so often surveyed with his glasses the white-tented city of the Union army spread out before us on the undulating plain below. A more peaceful scene could hardly be conceived than that which broke upon our view . . . as the rays of the morning sun fell upon the quiet, wide-spreading Union camp, with its thousands of smoke columns rising like miniature geysers, its fluttering flags marking, at regular intervals, the different divisions, its stillness unbroken save by an occasional drumbeat and the clear ringing notes of bugles sounding the familiar calls."

During his surveys of the Union camps, Lee was usually accompanied by several subordinates. One of the commander's parties included an exuberant young brigadier named John Pegram and a junior artillery officer, Robert Stiles, who had interrupted a career in law to embrace the Southern cause. Stiles relates: "While we continued to look at the Federal camps, two horsemen rode down to the other bank to water their horses. Pegram seemed much interested, and said he believed he would gallop down and interview 'those fellows.' As he started, General Lee said, in a deep voice, 'You'd better be careful, sir!'

"Pegram was a superb horseman and splendidly mounted, and I never saw a finer equestrian figure than he presented as he dashed off down the hill. . . . When he reached the flat [land] through which the river ran, the Federal horses raised their heads, and their riders shaded their eyes with their hands, gazing intently at the rapidly approaching horseman and striving to make him out. As he dashed into the stream amid a cloud of spray, they advanced rapidly to meet him, and we felt a shade of uneasiness.

"But the next moment we saw that the meeting was not only friendly but enthusiastic; and after the first fervors of the greeting had subsided the three sat on their horses in the middle of the stream and had a conference so long that we actually tired of waiting. When Pegram returned he told us, with a glowing countenance, that the troopers had belonged to his company in the old [United States] army, and that their hearts were [still] in the same place toward him. He was a noble gentleman, and no one suggested such a thing as military information acquired or divulged under such circumstances."

Another story having to do with Lee's observations of the Union lines is related by Edward Pollard, then associate editor of the *Richmond Examiner* and a close follower of the commander's career: "General Lee was . . . conversing with two of his officers, one of whom was

John B. Gordon

known to be not only a hard fighter and a hard swearer, but a cordial hater of the Yankees. . . . The latter officer, looking at the Yankees with a dark scowl on his face, exclaimed most emphatically, 'I wish they were all dead!' General Lee, with the grace and manner peculiar to himself, replied, 'How can you say so, General? Now, I wish they were all at home attending to their own business, and leaving us to do the same.' He then moved off, when the first speaker, waiting until he was out of earshot, turned to his companion and in the most earnest tone said, 'I would not say so before General Lee, but I wish they were all dead *and in hell!'*

"When this 'amendment' to the wish was afterwards repeated to General Lee, in spite of his goodness and customary reproof of profanity, he could not refrain from laughing heartily at the speech, which was so characteristic of [the offender], one of his favorite officers."

Returning to General John Gordon, the observer who depicted the tranquillity of the Union camps: "On the southern side of the Rapidan the scenes were, if possible, still less warlike. In every Confederate camp chaplains and visiting ministers erected religious altars, around which the ragged soldiers knelt and worshipped the Heavenly Father into whose keeping they committed themselves and their cause, and through whose all-wise guidance they expected ultimate victory.

"The religious revivals that ensued form a most remarkable and impressive chapter of war history. Not only on the Sabbath day but during the week, night after night for long periods, these services continued, increasing in attendance and interest until they brought under religious influence the great body of the army. Along the mountainsides and in the forests, where the Southern camps were pitched, the rocks and woods rang with appeals for holiness and consecration, with praises for past mercies and earnest prayers for future protection and deliverance. . . .

"General Lee, who was a deeply pious man, manifested a constant and profound interest in the progress of this religious work among his soldiers. He usually attended his own church when services were held there, but his interest was confined to no particular denomination. He encouraged all and helped all.

"Back of the army, on the farms, in the towns and cities, the fingers of Southern women were busy knitting socks and sewing seams of coarse trousers and gray jackets for the soldiers at the front. From Mrs. Lee and her daughters [in Richmond] to the humblest country matrons and maidens, their busy needles were stitching, stitching, stitching, day and night. The anxious commander thanked them for their efforts to bring greater comfort to the cold feet and shivering limbs of his half-clad men. He wrote letters expressing appreciation of the bags of socks and shirts as they came in. . . . His tributes were tender and constant to these glorious women for their labor and sacrifices for Southern independence."

Many of the women worked with heavy hearts, for the war had destroyed men who were close to them. Even now, during this winter lull, soldiers were dying of wounds received earlier, or of camp sicknesses such as typhoid fever and dysentery. A Richmond diarist, Mrs. Judith McGuire, made this lament: "We bury, one by one, the dearest, the brightest, the best of our domestic circles. . . . How can we escape the sadness of heart which will pervade the South when the war is over and we are again gathered together around our family hearths and altars, and find the circles broken? One and another gone. Sometimes the father and husband. . . . Again the eldest son and brother of the widowed home . . . or perhaps that bright youth on whom we had not ceased to look as still a child. . . . In all the broad South there will be scarcely a fold without its missing lamb, a fireside without its vacant chair. And yet we must go on. It is our duty to rid our land of invaders. We must destroy the snake which is endeavoring to entwine us in its coils, though it drain our heart's blood."

In another diary entry, Mrs. McGuire, a clerk in Richmond's Commissary Department, gives this vignette: "The Transportation Office is just opposite to us, where crowds of furloughed soldiers, returning to their commands, are constantly standing waiting for transportation. As I pass them on my way to the office in the morning, I always stop to have a cheerful word with them. Yesterday morning I said to them, 'Gentlemen, whom do you suppose I have seen this morning?' In answer to their inquiring looks, I said, 'General Lee.' 'General Lee!' they exclaimed, 'I did not know he was in town. God bless him!' And they looked excited. . . . 'And where do you suppose I saw him so early?' 'Where, Madame, where?' 'At prayer meeting, down upon his knees, praying for you and for the country.'

"In an instant they seemed subdued. Tears started to the eyes of many of those hardy sunburnt veterans. Some were utterly silent, while others exclaimed . . . 'God bless him!' 'God bless his dear old soul!' etc. As I walked away, some followed me to know where he was to be seen. One had never seen him at all, and wanted to see him 'monstrous bad.' Others had seen him often, but wanted to see him in town, 'just to look

Mrs. Robert E. Lee

at him.' I told them where his family residence was, but, as they feared that they could not leave the Transportation Office long enough to find Franklin Street, I dare say the poor fellows did not see General Lee."

Lee did not usually tarry long in Richmond. He preferred to share the privations of camp. "His unselfish solicitude for his men," says John Gordon, "was marked and unvarying. He sent to the suffering privates in the hospitals the delicacies contributed for his personal use. . . . If a handful of real coffee came to him, it went in the same direction, while he cheerfully drank from his tin cup the wretched substitute made from parched corn or beans."

According to Richmond editor Edward Pollard, Lee ate meat but twice a week. "His ordinary dinner consisted of a head of cabbage boiled in salt water, and a pone of corn bread. The story is jocosely told that on one occasion, a number of gentlemen having appointed to dine with him, he had ordered his servant to provide a repast of cabbage and middling [i.e., second-rate meat]. A very small bit of middling garnished the dish—so small that the polite guests all declined middling, and it remained on the dish when they rose from the table. Next day, the general, remembering the untouched meat, ordered his servant to 'bring that middling.' The man hesitated, scratched his head, and finally said, 'De fac is, mass'r Robert, dat ar middlin' was *borrid* middlin', and I done give it back to de man whar I got it from.' "

Like the Federals, Lee's troops did their share of drilling when the weather was favorable, and took their turns at picket duty in weather good or bad. Manual labor was also a part of their schedule. As recalled by J. F. J. Caldwell, a junior infantry officer from South Carolina: "We performed a rather laborious fatigue duty during a part of the winter, being compelled to cut and haul a sufficient number of logs to lay the plank road from Orange Court House to Liberty Mills, on the Rapidan, a distance of five miles. Other portions of the army hauled, broke, and laid stones in the streets of the town. . . .

"[Our] camps were kept very cleanly, and the health of the command was as good as could be desired. Good rations were issued to us, generally. There was rather too much cornmeal and far too little bacon (beef was a thing of the past now), but still we did not starve. . . .

"The first disturbance of our repose in winter quarters was caused by a movement of the enemy's cavalry in February. They attacked the Confederate cavalry on duty beyond the Rapidan [i.e., on the north side] and drove them in. They then moved up the river towards Liberty Mills. [Samuel] McGowan's and [James H.] Lane's brigades were sent across at Liberty Mills to meet them. Lane took a wide march from the Rapidan, so as to go around the enemy; we [of McGowan's brigade] moved down the river at a short distance from it. We marched on Sunday, the 7th of February. It was raining slowly . . . and the roads were extremely muddy.

"We moved rapidly, but never overtook the Federals. Whether they were frightened at our approach or had accomplished their object I do not know. They exchanged a few artillery shots with [Alfred M.] Scales' brigade at Barnett's Ford. Towards night, our cavalry passed in front of us and occupied their former position. We threw out pickets at night, but there being no appearance of the enemy then or the next morning, we returned to camp. . . .

"In February there was a general call for reenlistment in the Confederate armies. . . . Almost all the regiments organized in the summer of 1861 enlisted for 'three years or the war.' I always held the expression to mean a consent to serve three years, whether the war lasted so long or not; and to serve for the war, should it last even longer than three years. But as there was doubt about it . . . and as, above all things, the weary citizens at home needed encouragement, a renewal of enlistment and of allegiance to the Confederacy was invited. The army adopted the suggestion most cordially, and declared afresh their determination never to lay down their arms until the independence of the South should be achieved. . . .

"The weather continued cold and wet. . . . Snows were not so heavy nor so frequent as the winter previous, but they were not few; and the rains were constant. . . . I remember once standing for over twenty hours, on picket, in a continuous flood of water that chilled me to the very heart."

Adds a private from Georgia, G. W. Nichols: "Our picket post was at the fords on the Rapidan River near Clark's Mountain. . . . A regiment would have to go . . . and stay two days. One time when our regiment had to go the weather was very cold. The river was frozen over at least eight inches thick. We heard a terrible racket up the river and could not understand what it could be. The noise approached us rapidly, and we soon saw the cause. It was the river rising and breaking the ice. The rising water would break the ice and keep it piled up ahead on the solid ice three or four feet high. Large pieces which would have weighed one hundred or more pounds would be sliding along ahead of the breaking ice. Broken ice floated along all that day.

"That night I had to stand picket guard one hour. I came near freezing to death. When relief came I was so cold . . . I could hardly get back to the fire."

Private John O. Casler, a native Virginian, spent the winter serving as cook for a unit of pioneers, or construction workers. "The pioneer troops were divided into messes of twelve, and one of the twelve remained in camp to cook while the others went out to work. . . . I was cook for our mess. One day as they returned from work, Sam Nunnelly brought a pig along that he had caught in the road near some Negro shanties, and gave it to me to raise [for butchering]. I told him I did not want to be bothered with it, but he insisted we should keep it; and, as it was quite a pet, we adopted it and called it 'Susan Jane.'

"It would run around the quarters and eat the scraps and find some corn at the stables. . . . At night we would let it sleep in our shanty under the bunks; but when we got up every morning it would be lying in the fireplace in the ashes to keep warm. Every wash day we would wash it clean in the suds, and then make it stand up on the bed until it got dry. It was a white pig and improved rapidly, and was as tame as a dog and would follow anyone who called it. I had to tie a clog to it to keep it from following some of the soldiers to their camps.

"One day it got loose from the clog and I could not find it; but someone told me they had seen it following some Georgians who belonged to [Robert E.] Rodes' division. I hurried over to Rodes' division, which was camped about one-half mile from us, and just got there in time to save its throat from being cut and it being made a feast of by the Georgians.

"It was a great pet in camp, and I had to watch it continually to keep it from being stolen from me, as it would make good pork anytime. Everyone who knew it said they never saw a hog increase in weight so rapidly.

". . . [Finally] I concluded to butcher it and have a barbecue for the whole company, as it would weigh about two hundred pounds. . . . But we were all doomed to disappointment, for a few days before the slaughter was to take place 'Susan Jane' turned up missing, and we never saw her again. I always thought the Louisianians stole her, as they had made the attempt several times. Anyway, I lost my pork.

"Soldiers are very fond of pets, as I think all persons are who are isolated from home. Nearly every separate command had some kind of pet. The Louisiana brigade had a medium sized dog, black and white spotted, very intelligent, called 'Sawbuck.' Nearly everyone in the division knew the dog. He [had several times gone] into battle with the brigade, dashing up and down the line barking and making all the racket he could. One time he got wounded in the foreleg, and never would go in again. . . . If he would happen to get lost from the brigade when they went into camp after a day's march, he would station himself by the road and watch for the stragglers until he saw one belonging to his brigade, then follow him to camp. . . .

"My father came from Rockingham to see me in this camp and brought me a new pair of boots and some new clothing; also a box of good things to eat, which were relished by my mess. He remained with us several days and then went home.

"Some of the boys would get up parties and dances in the country, and have a houseful of ladies. We would take the musicians from camp; and, altogether, spent a pleasant time that winter.

". . . Every time it snowed the soldiers would turn out and have snowball battles. One day our division challenged Rodes' division to battle in a large field. They came out, and the battle raged with various success until towards evening, when a great many of our division got tired of it and went to camp. When Rodes' men saw our line weakened they brought up some fresh troops and made a charge and ran us into our quarters, and then fell back, formed a new line, and dared us out. It looked rather bad for us to be defeated in that way, so some of the boys went to General [James A.] Walker and got him to come out and take command.

"It was fun for Walker, so he mounted his horse, collected his staff, and sent conscript officers all over camp and forced the men out. We had signal corps at work, took our colors out in line, had the drummers and fifers beat the long roll, had couriers carrying dispatches, and everything done like in a regular engagement with the enemy. In the meantime, Rodes' men were making snowballs, and had piles of them along the crest of the ridge ready for us when we should charge. . . .

"When General Walker got everything in readiness, and the line formed, he ordered us to charge up close to Rodes' men and then wheel and fall back, so as to draw them after us away from the piles of snowballs they had made. When the drums beat we were to wheel again and charge them and run them over the hill and capture their snowballs.

"We did so, and the plan worked successfully. At the same time, the Louisiana brigade slipped around through the woods and struck them on the left flank by surprise, and the rout was complete. We ran them on to their camps and through them, and as some of the Louisianians were returning they stole some cooking utensils from Rodes' men and

The great Confederate snowball fight

kept them. We captured several stands of colors, but we had lost several in the earlier part of the fight. Officers would be captured and pulled off their horses and washed in the snow, but all took it in good part. After the fight was over we went out with a flag of truce and exchanged prisoners.

"It was probably the greatest snowball battle ever fought, and showed that 'men are but children of larger growth.' The Richmond papers had several columns each, giving an account of the battle. If all battles would terminate that way it would be a great improvement on the old slaughtering plan. . . .

"The Louisiana brigade and our brigade joined together and built a large log house, covered it with clapboards, erected a stage, organized a theatrical troupe of Negro minstrels [whites in blackface], and gave performances nearly every night to a crowded audience. 'Admission one dollar—net proceeds to be given to widows and orphans of Confederate soldiers.'

"Noble T. Johnson, of the 5th Virginia, was one of the end men, handled the bones, and was one of the most comical characters I ever saw. He could keep the house in a roar of applause all the time. Miller, of the 1st Louisiana, was banjoist, and a splendid performer.

"They would write some of their own plays, suitable to the times and occasion. One splendid piece was called 'The Medical Board,' a burlesque on the [army] surgeons. The characters were a number of surgeons sitting around a table playing cards, with a bottle of brandy on the table, which was passed around quite frequently, until one doctor inquired how they came to get such good brandy.

" 'Oh, this is some that was sent down from Augusta County for the sick soldiers, but the poor devils don't need it, so we'll drink it.' Then a courier would come in and inform them that there was a soldier outside badly wounded. 'Bring him in! Bring him in!' said the chief surgeon. When brought in, an examination would take place, with the result that his arm would have to be amputated. Then the poor fellow wanted to know if when that was done he could not have a furlough. 'Oh, no!' replied the surgeon.

"A further examination developed that his leg would have to be amputated. 'Then can I have a furlough?' said the soldier. 'By no means,' replied the surgeon, 'for you can drive an ambulance when you get well.' It was finally determined by the medical board, as he was wounded in the head, that his head would have to come off. 'Then,' says the soldier, 'I *know* I can have a furlough.'

Confederate theatricals

" 'No, indeed,' replied the surgeon, 'we are so scarce of men that your body will have to be set up in the breastworks to fool the enemy.'

"Many such pieces as the foregoing were acted—burlesques on the officers, quartermasters, and commissaries, or whatever was interesting and amusing. Taking it all together, we had splendid performances. . . . We had amongst us professional actors and musicians; and the theater became a great place of resort to while away the dull winter nights.

"As I was a shoemaker and had a few tools such as awl, claw-hammer, and pocketknife, I was prepared to half-sole the boys' shoes. I made my own pegs and a last. The next thing, and most important, was leather. Sometimes we could get government leather from the quartermaster; but in order to obviate that difficulty I formed a partnership with Sam McFadden, a messmate, of the 14th Louisiana. Sam [would] steal the leather, such as cartridge-box lids, saddle-skirts, and housings from the harness. . . . We would then charge five dollars in 'Confed' for half-soling, and divide, which kept us in spending money.

"One night, as we were returning from a visit to our brigade, in passing the tent of the colonel of the 2nd Virginia, we noticed his McClellan saddle hung up on the outside. Sam said that this was a good chance to lay in a stock of leather. . . . Consequently we clipped the skirts off and went on to our quarters. But, as there were several soldiers in our shanty who did not belong there, we concluded to leave the saddle skirts on the outside until the coast was clear, knowing full well the colonel would raise a racket in the morning about his saddle being cut. After the crowd had dispersed we went out to bring in our stock, but it was gone. Someone had stolen it from us. We never did hear of those skirts again, and were afraid to inquire for fear the colonel would hear of it and have us punished.

"Our division was not called out for any active service during the winter . . . until in March when the Federal cavalry crossed the Rappahannock under [Judson] Kilpatrick and [Ulric] Dahlgren on their raid [on] Richmond. They were repulsed. . . . Our corps was sent down to the old battlefield of Chancellorsville to head them off, but they did not return that way. After lying there one day, our corps returned to camp. As I was cook, I was left in camp and had charge of the camp in their absence. The boys reported that the old battleground was full of bones bleached white by exposure, as the bodies of the slain had been covered very shallow, and the rains had washed the dirt off."

As added by John H. Worsham, of the 21st Virginia Infantry, who accompanied the expedition: "It was an awful experience, even for soldiers, to lie down for rest at night after scraping the bones away."

For Worsham, this was not the winter's only jarring episode. "One afternoon the whole division was ordered out to witness the execution of three Confederate soldiers from another division. . . . The order to fire was given, and, at the report of the guns, two men were killed. . . . The third man, while shot, was not killed. One of the detail was ordered to place another gun against the man's breast and fire. This killed him instantly. This was the only execution I witnessed, and, if I live a thousand years, I will never be willing to see another."

For the most part, Worsham found the winter agreeable and interesting. "While we were in this camp, we received some of the Telescope rifles which were entrusted to a select body of men. On suitable occasions the men practiced shooting with them. At one of these practices they stood on one hill and shot at a target about half a mile off on another hill. The bottom between those hills was used as a grazing place for horses and mules belonging to our wagon train, and, during the shooting, they accidentally killed one of the mules. That mule was very fat, and not long after it was killed some of the men cut chunks of meat from him and carried them into camp to be cooked and eaten. Some officer, learning of this, had a guard stationed during the day near the mule to prevent it. That night [however] many had mule steak for supper. . . .

"The Negroes who accompanied their masters . . . were a source of much merriment as well as comfort to us. . . . Here is [a] tale of [a] Negro showing the feeling the Southerner had for him. My mess of about half a dozen . . . had a Negro slave as a cook who stayed about our tent during the day but slept in a cabin with other Negroes. He was taken sick with measles. We made him leave his quarters and come and stay in our tent, where we cooked for him and nursed him until he was well.

"I tried to keep clean while in the army, and made it a rule to take a bath once a week, and oftener when convenient. . . . Here is a winter day's experience in this camp. One day about noon, the sun shining brightly and little wind stirring, I thought I would take my bath. I walked over to Madison Run, a large stream about half a mile from camp. I found the stream frozen over solid. I got a large rock, walked to the middle of the stream, raised the rock over my head, and hurled it with all my force on the ice, but it made no impression. I repeated this eight or ten times without breaking the ice. I then returned to camp, got an ax, went back to the run, cut a large hole in the ice, which was about seven inches thick, cleared the hole of all floating ice, undressed, took a good bath, dressed, and when I returned to camp was in fine condition."

4

Grant Comes East

I t was early in March 1864 when Union General Ulysses Grant was summoned from his command in the West. According to Albert D. Richardson, a war correspondent for the *New York Tribune* who was acquainted with Grant and became one of his earliest biographers: "At five P.M. on the eighth of March he reached Washington, where he had never before spent more than a single day. After a hasty toilet, he entered the long dining hall at Willard's [Hotel] and sat down to dinner. A gentleman nearby asked his neighbor, 'Who is that major-general?' 'Why, that is *Lieutenant*-General Grant.'

"The news flew from table to table. Up sprang, and out spoke a Pennsylvania member of Congress, 'Ladies and gentlemen, the hero of Donelson, of Vicksburg, and of Chattanooga is among us. I propose the health of Lieutenant-General Grant!'

"Five hundred guests of both sexes were instantly on their feet, cheering, huzzaing, waving handkerchiefs and napkins—and a few enthusiasts dancing wildly, in reckless disregard of chairs, toes, and crockery. With evident embarrassment Grant bowed, shook hands with those who crowded around him, and then attempted to return to his muttons. But in vain. He could not take his meal in peace, and finally retired abashed before the crowd of loquacious men and showily dressed women."

As it happened, the President and Mrs. Lincoln had scheduled one of their regular public receptions for that evening, and Grant decided he had better stop by and pay his respects. He missed the first part of the affair. The early guests included Captain Horace Porter, a young

Ulysses S. Grant

Pennsylvanian (the son of David Rittenhouse Porter, governor of the state between 1839 and 1845) who had spent some time with Grant in the West but was presently on duty in Washington. Porter kept a copious record of his Civil War experiences, later turning this into a fine memoir. He says of the gathering:

"The President stood in the usual reception room, known as the 'Blue Room,' with several cabinet officers near him, and shook hands cordially with everybody as the vast procession of men and women passed in front of him. He was in evening dress and wore a turned-down collar a size too large. The necktie was rather broad and awkwardly tied. He was more of a Hercules than an Adonis. His height of six feet four inches enabled him to look over the heads of most of his visitors.

"His form was ungainly, and the movements of his long, angular arms and legs bordered at times upon the grotesque. His eyes were gray and disproportionately small. His face wore a general expression of sadness, the deep lines indicating the sense of responsibility which weighed upon him. But at times his features lighted up with a broad smile, and there was a merry twinkle in his eyes as he greeted an old acquaintance and exchanged a few words with him in a tone of familiarity. . . .

"Mrs. Lincoln occupied a position on his right. For a time she stood on a line with him and took part in the reception, but afterward stepped back and conversed with some of the wives of the cabinet officers and other personal acquaintances who were in the room.

"At about half-past nine o'clock a sudden commotion near the entrance to the room attracted general attention, and, upon looking in that direction I was surprised to see General Grant walking along modestly with the rest of the crowd [in the line] toward Mr. Lincoln. . . . Although these two historical characters had never met before, Mr. Lincoln recognized the general at once from the pictures he had seen of him. With a face radiant with delight, he advanced rapidly two or three steps toward his distinguished visitor, and cried out, 'Why, here is General Grant! Well, this is a great pleasure, I assure you,' at the same time seizing him by the hand and shaking it . . . with a vigor which showed the extreme cordiality of the welcome.

"The scene now presented was deeply impressive. Standing face to face for the first time were the two illustrious men whose names will always be inseparably associated in connection with the war of the rebellion. Grant's right hand grasped the lapel of his coat. His head was bent slightly forward, and his eyes upturned toward Lincoln's face. The

Pen and ink sketch of Abraham Lincoln

President, who was eight inches taller, looked down with beaming countenance upon his guest.

"Although their appearance, their training, and their characteristics were in striking contrast, yet the two men had many traits in common, and there were numerous points of resemblance in their remarkable careers. Each was of humble origin and had been compelled to learn the first lessons of life in the severe school of adversity. Each had risen from the people, possessed an abiding confidence in them, and always retained a deep hold upon their affections. . . . Both were conspicuous for the possession of that most uncommon of all virtues, common sense. Both despised the arts of the demagogue and shrank from posing for effect, or indulging in mock heroics. . . .

"The statesman and the soldier conversed for a few minutes, and then the President presented his distinguished guest to Mr. [William H.] Seward. The Secretary of State was very demonstrative in his welcome, and, after exchanging a few words, led the general to where Mrs. Lincoln was standing, and presented him to her. Mrs. Lincoln expressed much surprise and pleasure at the meeting, and she and the general chatted together very pleasantly for some minutes.

"The visitors had by this time become so curious to catch a sight of the general that their eagerness knew no bounds, and they became altogether unmanageable. Mr. Seward's consummate knowledge of the wiles of diplomacy now came to the rescue and saved the situation. He succeeded in struggling through the crowd with the general until they reached the large East Room, where the people could circulate more freely. This, however, was only a temporary relief. The people by this time had worked themselves up to a state of uncontrollable excitement. The vast throng surged and swayed and crowded until alarm was felt for the safety of the ladies.

"Cries now arose of 'Grant! Grant! Grant!' Then came cheer after cheer. Seward, after some persuasion, induced the general to stand upon a sofa, thinking the visitors would be satisfied with a view of him, and retire; but as soon as they caught sight of him their shouts were renewed, and a rush was made to shake his hand. The President sent word that he and the Secretary of War [Edwin M. Stanton] would await the general's return in one of the small drawing rooms. But it was fully an hour before he was able to make his way there, and then only with the aid of several officers and ushers."

Grant later said of his evening at the White House: "It was the hardest campaign I ever fought."

Mary Todd Lincoln, the President's wife

Returning to Horace Porter: "The next day, March 9, the general went to the White House, by invitation of Mr. Lincoln, for the purpose of receiving his commission from the hands of the President. Upon his return to Willard's Hotel, I called to pay my respects. . . . The act which created the grade of lieutenant general authorized a personal staff. . . . In our conversation the general referred to this circumstance and offered me one of the positions of aide-de-camp, which I said I would accept very gladly."

On March 10 Grant took the train to Brandy Station, Virginia, to look over the Army of the Potomac and to consult with General Meade. Returning to Washington the next day, Grant prepared to leave at once for a brief visit to the war's western theater for the purpose of organizing matters there.

Again in the words of Horace Porter: "While in Washington, General Grant had been so much an object of curiosity, and had been so continuously surrounded by admiring crowds when he appeared in the streets, and even in his hotel, that it had become very irksome to him. With his simplicity and total lack of personal vanity, he did not seem able to understand why he should attract so much attention. The President had given him a cordial invitation to dine that evening [the evening of the day he returned from Virginia] at the White House, but he begged to be excused for the reason that he would lose a whole day, which he could not afford at this critical period. 'Besides,' he added, 'I have become very tired of this show business.' "

An explanation of the general military situation at this time is given by Northern newsman William Swinton, who, ever as events developed, was formulating his *Campaigns of the Army of the Potomac*, which was to be published soon after the close of the war: "The elevation of General Grant to the lieutenant-generalship gave perfect satisfaction throughout the North—a sentiment arising not more from the conviction that it put the conduct of the war on a sound footing than from the high estimate held by the public of General Grant's military talent. The country had long ago awakened from its early dream of a coming 'Napoleon,' and there was no danger of its cherishing any such delusion respecting General Grant. But it saw in him a steadfast, pertinacious commander, one who faithfully represented the practical, patient, persevering genius of the North.

"As it was his happy fortune to reach the high office of general-in-chief at a time when the Administration and the people, instructed somewhat in war and war's needs, were prepared to give him an intelligent support, he was at once able, with all the resources of the country at his call, with a million men in the field, and a generous and patriotic people at his back, to enter upon a comprehensive system of combined operations. Moreover, the instrument with which he had to work was one highly tempered and brought to a fine and hard edge. The troops had become, by the experience of service, thoroughly inured to war. They could march, maneuver, and fight . . . and were . . . prepared to execute operations that at an earlier period would have been utterly impracticable.

"The lieutenant general was committed by the whole bent of his nature to vigorous action; and . . . he resolved upon a gigantic aggressive system that should embrace . . . the whole continental theater of war. His theory of action looked to . . . delivering a series of heavy and uninterrupted blows in the style of what the Duke of Wellington used to call 'hard pounding,' and of what General Grant . . . designated as 'continuous hammering.'

"The armed force of the Confederacy was at this time mainly included in the two great armies of [Joseph E.] Johnston and Lee—the former occupying an entrenched position at Dalton, Georgia, the latter ensconced within the lines of the Rapidan. These bodies were still almost as powerful in numbers as any the South had ever had in the field. Their intrinsic weakness lay in the fact that those reservoirs of strength from which armies must constantly draw to repair the never-ceasing waste of war were well-nigh exhausted; that the sustaining power of the Confederacy—the moral energy of the people—had so declined that what remained of the arms-bearing population in the South evaded rather than courted service in the field. Still, the existing armies presented a formidable and unabashed front, and by skilful conduct they might yet hope to do much.

"The immediate command of all the [Union] armies west of the Allegheny Mountains, and east of the Mississippi River, was committed to Major General W. T. Sherman, who was intrusted with the duty of acting against Johnston's force by a campaign having as its objective point Atlanta, the great railroad center of the middle zone. The lieutenant general [Grant] then established his headquarters with the Army of the Potomac, from where he designed to exercise general supervision of the movements of all the armies.

"This act was of itself a recognition of that primacy of interest and importance which belonged to that army. . . . General Grant saw that the task assigned the Army of the Potomac was no less momentous now than ever; for it still confronted, in Virginia, the foremost army of the Confederacy under the Confederacy's foremost military leader. After three years of colossal combat, that army . . . still continued to cover Richmond—a point which had been the first objective of the [Union] army's efforts, and which, though originally of no marked military importance, had come to acquire the kind of value that attaches to a national capital.

"Bearing on its bayonets the fate of the Confederacy, the Army of Northern Virginia stood erect and defiant, defending Richmond—threatening Washington. No man but knew that so long as it held the field, the Confederacy had lease on life. It was the *destruction* of this force that General Grant now undertook to accomplish. . . . He fixed his headquarters at Culpeper Court House during the last days of March, and sat down to study the difficult chessboard of Virginia."

The men of the Army of the Potomac, of course, found Grant's arrival a matter for busy speculation. Surprise at his physical appearance was the reaction of an unidentified private who saw the general for the first time in the company of several of his subordinates: "Of all the officers in the group . . . I should have selected almost anyone but him as the general who won Vicksburg. He was small and slim, even to undersize; very quiet, and with a slight stoop. But for his [starred] straps, which came down too far in front of his shoulders on his rusty uniform, I should have taken him for a clerk at headquarters rather than a general."

At first, according to Private Frank Wilkeson, a good part of the army viewed Grant's prospects with a certain skepticism: "Old soldiers who had seen many military reputations . . . melt before the battle fire of the Army of Northern Virginia . . . shrugged their shoulders carelessly, and said indifferently, 'Well, let Grant try what he can accomplish with the Army of the Potomac. He cannot be worse than his predecessors; and, if he is a fighter, he can find all the fighting he wants. We have never complained that Lee's men would not fight. . . . We welcome Grant. He cannot be weaker or more inefficient than the generals who have wasted the lives of our comrades during the past three years.'

". . . The enlisted men thoroughly discussed Grant's military capacity. Magazines, illustrated papers, and newspapers which contained accounts of his military achievements were sent for, and were eagerly and attentively read. I have seen an artillery private quickly sketch the water courses of the West in the sand with a pointed stick, and ridge up the earth with his hands to represent mountain chains, and then seize successive handfuls of earth and drop them in little piles to represent Forts Henry and Donelson, and Pittsburg Landing, Vicksburg, and Chattanooga. And then the enlisted men would gather around the sketch and take sides for and against Grant as the story of the battle was read aloud from a newspaper. These discussions were fruitless but combat-provoking, and frequently the wranglers adjourned to a secluded spot outside of the camp and fought it out with their fists. . . .

"With Grant came stricter discipline and recruits by the thousand. Throughout April there was great activity in all our camps along the Rapidan. . . . Many generals were sent to Washington for orders, and we saw no more of them. Staff officers constantly rode to and fro. Inspector-generals were busy. There was a . . . hum and bustle in all our camps. At all the railroad stations long trains of cars, filled with provisions and forage, were unloaded. White-capped wagons, loaded with hard bread and barrels of salted pork, rolled heavily into regimental and battery camps. We knew that battle was near."

As for Grant, his stock soon climbed. As explained by Augustus Buell, an enlisted man with the army's regular artillery: "His plain, unassuming appearance, his habit of going around among the camps frequently, and, above all, the rumors that he was occasionally subject to the besetting frailty of the soldier (injudicious drinking), all tended to popularize him with the men.

"There was also a different method of estimating the enemy in vogue. All through the early history of the Army of the Potomac the habit of its commanding officers was to exaggerate the strength of Lee's army . . . with a view, no doubt, to explain their frequent defeats or to excuse the butchery that resulted from their incompetency. But now all this was changed. We men in the ranks were informed that the Rebel army, though still strong no doubt, and very desperate, was inferior to us in numbers and equipment, and that we were expected to wind up its career that summer."

Newsman-historian Swinton says that Grant "adopted a kind of mixed plan of campaign, by which it was proposed to act with the main column on the overland route from the Rapidan to the James, but, at the same time, secure, by an independent force, some of the recognized advantages of a flank menace on the communications of Richmond. The latter operation was intrusted to General B. F. Butler, who, with an army of about thirty thousand men, was to ascend the James River from Fortress Monroe [at the mouth of the Chesapeake Bay], establish him-

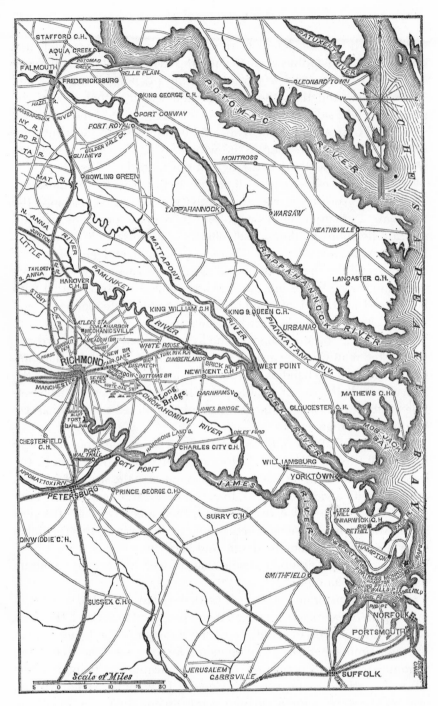

The waterways of the Chesapeake

self in an intrenched position near City Point, whence he was to operate against Richmond or its communications, or invest that city from the south side, or be in position to effect a junction with the Army of the Potomac coming down from the north. . . .

"General [Franz] Sigel, who held a considerable army for the protection of West Virginia and the frontiers of Maryland and Pennsylvania, was instructed to form his forces into two columns—the one . . . to move for the Kanawha [River] and operate against the Virginia and East Tennessee Railroad; the other . . . to advance as far [southward] as possible [in] the Shenandoah Valley, with the view to compel Lee to make detachments from his main force to meet this menace against his westward lines of supply.

"This was one of those combinations that are more specious in theory than successful in practice; for such outlying columns, moving against an enemy holding interior lines, are very liable to be beaten in detail, or, at least, to have their efforts neutralized and made of no avail.

"It is probable, however, that General Grant's main reliance was upon the Army of the Potomac. . . . At the time General Grant came to Virginia, it was reorganized into three corps—the Second, under Major General Winfield Scott Hancock; the Fifth, under Major General Gouverneur K. Warren; and the Sixth, under Major General John Sedgwick. The command of the army remained under General Meade, who had proved himself to be an excellent tactician.

"The three corps commanders were men of a high order of ability, though of very diverse types of character. Hancock may be characterized as the ideal of a soldier. Gifted with a magnetic presence and a superb personal gallantry, he was one of those lordly leaders who, upon the actual field of battle, rule the hearts of troops with a potent and irresistible mastery. Warren, young in the command of a corps, owed his promotion to the signal proofs of ability he had given, first as a brigadier, then as chief-engineer of the army, and latterly as the temporary commander of the Second Corps [while Hancock was recovering from a wound received at Gettysburg]. Of a subtle, analytical intellect, [Warren was] endowed with an eminent talent for details . . . and a fiery concentrated energy. . . . Sedgwick . . . was the exemplar of steadfast soldierly obedience to duty. Singularly gentle and child-like in character, he was . . . loved . . . throughout the army.

"A fit leader for the cavalry corps had long been wanting. This disideratum was fully filled by the appointment of Major General P. H. Sheridan. Although his experience had been confined to that of a divi-

Winfield S. Hancock

sional general of infantry in the West, enough was known of his character to justify the nomination."

Sheridan's train from the West reached Washington on April 4.
Horace Porter depicts the general, who was in his early thirties, as
"worn down almost to a shadow by hard work and exposure in the field.
He weighed only a hundred and fifteen pounds, and, as his height was
but five feet six inches, he looked anything but formidable as a candidate for a cavalry leader. He had met the President and the officials at
the War Department that day for the first time, and it was his appearance on this occasion which gave rise to a remark made to General
Grant the next time he visited the department, 'The officer you brought
in from the West is rather a little fellow to handle your cavalry.' To
which Grant replied, 'You will find him big enough for the purpose
before we get through with him.' "

Just before the campaign opened, the Army of the Potomac received a considerable reinforcement from Maryland. In the words of
Charles Carleton Coffin, field correspondent for the *Boston Journal:* "I
was in Washington on the last days of April [when] I heard the drum
beat and beheld a long column of troops passing down Pennsylvania
Avenue. Unheralded, the Ninth Corps [under General Ambrose E.
Burnside] had marched from Annapolis. The veteran regiments, which
had seen service in North Carolina and Tennessee, had full ranks once
more. There was a division of colored troops. It was an army of nearly
thirty thousand men. So well had General Grant kept his own counsel
that even General Burnside knew nothing positively as to his destination till the order came for him to break camp and make a rapid march
through Washington and join the Army of the Potomac."

Even while he was watching the troops pass, Coffin wrote in his
notebook: "The bright sunshine gleams from their bayonets. Above
them wave their standards, tattered by the winds, torn by cannon ball
and rifle shot, stained by the blood of dying heroes. . . . I see upon those
banners as they flutter in the breeze, 'Bull Run, Ball's Bluff, Roanoke,
Newbern, Gainesville, Mechanicsville, Seven Pines, Savage's Station,
Malvern Hill, Fredericksburg, Chancellorsville, Antietam, South Mountain, Knoxville, Vicksburg, Port Hudson, Gettysburg.' All those names
are there in golden letters, and others so torn and defaced that I cannot
read them.

"The streets are lined with men, women, and children. The grave
Senators have left their chambers, and the members of the House of
Representatives have taken a recess to gaze upon the defenders of their

Philip H. Sheridan

country . . . as they pass through the city—many of them, alas, never to return. There is the steady tramping of the thousands, the deep, heavy jar of the gun carriages on the pavement, the clattering of hoofs, the clanking of sabers, the drumbeat, the bugle call, and the music of the military bands.

"Pavement, sidewalk, windows, and roofs are occupied by the people. Upon the balcony of [a] hotel is their corps commander, General Burnside, and by his side the President of the United States, pale, careworn, returning the salutes of the officers and acknowledging those of the soldiers.

"A division of veterans pass. [Next in line], with full ranks, platoons extending from sidewalk to sidewalk, are brigades [of blacks] which never have been in battle. But, at the call of their country, they are going forth to crush the rebellion. *Their country!* They never had a country till the tall man on the balcony . . . gave them one. For the first time they behold their benefactor. They are darker hued than their veteran comrades who have gone before, but they can cheer as heartily as they. 'Hurrah for Uncle Abe! Hurrah for Massa Linkun! Three cheers for the President! Hurrah, hurrah, hurrah!' There is a swinging of caps, a clapping of hands, a waving of handkerchiefs and banners. There are no cheers more lusty than those given by the redeemed sons of Africa. There are no responses more hearty than those in return from the admiring multitude. Regiment after regiment of stalwart men, slaves once, but freemen now, with steady step, closed-up file, and even rank, pass down the street, moving on to Old Virginia."

Although Culpeper was Grant's center of operations, he made frequent trips to Washington. Horace Porter (who was now serving as a full-time aide to the general and bore the rank of lieutenant colonel) reveals that Grant's final visit to the capital almost had a very unhappy ending: "On his return . . . when his special train reached Warrenton Junction, he saw a large cloud of dust to the east of the road. Upon making inquiries of the station master as to its cause, he learned that Colonel Mosby [the Confederate cavalry leader] . . . had just passed, driving a detachment of our cavalry before him.

"If the train had been a few minutes earlier, Mosby, like Christopher Columbus upon his voyage to this country, would have discovered something which he was not looking for. As the train carried no guard, it would not have been possible to make any defense. In such case the Union commander would have reached Richmond a year sooner than he finally arrived there, but not at the head of an army."

Grant's wife, Julia, was with him at Culpeper, and, according to newsman-biographer Albert Richardson, it was about this time that "a party of ladies asked Mrs. Grant's opinion of her husband's new responsibilities and prospects. 'Mr. Grant has succeeded thus far,' she answered, 'wherever the Government has placed him; and he will do the best he can.' 'Do you think he will capture Richmond?' 'Yes, before he gets through. Mr. Grant always was a very obstinate man.'"

Narrator Richardson goes on to give another bit: "To take the rebel capital—that had been the supreme desire of three blood-stained years. A gentleman, wishing to enter the enemy's lines on business, asked the President for a pass to Richmond. 'I should be glad to oblige you,' replied Father Abraham, 'but my permits are not respected. I have given a quarter of a million men passes to Richmond, and not one has ever got there, except as a prisoner of war.'"

The final preparations for the campaign included the pageantry of reviews. As recalled by George Stevens, the surgeon from New York: "Our corps [the Sixth, under John Sedgwick] was reviewed by General Grant; by [a] Russian admiral and suite, who, for the amusement of the soldiers, performed some most ludicrous feats in horsemanship; and by a body of English officers. Never had such general good health prevailed among our camps, and never were the men so well contented or in such good spirits."

On May 1 the fragments of the army that lay to the north of the main encampments were drawn in. Among these units was the brigade to which Private Theodore Gerrish belonged. "It was an inspiring scene at Rappahannock Station . . . when we broke camp and marched forth to enter upon the spring campaign. Several regiments had been added to our brigade, which was commanded by General [Joseph J.] Bartlett. Our division was under the command of General [Charles] Griffin, while General Warren commanded the corps. It was a beautiful morning. . . . The sun shone warm and bright from the soft blue sky, the air was warm and balmy, the birds were singing their sweetest songs. . . . Man, who prides himself as being the noblest work of the Creator, was the only being that seemed to be out of harmony. . . . He was preparing for strife and sorrow.

"On every hand were indications of the bloody struggle about to open. Bands were playing warlike music; the shrill, keen notes of the bugles were ringing out over the hillsides and down through the meadows; long lines of soldiers were forming the ranks of war; banners were waving, and soldiers cheering as the general officers rode along the lines.

"Our brigade . . . marched to a camping ground east of Brandy Station, where the Fifth Corps, now composed of thirty thousand men, was being concentrated. . . . Our men were anxious for the campaign to open, hoping it would be the last one of the war."

5

A Lion at Bay

General Lee, of course, had been keeping abreast of the developments north of the Rapidan. As early as April 6 he wrote President Jefferson Davis in Richmond: "All the information I receive tends to show that the greatest effort of the enemy in this campaign will be made in Virginia. . . . Reinforcements are certainly daily arriving to the Army of the Potomac. . . . The tone of the Northern papers, as well as the impression prevailing in their armies [known to Lee through spies and Union deserters], go to show that Grant with a large force is to move against Richmond."

Lee's biggest concern as the campaign drew near was pointed up in a letter he wrote Davis on April 12: "My anxiety on the subject of provisions for the army is so great that I cannot refrain from expressing it to Your Excellency. I cannot see how we can operate with our present supplies. Any derangement in their arrival, or disaster to the railroad, would render it impossible for me to keep the army together. . . . There is nothing to be had in this section for men or animals. We have rations for the troops today and tomorrow. I hope a new supply arrived last night, but I have yet had no report. Every exertion should be made to supply the depots at Richmond and at other points. All pleasure travel [by train] should cease, and everything be devoted to necessary wants."

In a private letter, Lee wrote: "The indications at present are that we shall have a hard struggle. General Grant is with the Army of the Potomac. All the officers' wives, sick, etc., have been sent to Washington. No ingress into, or egress from the lines is now permitted, and no papers [i.e., Northern newspapers and news sheets printed in camp] are allowed to come out."

Jefferson Davis

The month of April was a time of unease and apprehension among the people of Richmond. Mrs. Sarah A. "Sallie" Putnam, an acute observer and a skillful chronicler, gives this picture: "Friend looked into the face of friend to read a tale of anxiety and sorrow, while sighs usurped the place of smiles. . . . Ever busy Rumor circulated stories . . . in the Confederate Capital, and . . . we heard the ominous word, 'Evacuation!' It was reported that the government had appropriated a sum for the removal of the noncombatants from the city in order to allow a more thorough opportunity for its defense in the event of assault. . . .

"Every day the teeming population of women and children and the infirm and aged expected to be sent forth as wanderers, they knew not whither, over the wasted territory of the Southern Confederacy.

"In a few days, corrected reports and satisfactory explanations sufficed to silence these rumors and to restore confidence. Yet nought could lift from our hearts the heavy gloom of impending terror in the immense preparations made by the enemy for our destruction. The monster 'Anaconda' [i.e., the constricting snake chosen to symbolize a Northern plan for surrounding the South by land and sea], of which we had been hearing from the commencement of the war, which was to crush us in its fatal coil, was reported by our enemies to be in a fair way to have his 'tail in his mouth.' Once surrounded in his murderous embrace, there was little chance for our freedom. . . .

"But we listened to these ominous warnings as we listened to the whisperings of the wind. They came from the North to dampen our ardor, to discourage our fortitude, to dismay our souls, but they failed of effect. Defeat was nowhere written on our future prospects. Discouragement might be, but defeat nowhere! And we once more hugged to our bosoms the phantom of hope, and it sang a lullaby to our fears, and the Confederate metropolis pursued its usual busy routine and contented itself with the thought that 'the end is not.' But the bright genial airs of spring, the perfume of the flowers, the carolling of the feathered musicians, awoke in our hearts little feeling of pleasure."

City resident Judith McGuire appraised the situation in her diary. "April 25: The enemy threatens Richmond, and is coming against it with an immense army. They boast that they can and will have it this summer; but, with the help of God, we hope to drive them back again. Our Government is making every effort to defeat them. I don't think that anyone doubts our ability to do it; but the awful loss of life necessary upon the fights is what we dread. April 27: Another day and night have passed, and nothing of importance has occurred to the country. We are expecting movements in every direction. O God! Direct our leaders. . . . April 29: The country seems to continue quiet, but the campaign on the Rapidan is expected to open every day. Oh, how I dread it! The morning is bright and beautiful. It seems hardly possible that such strife is abroad in the land."

Adjunctive to the strife, and affecting the people of the South and the North alike, were the usual personal crises and tragedies that plague mankind in all seasons, in wartime and peacetime. These ills tend to be hardest on persons in positions of leadership, who must somehow rise above their anguish in favor of their public duties. Early in the war, Abraham Lincoln and his wife, Mary, had been staggered by the loss of a young son to illness; and now it was the lot of Jefferson and Varina Davis to lose a child through an accident, the tragedy occurring in the presidential mansion. Varina tells the story:

"On April 30, when we were threatened on every side, and encompassed so perfectly that we could only hope by a miracle to overcome our foes, Mr. Davis's health declined from loss of sleep so that he forgot to eat, and I resumed the practice of carrying him something at one o'clock [in the afternoon]. I left my children quite well, playing in my room, and had just uncovered my basket in his office when a servant came for me. The most beautiful and brightest of my children, Joseph Emory, had, in play, climbed over the connecting angle of a bannister and fallen to the brick pavement below. He died a few minutes after we reached his side.

"This child was Mr. Davis's hope, and greatest joy in life. At intervals, he ejaculated, 'Not mine, oh, Lord, but thine.' A courier came with a dispatch [related to military affairs]. He took it, held it open for some moments, and looked at me fixedly. . . . I saw his mind was momentarily paralyzed by the blow, but at last he tried to write an answer, and then called out, in a heartbroken tone, 'I must have this day with my little child!' Somebody took the dispatch to [a subordinate] and left us alone with our dead."

Along the line of the Rapidan, with his headquarters near Orange Court House, General Lee concluded his preparations for the campaign. His army comprised three corps, the First under James Longstreet, the Second under Richard S. Ewell, and the Third under Ambrose P. Hill. The cavalry was headed by James Ewell Brown Stuart. All four commanders were veterans of many actions.

James Longstreet, whom Lee called his "old war horse," was big, strong-limbed, and full-bearded, and he possessed a confidence that led him to believe he was at least Lee's equal, and perhaps his superior, as a strategist, which was not the case. He did, however, have a sound preconception of the forthcoming campaign, as illustrated by a conversation he had with an officer who believed that Grant would be easy to defeat. Longstreet asked, "Do you know Grant?" Upon getting a negative reply, he said, "Well, I do. I was in the corps of cadets with him at West Point for three years, I was present at his wedding, I served in the same army with him in Mexico, I have observed his methods of warfare in the West, and I believe I know him through and through; and I tell you that we cannot afford to underrate him and the army he now commands. We must make up our minds to get into line of battle and to stay there; for that man will fight us every day and every hour till the end of this war."

Richard Ewell was oddly birdlike in appearance, having a jutting nose, a bald head, and an animated manner that had survived his loss of a leg at Groveton in 1862 and a resulting decline in his health. A. P. Hill, though he too had health concerns, was a leader of signal magnetism and popularity. Both Ewell and Hill had been dazzling fighters early in the war, but had lost much of their original fire. Their low vitality was probably only part of the problem. It is likely their faith in victory had waned. Jeb Stuart, the South's "gay cavalier," had lost some of his luster after his questionable performance in the critical Gettysburg Campaign; but, thanks to his early exploits and his colorful style, he had become a legendary figure and was admired even in the North.

James Longstreet's corps was not with Lee's main encampments along the line of the Rapidan, but in the Gordonsville area, about ten miles farther south. As April closed, Lee set aside a day for a formal visit to the isolated forces. According to D. Augustus Dickert, a junior officer with Joseph P. Kershaw's division of Longstreet's corps, the announcement that the troops were to be reviewed precipitated a flurry of preparations. "Everything possible that could add to our looks and appearances was done to make an acceptable display before our commander in chief. Guns were burnished and rubbed up, cartridge boxes and belts polished, and the brass buttons and buckles made to look as bright as new. Our clothes were patched and brushed up, so far as was in our power, boots and shoes greased, the tattered and torn old hats were given here and there 'a lick and a promise,' and on the whole I must say we presented not a bad-looking body of soldiers.

"Out a mile or two was a very large old field of perhaps one hundred

James Longstreet

Richard S. Ewell

acres or more, in which we formed in double columns. The artillery stationed on the flank fired thirteen guns, the salute to the commander in chief, and as the old warrior rode out into the opening, shouts went up that fairly shook the earth. Hats and caps flew high in the air, flags dipped and waved to and fro, while the drums and fifes struck up 'Hail to the Chief.' General Lee lifted his hat modestly from his head in recognition of the honor done him, and we knew the old commander's heart swelled with emotion at this outburst of enthusiasm . . . on his appearance. If he had any doubts before as to the loyalty of his troops, this old 'Rebel yell' must have soon dispelled them.

"After taking his position near the center of the columns, the command was broken in columns of companies and marched by him, each giving a salute as it passed. It took several hours to pass in review, Kershaw leading with his division, [Micah] Jenkins following. The line was again formed, when General Lee and staff, with Longstreet and his staff, rode around the troops and gave them critical inspection. No doubt Lee was then thinking of the bloody day that was soon to come, and how well these brave, battle-scarred veterans would sustain the proud prestige they had won.

"Returning to our camp, we were put . . . in active fighting trim, and the troops closely kept in camp. All were now expecting every moment the summons to the battlefield. . . . The two military giants of the nineteenth century were about to face each other and put to the test the talents, tactics, and courage of their respective antagonists. Both had been successful beyond all precedent, and both considered themselves invincible in the field. Grant had . . . tenacity, with an overwhelming army behind him. Lee had talent, impetuosity, and boldness, with an army of patriots at his command who had [seldom] known defeat, and considered themselves superior in courage and endurance to any body of men on earth.

"Well might the clash of arms . . . of these mighty giants cause the civilized world to watch and wonder. Lee stood like a lion in the path— his capital behind him, his army at bay—while Grant, with equal pugnacity, sought to crush him by sheer force of overwhelming numbers."

Adds one of Longstreet's brigade commanders, General E. M. Law: "On the second of May, 1864, a group of officers stood at the Confederate signal station on Clark's Mountain, Virginia, south of the Rapidan, and examined closely through their fieldglasses the position of the Federal army then lying north of the river in Culpeper County. The central figure of the group was the commander of the Army of Northern Virginia, who had requested his corps and division commanders to meet him there. Though some demonstrations had been made in the direction of the upper fords, General Lee expressed the opinion that the Federal army would cross the river at Germanna or Ely's."

6

Pontoons across the Rapidan

During the afternoon of May 3, mounted couriers from Grant's headquarters circulated among the Union camps presenting the high commanders with sealed packets: orders for a general movement of the army. As recalled by Frank Wilkeson, the artillery private: "[In] the evening . . . we fell in for dress parade. Up and down the immense camp we could see regiment after regiment, battery after battery, fall into line. The bugles rang out clearly in the soft spring air, distant drums beat, and trumpets blared. Then there was silence most profound.

"We listened attentively to the orders to march. To the right, to the left, in the distance before us, and far behind us, cheers arose. Battery after battery, regiment after regiment, cheered until the men were hoarse. My comrades did not cheer. They seemed to be profoundly impressed, but not in the least elated.

"The wonted silence of the evening was repeatedly broken by the resounding shouts of distant troops who could not contain their joy that the season of inactivity was over, and the campaign, which we all hoped would be short and decisive, was opened. . . . Many unwonted fires burned, and we knew that the veteran troops were destroying the camp equipage which they did not intend to carry."

Narrator Wilkeson himself was not a veteran campaigner, and therefore became a subject for counsel. "Jellet, the gunner of the piece I served on, came to me that evening and kindly looked into my knapsack, and advised me as to what to keep and what to throw away. He cut my kit down to a change of underclothing, three pairs of socks, a pair of spare shoes, three plugs of navy tobacco, a rubber blanket, and a pair of woolen blankets.

" 'Now, my lad,' Jellet said, 'do not pick up anything excepting food and tobacco, while you are on the march. Get hold of all the food you can. Cut haversacks from dead men. Steal from the infantry if you can. Let your aim be to secure food and food and still more food, and keep your eyes open for tobacco. Do not look at clothing or shoes or blankets. You can always draw those articles from the quartermaster. Stick to your gun [i.e., artillery piece] through thick and thin. Do not straggle. Fill your canteen at every stream we cross and wherever you get a chance elsewhere. Never wash your feet until the day's march is over. If you do, they will surely blister.' "

The great movement began that night. Union newsman Charles Carleton Coffin was on the scene. "There was no drumbeat, but a quiet mustering of troops, a folding of tents, and then the column of men and long lines of white-topped wagons disappeared, moving southeast towards the fords of the Rapidan [ten or fifteen miles distant]. The cavalry, under Sheridan, were in the advance, then a long train of wagons and pontoons—the Engineer Corps, hastening to Germanna Ford, where they quickly constructed two bridges of boats, and two more at Ely's, and one at Culpeper Mine. . . . The most difficult part of Grant's plan was the movement of the four thousand wagons. A wagon train, at best, cannot get on very fast. An obstinate mule, the breaking of a trace or strap, stops the whole train. The trains must be protected by the troops."

By midnight the march was well under way. There was a good deal of enthusiasm and jocularity in the ranks, but, according to Warren Goss, the private from Massachusetts, the spirit of some of the men of longest service "had been tempered and modified . . . by many weary marches, many a terrible battle and humiliating defeat. Their thoughts were moulded by former experiences. Did their footsteps tend to victory or defeat? Would [events] give them mutilation, unknown graves, or honors and a safe return to happy homes? A careless indifference, outwardly, with an undercurrent of saddened forebodings often accompany the intelligent veteran soldier when starting out for the uncertain adventures of the battlefield."

It wasn't long before many of the men who were plodding through the starlit night found their loads becoming heavy. "The beginning of this campaign," explains Captain Henry Blake, "was like all those which had preceded it; and thousands of overcoats and blankets were scattered in the woods and fields through which the soldiers passed."

Grant remained at his Culpeper headquarters during the first phase

Union supply wagons

of the march, and some of the army's newsmen also lingered in the area. "There was little sleep that night," observes William Swinton, "for during all its hours the air was filled with the tramp of armed men and the rumble of wagons—and indeed the anticipations of the morrow were too exciting to permit slumber."

As related by Grant's aide, Horace Porter: "The night of May 3 will always be memorable in the recollection of those who assembled in the little front room of the house occupied as headquarters at Culpeper. The eight senior members of the staff seated themselves . . . about their chief to receive their final instructions, and participated in an intensely interesting discussion of the grand campaign, which was to begin next morning with all its hopes, its uncertainties, and its horrors.

"Sherman had been instructed to strike Joseph E. Johnston's army in northwest Georgia, and make his way to Atlanta. [Nathaniel P.] Banks was to advance up the Red River [in Louisiana] and capture Shreveport. Sigel was ordered to make an expedition down the valley of Virginia [i.e., to march southward in the Shenandoah] and endeavor to destroy a portion of the East Tennessee, Virginia, and Georgia Railroad. His movement was expected to keep Lee from withdrawing troops from the valley and reinforcing his principal army. . . . Butler was directed to move up the James River and endeavor to secure Petersburg and the railways leading into it, and, if opportunity offered, to seize Richmond itself. Burnside, with the Ninth Corps, which had been moved from Annapolis into Virginia, was to support the Army of the Potomac. The subsequent movements of all the forces operating in Virginia were to depend largely upon the result of the first battle between the Army of the Potomac and the Army of Northern Virginia. . . .

"The general sat for some time preparing a few final instructions in writing. After he had finished, he turned his back to the table, crossed one leg over the other, lighted a fresh cigar, and began to talk of the momentous movement which in a few hours was to begin. He said, 'I weighed very carefully the advantages and disadvantages of moving against Lee's left and moving against his right. The former promised more decisive results if immediately successful, and would best prevent Lee from moving north to make raids, but it would deprive our army of the advantages of easy communication with a water base of supplies [i.e., the Potomac River and Chesapeake Bay], and compel us to carry such a large amount of ammunition and rations in wagon trains, and detach so many troops as train guards, that I found it presented too many serious difficulties; and when I considered especially the sufferings of the wounded in being transported long distances overland, instead of being carried by short routes to water, where they could be comfortably moved by boats, I had no longer any hesitation in deciding to cross the Rapidan below the position occupied by Lee's army, and move by our left. This plan will also enable us to cooperate better with Butler's forces, and not become separated too far from them. I shall not give my attention so much to Richmond as to Lee's army. . . .'

"To use Grant's own language to Meade [who, it will be recalled, had been retained in his position as commander of the Army of the Potomac], 'Wherever Lee goes, there you will go also.' He of course thought it likely that Lee would fall back upon Richmond in case of defeat, and place himself behind its fortifications, for he said to Meade in his instructions to him, 'Should a siege of Richmond become necessary, ammunition and equipments can be got from the arsenals at Washington and Fort Monroe.' And during the discussion that evening he rose from his seat, stepped up to a map hanging upon the wall, and with a sweep of his forefinger indicated a line around Richmond and Petersburg [i.e., a semicircle east of these places] and remarked, 'When my troops are there, Richmond is mine. Lee must retreat or surrender.'

". . . He said he would locate his headquarters near those of Meade, and communicate his instructions through that officer, and through Burnside, whose command at this time was independent of the Army of the Potomac; but that emergencies might arise in which he himself would have to give immediate direction to troops when actually engaged in battle. . . . His calm confidence communicated itself to all who listened to him, and inspired them with a feeling akin to that of their chief.

"The discussion did not end till long past midnight. As usual on the eve of battle, before the general retired he wrote a letter to Mrs. Grant. . . . The letters . . . always contained words of cheer and comfort, expressed an abiding faith in victory, and never failed to dwell upon the sad thought which always oppressed him when he realized that many human lives would have to be sacrificed, and great sufferings would have to be endured by the wounded. The general's letters to his wife were very frequent during a campaign, and no pressure of official duties was ever permitted to interrupt this correspondence. . . .

"The Army of the Potomac . . . [plus] Burnside's separate command . . . numbered in all about 116,000 present for duty, equipped.

George G. Meade

Julia Dent Grant, the general's wife

The Army of Northern Virginia consisted of . . . about 70,000 present for duty, equipped. . . .

"Those familiar with military operations and unprejudiced in their opinion, will concede that, notwithstanding Lee's inferiority in numbers, the advantages were, nevertheless, in his favor in the approaching campaign. Having interior lines, he was able to move by shorter marches and to act constantly on the defensive at a period of the war when troops had learned to intrench themselves with marvelous rapidity, and force the invading army continually to assault fortified positions.

"The task to be performed by the Union forces was that of conducting a moving siege. The field of operations, with its numerous rivers and creeks difficult of approach, its lack of practicable roads, its dense forests, its impassable swamps, and its trying summer climate, debilitating to Northern troops, seemed specially designed by nature for purposes of defense. Lee and his officers were familiar with every foot of the ground, and every inhabitant was eager to give them information. His army was in friendly country . . . and few troops had to be detached to guard lines of supply.

"The Union army, on the contrary, was unfamiliar with the country, was without accurate maps, could seldom secure trustworthy guides, and had to detach large bodies of troops from the main command to guard its long lines of communication, protect its supply trains, and conduct the wounded to points of safety. . . .

"Since Lee had taken command [in 1862] he had not lost a single battle fought in the State of Virginia, and the prestige of success had an effect upon his troops the importance of which cannot easily be overestimated. His men were made to feel that they were fighting for their homes and firesides. The pulpit, the press, and the women were making superhuman efforts to 'fire the Southern heart.' Disasters were concealed, temporary advantages were magnified into triumphant victories, and crushing defeats were hailed as blessings in disguise.

"In the North there was a divided press, with much carping criticism on the part of journals opposed to the war, which was fitted to discourage the troops and destroy their confidence in their leaders. There were hosts of Southern sympathizers, constituting a foe in the rear, whose threats and overt acts often necessitated the withdrawal of troops from the front to hold them in check. In all the circumstances, no just military critic will claim that the advantage was on the side of the Union army merely because it was numerically larger.

"The campaign in Virginia was to begin by throwing the Army of the Potomac with all celerity to the south side of the Rapidan, below Lee's position. . . .

"At 8 A.M. the general-in-chief, with his staff, started from headquarters and set out for Germanna Ford, following Warren's troops. He was mounted on his bay horse 'Cincinnati,' equipped with a saddle of the Grimsley pattern, which was somewhat the worse for wear, as the general had used it in all his campaigns from Donelson to the present time. . . . Grant was dressed in a uniform coat and waistcoat, the coat being unbuttoned. On his hands were a pair of yellowish-brown thread gloves. He wore a pair of plain top-boots reaching to his knees, and was equipped with a regulation sword, spurs, and sash. On his head was a slouch hat of black felt with a plain gold cord around it. His orderly carried strapped behind his saddle the general's overcoat, which was that of a private soldier of cavalry.

"A sun as bright as the 'sun of Austerlitz' [where Napoleon fought the Russian and Austrian armies in 1805] shone down upon the scene. Its light brought out in vivid colors the beauties of the landscape which lay before us, and its rays were reflected with dazzling brilliancy from the brass field-pieces and the white covers of the wagons as they rolled lazily along in the distance. The crisp, bracing air seemed to impart to all a sense of exhilaration. As far as the eye could reach, the troops were wending their way to the front [i.e., toward the Rapidan]. Their war banners, bullet-riddled and battle-stained, floated proudly in the morning breeze. The roads resounded to the measured tread of the advancing columns, and the deep forests were lighted by the glitter of their steel.

"The quick, elastic step and easy, swinging gait of the men, the cheery look upon their faces, and the lusty shouts with which they greeted their new commander as he passed, gave proof of the temper of their metal and the superb spirit which animated their hearts. If the general's nature had been as emotional as that of Napoleon, he might have been moved to utter the words of the French emperor as his troops filed past him in moving to the field of Waterloo, 'Magnificent! Magnificent!' But as General Grant was neither demonstrative nor communicative, he gave no expression whatever to his feelings."

The light artillery unit to which Private Frank Wilkeson belonged made the march just behind the German regiment that Wilkeson had found so fascinating a study during the long encampment. "We light artillerymen laughed to see the burdens these sturdy men had on their backs. All of the enlisted men of that regiment had one knap-sack . . . and many of them had two. . . . We were in high spirits. Indeed, we were frisky, and walked along gayly. The men talked of the coming battle, and they sang songs about the soul of John Brown, alleged to be marching on, [and] songs indicative of a desire to hang Jeff Davis to a sour apple tree. The Germans were, as usual, full of song and exceedingly noisy. . . .

"We marched toward Ely's Ford. . . . As we drew near it, we saw that the troops were beginning to jam around its approaches. They were being massed quicker than they could cross. We halted at a short dis-tance from the ford and impatiently waited for our turn to cross. . . . I noticed that the Germans in our front were sitting on their knapsacks engaged in mopping their faces with red handkerchiefs. And I also noticed that as the sun swung higher and higher toward the zenith their songs retired within their hairy throats. I mentioned these, to me, interesting facts to Jellet, and he tapped his nose significantly with his index finger and said, 'Wait a bit. We will lay in provisions from those fellows soon.'

". . . We crossed the Rapidan on a pontoon bridge, and filled our canteens and drank deeply as we crossed. Then we marched over a narrow strip of valley land. Then came a long, steep hill that led up to the comparatively level tableland of the Wilderness. This was the hill that caused the Germans to part with their personal property. Spare knapsacks, bursting with richness, were cast aside near its base. Blan-kets, musical instruments, spare boots, and innumerable articles of doubtful utility outcropped about halfway up the hill. . . . Near the top of the hill we found many well-filled haversacks, and we picked up every one of them and hung them on the limbers and caissons and guns. The mine was rich, and we worked it thoroughly. . . .

"On the upland we marched briskly. I saw no inhabitants in this region. They had fled before our advance, abandoning their homes. The soil was poor and thin, and the fields were covered with last year's dead grass, and this grass was burning as we passed by. I saw the burning grass [set fire to] fences and sweep into the woods, and I wondered, as tiny whirlwinds formed and carried revolving columns of sparks through the battery, if the caissons and limber chests were spark-tight. As none of the men seemed to be in the least alarmed at the near presence of fire, I ceased to worry, willing to take my chances if an explosion occurred."

It was a little before noon, according to Horace Porter, when Grant

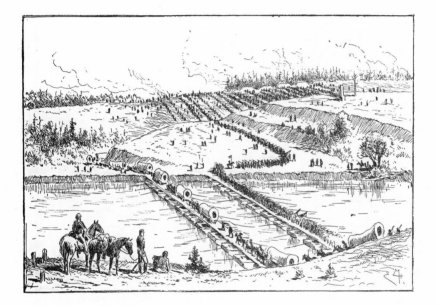

Federals crossing the Rapidan on pontoons

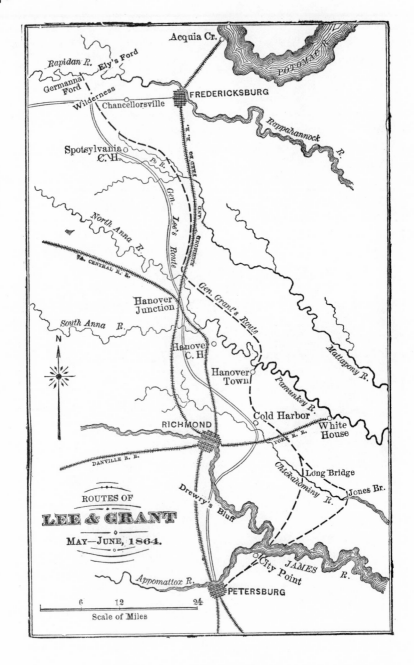

Acquia Cr.

Rapidan R. Ely's Ford

Germanna Ford

Wilderness

Chancellorsville

POTOMAC R.

FREDERICKSBURG

Rappahannock R.

Spotsylvania C. H.

Fo. R.

Gen. Lee's Route

North Anna R.

CENTRAL R. R.

Gen. Grant's Route

South Anna R.

Hanover Junction

Hanover C. H.

Hanover Town

Mattapony R.

Pamunkey R.

N

RICHMOND

Cold Harbor

White House

York R. R.

DANVILLE R. R.

Long Bridge

Chickahominy R.

Jones Br.

ROUTES OF

LEE & GRANT

MAY—JUNE, 1864.

Drewry's Bluff

JAMES R.

City Point

Appomattox R.

PETERSBURG

6   12   24

Scale of Miles

"crossed one of the pontoon bridges at Germanna Ford to the south side of the Rapidan, rode to the top of the bluff overlooking the river, and there dismounted and established temporary headquarters at an old farmhouse with Dutch gables and porch in front. It was rather dilapidated in appearance, and looked as if it had been deserted for some time. The only furniture it contained was a table and two chairs. Meade's headquarters were located close by.

"General Grant sat down on the steps of the house, lighted a cigar, and remained silent for some time, quietly watching Sedgwick's men passing over the bridge. After a while he said, 'Well, the movement so far has been as satisfactory as could be desired. We have succeeded in seizing the fords and crossing the river without loss or delay. Lee must by this time know upon what roads we are advancing, but he may not yet realize the full extent of the movement. We shall probably soon get some indications as to what he intends to do.'

"A representative of a newspaper . . . now stepped up to him and said, 'General Grant, about how long will it take you to get to Richmond?' The general replied at once, 'I will agree to be there in about four days—that is, if General Lee becomes a party to the agreement. But if he objects, the trip will undoubtedly be prolonged.' "

7

Lee Accepts the Challenge

As pointed out by Confederate General John Gordon: "This advance by General Grant inaugurated the seventh act in the 'On to Richmond' drama played by the armies of the Union. The first advance, led by General McDowell, had been repelled by Beauregard and Johnston at Bull Run; the next five, under the leadership respectively of McClellan, Pope, Burnside, Hooker, and Meade, had been repelled by Lee."

The Confederate chief did not hesitate to meet the new challenge. As explained by brigade commander E. M. Law: "When the Federal army was known to be in motion, General Lee prepared to move [eastward] upon its flank with his whole force as soon as his opponent should clear the river and begin the march southward. The route selected by General Grant led entirely around the right of Lee's position. . . . Grant's passage of the Rapidan was unopposed. . . . Two roads lead from Orange Court House [where Lee was headquartered] down the Rapidan. . . . They follow the general direction of the river, and are almost parallel to each other, the [Orange] Turnpike nearest the river, and the [Orange] Plank Road a short distance south of it. [See map "The regions of the Rapidan" on page 5.] The route of the Federal army lay directly across these two roads, along the western border of the famous Wilderness."

Robert Stiles, the Confederate artillery officer, makes this assessment: "Lee's ready acceptance of the gage of battle flung down by Grant . . . while it appeared to be the height of reckless audacity, was really the dictate of the wisest and most balanced prudence. In such a country, the advantage of Grant's overwhelming preponderance of numbers was reduced to a minimum, and his great parks of artillery were absolutely useless. [Actually, not "absolutely" but "very nearly" useless.] Besides, to retire and fall back upon an inner line [one nearer Richmond] was just what Grant desired and expected Lee to do, and would have been in exact furtherance of Grant's plans. In this instance, as usual, Lee's audacity meant the exercise of his unerring military instinct and judgment."

In the words of J. F. J. Caldwell, the lieutenant from South Carolina: "On the 4th of May . . . about eleven o'clock in the morning, we received orders to cook rations immediately and prepare for the march. We at once set to work, but before half the bread could be baked the command was given to fall in. A universal stir ensued. . . . The officers' tents were torn down. . . . Knapsacks were packed, blankets rolled up, half-cooked dough or raw meal thrust into haversacks, the accumulated plunder of nine months thrown into the streets, accoutrements girded on, arms taken, and in half an hour we were on the march."

The accoutrements of most of the marchers were remarkably light, as one of them ventures to explain: "The blanket, rolled lengthwise, the ends brought together and strapped, hung from left shoulder across under right arm. The haversack—furnished with towel, soap, comb, knife and fork in various pockets, a change of underclothes in the main division, and whatever rations we happened to have in the other—hung on the left hip. The canteen, cup, and plate, tied together, hung on the right. Toothbrush . . . [was] stuck in two buttonholes of jacket or in haversack, tobacco bag hung to a breast button, pipe in pocket. In this rig, into which a fellow could get in just two minutes from a state of rest, the Confederate soldier considered himself all right and all ready for anything. In this he marched, and in this he fought. Like the terrapin, 'all he had he carried on his back.' And this 'all' weighed about seven or eight pounds."

The mood of the troops at this time is analyzed by Robert Stiles, who makes his point by using the retrospections of a friend, "Billy," who returned from a furlough just before the movement began, and could therefore view the army with a certain objectivity. "His recollection is that he was deeply impressed with the change. . . . He did not detect any depression, or apprehension of disaster, or weakness of pluck or purpose; but he says he did miss the bounding buoyant spirit, the effervescent outbursts, the quips, the jests, the jokes, the jollities, such as had usually characterized the first spring rousings of the army and the first meetings and minglings of the different commands as they shouted their tumultuous way to battle.

"He says that there seems to have sifted through the ranks the conviction that the struggle ahead of us was of a different character from any we had experienced in the past—a sort of premonition of the definite mathematical calculation in whose hard, unyielding grip it was intended our future should be held and crushed. . . . I am inclined to think . . . that Billy is right—that in the spring of 1864 there was very generally diffused throughout the army a more or less definite realization or consciousness that a new stage in the contest had been reached and a new theory broached: the mathematical theory that if one army outnumbers another . . . and the larger can be indefinitely reinforced and the smaller not at all, then if the stronger side will but make up its mind to stand all the killing the weaker can do, and will keep it so made up, there can be but one result.

"Billy says the realization of this new order of things did not affect the resolution of the men, but that it did affect their spirits. I can only say I believe he is exactly correct."

Early afternoon of May 4 found Ewell's Second Corps marching eastward by way of the Turnpike, while A. P. Hill's Third Corps traveled a parallel course on the Plank Road. The columns were preceded by elements of Jeb Stuart's cavalry. Orders had been sent to Longstreet to bring his First Corps up from the southwest and join the movement. Longstreet was fortunate in securing as a guide one James Robinson, a former Orange County sheriff who had spent much of his life in the Wilderness.

The Union army, meanwhile, was still in the process of crossing the Rapidan. Newsman-historian William Swinton says that "the scene . . . throughout all the afternoon . . . was wonderfully imposing—the long columns winding down to the river's brink, traversing the bridges, and then spreading out in massive array over the hill slopes and subjacent valleys of the south bank. Before the afternoon was spent the whole army was across, and the heads of the columns, plunging into the depth of the forest, were lost to view. Hancock pushed out to Chancellorsville, . . . Warren advanced southward by the Stevensburg Plank Road . . . to Old Wilderness Tavern. Sedgwick remained close to the river. Burnside had orders to hold Culpeper Court House [north of the Rapidan] for twenty-four hours, and then follow in the path of the other corps."

Frank Wilkeson, the artillery private, was with the column that headed for Chancellorsville. "We marched steadily until the old Chan-

A Confederate straggler

cellorsville House was in sight. Many of the trees standing around us
were bullet scarred [from the battle fought in 1863]. We stood idly in
the road for some time, then went on for a few hundred yards and
parked in a field by the road, with the Germans in camp ahead of us.
Beyond them brigades of troops lay restfully around their campfires.
Other troops marched by rapidly. . . .

"During the day we had occasionally heard the faint report of distant rifles or the heavy, muffled report of a gun, and we suspected that
our cavalry was feeling of Lee's men. . . . All of the enlisted men hoped
that they would get through the Wilderness—a rugged, broken area of
upland that extended from the Rapidan River close to Spotsylvania—
without fighting. The timber is dense and scrubby, and the whole region is cut up by a labyrinth of roads which lead to clearings of charcoal
pits, and there end. Deep ravines, thickly clad with brush and trees,
furrow the forest. The Confederates knew the region thoroughly.
. . . We knew nothing, except that the Army of the Potomac, under
Hooker, had once encountered a direful disaster on the outskirts of this
desolate region. On all sides I heard the murmur of the enlisted men
as they expressed the hope that they would not have to fight in the
Wilderness.

"In the evening after supper, I walked with a comrade to the spot
where [Union General Alfred] Pleasonton had massed his guns and
saved the army under Hooker from destruction by checking the impetuous onslaught of Stonewall Jackson's Virginian infantry, fresh from the
pleasures of the chase of the routed Eleventh Corps. We walked to and
fro over the old battlefield, looking at bullet-scarred and canister-riven
trees.

"The men who had fallen in that fierce fight had apparently been
buried where they fell, and buried hastily. Many polished skulls lay on
the ground. [Some of these held wasp nests, and at least one was host
to a nest of bird eggs.] Leg bones, arm bones, and ribs could be found
without trouble. Toes of shoes and bits of faded, weather-worn uniforms, and occasionally a grinning, bony, fleshless face peered through
the low mound that had been hastily thrown over these brave warriors.

"As we wandered to and fro over the battleground, looking at the
gleaming skulls and whitish bones, and examining the exposed clothing
of the dead to see if they had been Union or Confederate soldiers, many
infantrymen joined us. It grew dark, and we built a fire, at which to light
our pipes, close to where we thought Jackson's men had formed for the
charge, as the graves were thickest there, and then we talked of the

battle of the preceding year. We sat on long, low mounds. The dead were all around us. Their eyeless skulls seemed to stare steadily at us. The smoke drifted to and fro among us. The trees swayed and sighed gently in the soft wind.

"One veteran told the story of the burning of some of the Union soldiers who were wounded during Hooker's fight around the Wilderness as they lay helpless in the woods. It was a ghastly and awe-inspiring tale as he vividly told it to us as we sat among the dead. This man finished his story by saying shudderingly, 'This region,' indicating the woods beyond us with a wave of his arm, 'is an awful place to fight in. The utmost extent of vision is about one hundred yards. Artillery cannot be used effectively. The wounded are liable to be burned to death. I am willing to take my chances of getting killed, but I dread to have a leg broken and then to be burned slowly; and these woods will surely be burned if we fight here. I hope we will get through this chapparal without fighting.' And he took off his cap and meditatively rubbed the dust off of the red clover leaf which indicated the division and corps he belonged to.

"As we sat silently smoking and listening to the story, an infantry soldier who had, unobserved by us, been prying into the shallow grave he sat on with his bayonet, suddenly rolled a skull on the ground before us, and said in a deep, low voice, 'That is what you are all coming to, and some of you will start toward it tomorrow.' "

General Grant had spent the afternoon and evening at his temporary headquarters on the south bank of the Rapidan at Germanna Ford. The Dutch-gabled house had been abandoned in favor of a cluster of newly raised tents. One of the newsmen at headquarters was Charles Carleton Coffin, who relates: "When supper was finished, General Grant sat on a camp stool . . . smoking his cigar, silent, absorbed in thought, looking out upon the gleaming campfires of a division of the Sixth Corps, forming the right wing of the army in this movement.

"The great religious interest manifest in the army during the winter had not lost its force. The soldiers of an entire brigade were holding a prayer meeting. The sky was without a cloud, and the gleaming stars looked down upon them, while the glimmering bivouac fires brought out in bold relief the kneeling throng. This was to be their last meeting before the beginning of the terrific struggle. Before another sunset the lips of many of that congregation would be silent evermore. The prayers finished, they stood erect and then joined in their parting hymn, the mighty chorus of manly voices mingling with the tattoo of the evening

Grant's headquarters at Germanna Ford

drumbeat, swelling out in the melody and harmony of Old Hundred, the music of Martin Luther, the great apostle of Liberty: 'Eternal are thy mercies, Lord, / Eternal truth attends thy word; / Thy praise shall sound from shore to shore / Till suns shall rise and set no more.' "

There was a parley at Grant's headquarters that night. Horace Porter gives the details: "General Meade came over . . . and took a seat upon a folding camp-chair by our fire, and he and General Grant entered into a most interesting discussion of the situation and the plans for the next day. The general in chief offered Meade a cigar. The wind was blowing, and he had some difficulty in lighting it, when General Grant offered him his flint and steel, which overcame the difficulty. . . . While the two generals were talking, and a number of staff officers sitting by listening, telegrams were received from Washington saying that Sherman had advanced in Georgia, Butler had ascended the James River, and Sigel's forces were moving down the valley of Virginia. These advances were in obedience to General Grant's previous orders. He said, 'I don't expect much from Sigel's movement. It is made principally for the purpose of preventing the enemy in his front from withdrawing troops to reinforce Lee's army. . . . It is very gratifying to know that Hancock and Warren have made a march today of over twenty miles, with scarcely any stragglers from their commands.'

"Telegrams were now sent to Washington announcing the entire success of the crossing of the Rapidan, and saying that it would be demonstrated before long whether the enemy intended to give battle on that side of Richmond. Meade soon after retired to his headquarters, and a little while before midnight General Grant entered his tent and turned in for the night."

At Chancellorsville, Private Frank Wilkeson was still at his fireside. "A few of us . . . sat by the dying embers and smoked. As we talked we heard picket firing, not brisk—but, at short intervals, the faint report of a rifle quickly answered. And we reasoned correctly that a Confederate skirmish line was in the woods, and that battle would be offered in the timber. The intelligent enlisted men of the Second Corps with whom I talked that night listened attentively to the firing, now rising, now sinking into silence, to again break out in another place. All of them said that Lee was going to face Grant in the Wilderness, and they based their opinion on the presence of a Confederate skirmish line in the woods. And all of them agreed that the advantages of position were with Lee, and that his knowledge of the region would enable him to face our greatly superior army . . . with a fair prospect of success. But every

infantry soldier I talked with was resolute in his purpose to fight desperately and aid to win a victory that would end the war, if it was possible
to win it. . . .

"It was past midnight when I crept under the caisson of my gun and
pillowed my head on my knapsack. The distant rifle shots on the picket
line grew fainter and fainter, then were lost in the nearer noises of the
camps, and I slept."

8

The Contest Begins

General Lee had established his night encampment with A. P. Hill's Third Corps on the Plank Road at New Verdiersville, about ten miles west of the right flank of the Union army. Brigadier General Armistead L. Long, formerly Lee's military secretary and now a senior artillery officer, spent the night with the commander in chief and had breakfast with him. "The general," Long relates, "displayed the cheerfulness which he usually exhibited at meals, and indulged in a few pleasant jests at the expense of his staff officers, as was his custom on such occasions. He expressed himself surprised that his new adversary had placed himself in the same predicament as 'Fighting Joe' had done the previous spring. He hoped the result would be even more disastrous to Grant than that which Hooker had experienced. He was in the best of spirits, and expressed much confidence in the result—a confidence which was well founded, for there was much reason to believe that his antagonist would be at his mercy while entangled in the pathless thickets."

Lee's columns went forward at daybreak, passing roadside grasses that were heavy with dew. A blanketing mist obscured the sun's ascent, but was soon dispelled by its burgeoning warmth. Hill continued in his right-wing position on the Plank Road, and Ewell, as before, moved on the left by way of the Turnpike. Longstreet was on the march from the southwest. Hill and Ewell were only a few miles from Grant's army, while Longstreet was still a good distance away, and his roads were indirect.

One of the men on the Turnpike was artillery officer Robert Stiles.

"Early on the morning of the 5th of May, while riding ahead of the battalion, I came upon my old friend, General Ewell, crouching over a low fire at a crossroads in the forest, no one at the time being nigh except two horses and a courier who had charge of them and [Ewell's] two crutches. The old hero . . . could not mount his horse alone, and never rode without at least one attendant who always followed close after him, carrying his . . . 'tripod pegs.'

". . . The general was usually very thin and pale—unusually so that morning—but bright and alert. He was accustomed to ride a flea-bitten gray named Rifle, who was singularly like him—so far as a horse could be like a man. I knew Rifle well, and noted that both he and his master looked a little as if they had been up all night and had not had breakfast. . . .

". . . The general . . . asked me to dismount and take a cup of coffee with him. . . . While we were drinking our coffee, I asked him if he had any objection to telling me his orders, and he answered briskly, 'No, sir; none at all—just the orders I like—to go right down the [Turnpike] and strike the enemy wherever I find him.' "

Robert Stiles soon moved on, and Ewell sought his staff. "I sent Major Campbell Brown . . . to General Lee to report my position. In reply he instructed me to regulate my march by General A. P. Hill, whose progress down the Plank Road I could tell by the firing at the head of his column [the troops were skirmishing with a regiment of Union cavalry], and informed me that he preferred not to bring on a general engagement before General Longstreet came up."

When Union General Grant lay down to sleep the previous night he had no knowledge of Lee's intentions. Grant had sent no orders for the interruption of the two-pronged march toward Richmond. In the words of newsman-historian William Swinton: "At headquarters we were up long before dawn of the 5th of May, and rode southward from Germanna Ford to reach Warren's position at Old Wilderness Tavern. We found the road filled with Sedgwick's corps faring forth in the same direction. The sun blazed hotly and fiery red. . . . After a few hours' ride we reached Old Wilderness Tavern. We found that Warren's corps had bivouacked here during the night—one division [that of Charles Griffin] being thrown out on the Orange Turnpike about a mile to the westward to guard the approaches by which the enemy would advance if he was minded to risk battle.

"Warren's orders had been to resume the march early that morning and advance by a wood road running southwesterly from Wilderness

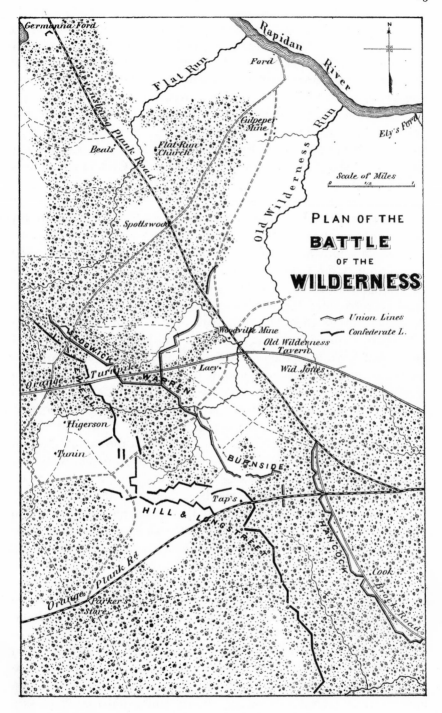

Germanna Ford

Rapidan River

Flat Run

Ford

Culpeper Mine

Beals

Flat Run Church

Old Wilderness Run

Ely's Ford

Ravensburg Plank Road

Spottswood

Scale of Miles

PLAN OF THE
BATTLE
OF THE
WILDERNESS

Woodville Mine

~~~ Union Lines
~~~ Confederate L.

SEDGWICK

Old Wilderness Tavern

Orange & Turnpike

EWELL

WARREN

Lacy

Wid Jones

Higerson

Tunin

BURNSIDE

Tap's

HILL & LONGSTREET

Plank Rd

HANCOCK

Cook

Orange Plank Rd

Parker Store

Brock Road

Tavern to Parker's Store. . . . [The store was located where the wood road crossed the Plank Road, upon which A. P. Hill was marching.] Accordingly at daybreak [Samuel W.] Crawford's division, followed by the divisions of [James S.] Wadworth and [John C.] Robinson moved forward to attain that point—Griffin's division being still held on the Turnpike. But when Crawford's division had neared Parker's Store it found a Union cavalry body that had been sent forward to preoccupy that point being driven out by a hostile column which was pushing rapidly down the Plank Road. And at the same time Griffin's skirmishers on the Turnpike became engaged with another body of the enemy.

"It happened that just as we reached Old Wilderness Tavern, about 8 A.M. of the 5th, the tidings came that Griffin had encountered a Confederate force moving down the Turnpike. Now, there was here an *appearance* and a *fact.* And it is necessary to explain both how the commander [Grant] construed the circumstances, and what the circumstances actually were, for they differed most materially—and indeed, thereby hangs the Battle of the Wilderness.

"When, on the 4th of May, the Army of the Potomac, by its successful passage of the Rapidan at Germanna and Ely's Fords, had turned Lee's right flank, it seemed a warrantable inference to conclude that the Confederate commander, finding his river line now become obsolete, would not attempt to join battle near the Rapidan, but that he would be compelled, in view of the wide dispersion of his corps, to choose a point of concentration nearer Richmond. Grant and Meade therefore had no thought of being interrupted in the march through the Wilderness, and their purpose was by a rapid march southwestward to throw themselves between Lee and his capital, or at least to catch the Confederate corps divided, and beat them in detail.

"It was in execution of this purpose that on the morning of the 5th, Warren was directed on Parker's Store, and that Hancock, whose corps had bivouacked at Chancellorsville, was ordered . . . to move to Shady Grove Church, six miles south of Parker's Store. By launching [the two columns] forward in the same southwesterly direction, it was supposed that the Union army would, in a few vigorous marches, bring Lee to battle somewhere between Gordonsville and Louisa Court House [below the North Anna River].

"Now, when on the morning of the 5th, Warren reported that Griffin had encountered a hostile force pressing down upon him on the Orange Turnpike, Grant and Meade, fully believing that Lee was executing a movement of retreat [toward the North Anna], did not attach any importance to the fact. It was concluded that the force which now faced Griffin was only some part of the Confederate right . . . left behind as a rear guard while the mass of Lee's army concentrated far below. . . .

"I put down in my notebook an observation which, while standing beside General Meade shortly after our arrival at Wilderness Tavern, I heard that officer make to Generals Sedgwick and Warren. 'They [the enemy],' said he, 'have left a division to fool us here while they concentrate and prepare a position toward the North Anna. And what I want is to prevent those fellows getting back to Mine Run [i.e., from making their escape].' Acting on this hypothesis, the order was given to Warren to attack the enemy on the Turnpike.

"Such were appearances. The reality, as has been seen, was very different. Lee, instead of falling back on learning of Grant's advance, had no sooner detected the nature of the maneuver than he resolved to assume the offensive. . . . The force that encountered Griffin [on the Turnpike] on the morning of the 5th was Ewell's van. The column seen by Crawford hastening down the Plank Road was that of [Hill]. Lee had met Grant's move with another equal in dexterity and surpassing it in boldness.

"That the hope of getting between Lee and Richmond was futile soon became apparent to the Union commander, for, as the forenoon wore away, the pressure on Griffin's front became more and more weighty, and on the Plank Road an endless column of the enemy was seen [coming on] with swift strides. It was now imperative to form new combinations. Hancock . . . must be recalled from his march southwards towards Shady Grove Church, and brought up into position with the rest of the army. If indeed it were only possible that he should get up in time, for the enemy was gathering so strongly on the Plank Road, and pushing forward so strenuously, that it was doubtful whether he would not sever connection between Hancock and the rest of the army!"

Hancock interjects: "My advance was about two miles beyond Todd's Tavern, when, at 9 A.M., I received a dispatch . . . to halt at the tavern, as the enemy had been discovered in some force on the Wilderness [Turn]pike. Two hours later I was directed to move my command [northwestward on] the Brock Road to its intersection with the Orange Plank Road. I immediately gave orders for the troops to march toward the point designated."

Returning to William Swinton: "To prevent Hill's attaining this all-important intersection, and allow Hancock . . . to come up into position on the left of Warren, [George W.] Getty's division of the Sixth Corps

was sent to the junction of the Brock Road and the Orange Plank Road
to hold it at all hazards; and, meanwhile, Warren was to attack Ewell
on the Turnpike with all his force, Sedgwick assisting on his right.
. . . Griffin's division [straddled] the Turnpike. Wadsworth's division was
to go in and take position on the left of Griffin, with Robinson's division
in support. . . . One brigade of Crawford's division . . . was put in on the
left of Wadsworth."

While the deployments were progressing, Grant and Meade established their headquarters on a knoll west of Wilderness Tavern (which
was actually a deserted building surrounded by weeds) and north of the
Lacy farmhouse, where the road from Germanna crossed the Turnpike.
"The knoll," says staff officer Horace Porter, "was high enough to afford
a view for some little distance, but the outlook was limited in all directions by the almost impenetrable forest with its interlacing trees and
tangled undergrowth. . . . General Grant lighted a cigar, sat down on
the stump of a tree, took out his penknife, and began to whittle a stick.
He kept on his brown thread gloves. . . . Everything was comparatively
quiet until the hour of noon, when the stillness was suddenly broken by
the sharp rattle of musketry and the roar of artillery. These sounds were
the quick messengers which told that Warren had met the enemy and
begun the conflict."

9

Events on the Turnpike Front

Grant's thrust against Ewell on the left of Lee's line (his northern wing) ended the Confederate chief's hope of keeping the fight on a low key until Longstreet's arrival. The hope had been a frail one at any rate, since Longstreet, marching his difficult route, showed no promise of reaching the field that day. Only Union General Getty, in front of A. P. Hill on Lee's right (his southern wing) was willing to keep matters light for a time. He needed Hancock's backing, and Hancock was still a few miles to the south. As for Ewell, he was obliged to begin the battle with an incomplete command, for the rear of his column was not yet up. He was lucky in that Union General Sedgwick's Sixth Corps, which had been ordered to cooperate with Warren's attack from a position north of the Turnpike (a position facing Ewell's left flank), was not yet on line when Warren advanced.

Among the units with Warren was the Maine regiment (led by Major Ellis Spear) to which Private Theodore Gerrish belonged. "Seldom, if ever," Gerrish asserts, "was a battle fought under such circumstances. The rebels evidently knew but little of our force, position, and intention; and it is safe to say we knew less of theirs. And thus the two great masses of men were hurled against each other. The rebels fought like demons, and under cover of the dense underbrush poured deadly volleys upon us. The air was filled with lead. Minie bullets [more correctly, minié balls, but given variously] went snapping and tearing through the pine limbs; splinters flew in every direction; trees were completely riddled with bullets in a moment's time; blood ran in torrents; death lost its terror; and men for a time seemed transformed to beings that had no fear."

Largely absent from the battle was the sound of artillery, for neither side could find enough open ground to employ more than a few guns. Many an artillerist chafed at remaining idle in the rear, and Union Private Frank Wilkeson, on his first battlefield, found the situation unendurable. "I was quite wild with curiosity, and, confident that the artillery would remain in park, I decided to go to the battle line and see what was going on. . . . I walked out of camp and up the road. The wounded men were becoming more and more numerous. I saw men—faint from loss of blood—sitting in the shade cast by trees. Other men were lying down. All were pale, and their faces expressed great suffering.

"As I walked, I saw a dead man lying under a tree which stood by the roadside. He had been shot through the chest and had struggled to the rear; then, becoming exhausted or choked with blood, he had lain down on a carpet of leaves and died. His pockets were turned inside out. . . .

"I went on. There was a very heavy firing to the left of the road in a chaparral of brush and scrubby pines and oaks. There the musketry was a steady roar, and the cheers and yells of the fighters incessant. I left the road and walked through the woods toward the battleground, and met many wounded men who were coming out. They were bound for the rear and the hospitals.

"Then I came on a body of troops lying in reserve. . . . I heard the hum of bullets as they passed over the low trees. Then I noticed that small limbs of trees were falling in a feeble shower in advance of me. It was as though an army of squirrels were at work cutting off nut and pinecone-laden branches preparatory to laying in their winter's store of food.

"Then, partially obscured by a cloud of powder smoke, I saw a straggling line of men clad in blue . . . not standing as if on parade, but . . . taking advantage of the cover afforded by trees, and they were firing rapidly. Their line officers were standing behind them or in line with them. The smoke drifted to and fro, and there were many rifts in it. I saw scores of wounded men. I saw many dead soldiers lying on the ground, and I saw men constantly falling on the battle line.

"I could not see the Confederates, and, as I had gone to the front expressly to see a battle, I pushed on, picking my way from protective tree to protective tree until I was about forty yards from the battle line. The uproar was deafening; the bullets flew through the air thickly. Now our line would move forward a few yards, now fall back. I stood behind

Fighting in the Wilderness. Federals in foreground

a large oak tree and peeped around its trunk. I heard bullets spat into this tree, and I suddenly realized that I was in danger. My heart thumped wildly for a minute; then my throat and mouth felt dry and queer.

"A dead sergeant lay at my feet, with a hole in his forehead just above his left eye. Out of this wound bits of brain oozed and slid on a bloody trail into his eye, and thence over his cheek to the ground. I leaned over the body to feel of it. It was still warm. He could not have been dead for over five minutes. As I stooped over the dead man, bullets swept past me, and I became angry at the danger I had foolishly gotten into.

"I unbuckled the dead man's cartridge belt, and strapped it around me; and then I picked up his rifle. . . . Standing behind the large oak tree, [I dropped] the ramrod into the rifle to see if it was loaded. It was not. [The ramrod found only a hollow space where a cartridge and ball might have been.] So I loaded it, and, before I fairly understood what had taken place, I was in . . . the battle line . . . bareheaded and greatly excited, and blazing away at an indistinct, smoke-and-tree-obscured line of men clad in gray, and slouch-hatted. . . . The fire was rather hot, and the men were falling pretty fast. Still it was not anywhere near as bloody as I had expected a battle to be.

"As a grand, inspiring spectacle it was highly unsatisfactory, owing to the powder smoke obscuring the vision. At times we could not see the Confederate line, but that made no difference; we kept on firing just as though they were in full view. We gained ground at times, and then dead Confederates lay on the ground as thickly as dead Union soldiers did behind us. Then we would fall back, fighting stubbornly, but steadily giving ground, until the dead were all clad in blue. . . .

"I saw a youth of about twenty years skip and yell, stung by a bullet through the thigh. He turned to limp to the rear. After he had gone a few steps he stopped, then he kicked out his leg once or twice to see if it would work. Then he tore the clothing away from his leg so as to see the wound. He looked at it attentively for an instant, then kicked out his leg again, then turned and took his place in the ranks and resumed firing.

"There was considerable disorder in the line, and the soldiers moved to and fro—now a few feet to the right, now a few feet to the left. One of these movements brought me directly behind this wounded soldier. I could see plainly from that position, and I pushed into the gaping line and began firing. In a minute or two the wounded soldier dropped his rifle, and, clasping his left arm, exclaimed, 'I am hit again!' He sat down behind the battle ranks and tore off the sleeve of his shirt. The wound was very slight—not much more than skin deep. He tied his handkerchief around it, picked up his rifle, and took position alongside of me.

"I said, 'You are fighting bad luck today. You had better get away from here.' He turned his head to answer me. His head jerked, he staggered, then fell, then regained his feet. A tiny fountain of blood and teeth and bone and bits of tongue burst out of his mouth. He had been shot through the jaws. The lower one was broken and hung down. I looked directly into his open mouth, which was ragged and bloody and tongueless. He cast his rifle furiously on the ground and staggered off."

Switching back to that part of the field where Union Private Theodore Gerrish was fighting: "Major Spear, aided by the field and line officers, gallantly led the regiment on. Our lines were broken. It was a disorganized battle; every man fought for himself and by himself, but all faced the enemy with heroic daring, and were determined that the tide of victory should set on the Union side. With remorseless determination the rebels poured their deadly fire upon our men, and they, with irresistible power, pressed back the foe.

"The rebels retreated across a small field that had been cleared in the heart of the great forest, and, reforming their lines in the edge of the woods, prepared to receive us. By this time our regiment had worked its way well up to the front line. General [Joseph J.] Bartlett, in person, led our brigade. . . . As we stood for a moment and looked upon that field, and saw where the bullets were falling into the dried soil, and the little clouds of dust arising so thickly, we were reminded of heavy drops of rain falling just before the shower comes in its full force.

"The order was given to charge. The right of our regiment now rested upon the Turnpike; and across the field we dashed. Zip, zip, zip came the bullets on every side. The field was nearly crossed. We dashed up a little swell of land on its farthest side and were under the shadow of the trees. A red volcano [of muzzle flashes] yawned before us and vomited forth . . . lead and death. Our lines staggered for a moment, but with desperate resolution our men threw themselves upon the enemy's guns. It was . . . like a conflict of giants. North and South arrayed against each other, man against man. The sons of the Pine Tree State crossed bayonets with those who were reared under the orange groves of the far South. The rifle barrels touched, as from their muzzles they poured death into each others' faces; the ground shook with the roar of musketry; the forest trees were flaming with fire, and the air was loaded with death.

"Foot after foot the rebels retreated, their gray forms mantled with fire as they went. Slowly and steadily we advanced, giving blows with a mailed hand as we pursued the foe. What a medley of sounds—the incessant roar of the rifle; the screaming of bullets; the forest on fire; men cheering, groaning, yelling, swearing, and praying!"

By intention, Confederate General Ewell (in agreement with his original orders from Lee) had been fighting a battle of tactics that were largely retrograde. He had been making no sustained effort to keep the Federals at bay or drive them back. But now a crisis beset him. He found himself pressed in a manner that threatened his front with collapse.

Meanwhile, Confederate General John Gordon's brigade of Jubal Early's division, the rear guard of Ewell's Turnpike column, was approaching the field. Gordon relates: "Long before I reached the point of collision, the steady roll of small arms left no doubt as to the character of the conflict in our front. Despatching staff officers to the rear to close up the ranks in compact column, so as to be ready for any emergency, we hurried with quickened step toward the point of heaviest fighting. Alternate confidence and apprehension were awakened as the shouts of one army or the other reached our ears. So distinct in character were these shouts that they were easily discernible. At one point the weird 'Confederate yell' told us plainly that Ewell's men were advancing. At another the huzzas, in mighty concert, of the Union troops warned us that they had repelled the Confederate charge; and as these ominous huzzas grew in volume we knew that Grant's lines were moving forward.

"Just as the head of my column came within range of the whizzing Miniés, the Confederate yells grew fainter, and at last ceased; and the Union shout rose above the din of battle. I was already prepared by this infallible admonition for the sight of Ewell's shattered forces retreating in disorder. . . . These retreating divisions, like broken and receding waves, rolled back against the head of my column while we were still rapidly advancing along the narrow road. The repulse had been so sudden and the confusion so great that practically no resistance was now being made to the Union advance; and the elated Federals were so near me that little time was left to bring my men from column into line in order to resist the movement or repel it by a countercharge.

"At this moment of dire extremity I saw General Ewell . . . notwithstanding the loss of his leg, riding in furious gallop toward me, his [mount] bounding like a deer through the dense underbrush. With a quick jerk of his bridle-rein just as his wooden leg was about to come into unwelcome collision with my knee, he checked his horse and rapped out his few words with characteristic impetuosity. He did not stop to explain the situation; there was no need of explanation. The disalignment, the confusion, the rapid retreat of our troops, and the raining of Union bullets as they whizzed and rattled through the scrub-oaks and pines rendered explanations superfluous, even had there been time to make them.

"The rapid words he did utter were electric and charged with tremendous significance. 'General Gordon, the fate of the day depends on you, sir!' he said. 'These men will save it, sir,' I replied, more with the purpose of arousing the enthusiasm of my men than with any well-defined idea as to how we were to save it. Quickly wheeling a single regiment into line, I ordered it forward in a countercharge, while I hurried the other troops into position. The sheer audacity and dash of that regimental charge checked, as I had hoped it would, the Union advance for a few moments, giving me the essential time to throw the other troops across the Union front. Swiftly riding to the center of my line, I gave in person the order, 'Forward!' "

As interjected by Confederate Private G. W. Nichols: "Just as we were ordered forward, Irvin Spivy, of the 26th Georgia Regiment, hallooed. He could halloo the queerest that I ever heard anyone. It was a kind of a scream or [a] low, like a terrible bull, with a kind of neigh mixed along with it, and it was nearly as loud as a steam whistle. We called him 'The 26th Georgia's Bull,' and the Yankees called him 'Gordon's Bull.' He would always halloo this way when we charged the enemy, and we were informed that the Yankees understood it as a signal for them to move back."

Spivy's halloo was followed by a general yell that, General Gordon declares, "must have been heard miles away. . . . The shock of [our] furious onslaught shattered into fragments all that portion of the compact Union line which confronted [us]. At that moment was presented one of the strangest conditions ever witnessed upon a battlefield. My command covered only a small portion of the long lines in blue, and not a single regiment of those stalwart Federals yielded except those which had been struck by the Southern advance. On both sides of the swath cut by this sweep of the Confederate scythe the steady veterans of Grant were unshaken and still poured their incessant volleys into the retreating Confederate ranks. My command had cut its way through the Union center, and at that moment it was in the remarkably strange position of being on identically the same general line with the enemy, the Confederates facing in one direction, the Federals in the other. Looking down that line from Grant's right toward his left, there would first have been seen a long stretch of blue uniforms, then a short stretch of gray, then another still longer of blue, in one continuous line. The situation was both unique and alarming. . . .

"In such a crisis, when moments count for hours, when the fate of a command hangs upon instantaneous decision, the responsibility of the commander is almost overwhelming; but the very extremity of the danger electrifies his brain to abnormal activity. . . . As soon as my troops had broken through the Union ranks, I directed my staff to halt the command; and, before the Union veterans could recover from the shock, my regiments were moving at double quick from the center into file right and left, thus placing them in two parallel lines, back to back, in a position at a right angle to the one held a moment before.

"This quickly executed maneuver placed one half of my command squarely upon the right flank of one portion of the enemy's unbroken line, and the other half facing in exactly the opposite direction, squarely upon the left flank of the enemy's lines. . . . This done, both these wings were ordered forward, and, with another piercing yell, they rushed in opposite directions upon the right and left flanks of the astounded Federals, shattering them as any troops that were ever marshalled would have been shattered, capturing large numbers and checking any further effort by General Grant on that portion of the field. Meantime, while this unprecedented movement was being executed, the Confederates who had been previously driven back rallied and moved in spirited charge to the front. . . ."

At one spot, according to Confederate soldier John Worsham, the ensuing action waged back and forth across a field that had a deep and rugged gully spanning its center. The contenders finally posted themselves in the woods at opposite ends of the field and began exchanging volleys across the gulley. During the earlier fighting, two men, a Federal and a Confederate, had taken refuge in the gully, neither in sight of the other, and they were still there. As the bullets zipped over their heads and they began moving about, considering courses of action, the two suddenly came face to face. Worsham tells what happened:

"They . . . commenced to banter one another. Then they decided that they would go into the road and have a regular fist and skull fight, the best man to have the other as his prisoner. When the two men came into the road about midway between the lines of battle, in full view of both sides . . . they surely created a commotion. . . . Both sides ceased firing! When the two men took off their coats and commenced to fight with their fists, a yell went up along each line, and men rushed to the edge of the opening for a better view. The Johnny soon had the Yank down, who surrendered, and both quietly rolled into the gulley. . . . The disappearance of the two men was the signal for the resumption of firing!"

At most points along Ewell's front, the Confederates were now either holding their own or beginning to make advances. Union General Sedgwick's Sixth Corps was still not in position to support Warren on his right, and Warren's men were obliged to begin withdrawing toward breastworks they had thrown up in the morning before the battle started.

Union Private Gerrish describes the retreat as it was experienced by the 20th Maine: "The brigade upon our right had fallen back, and the enemy was in our rear. Our only way of escape was by the left flank. . . . It was a very narrow escape for us, and it was only by a quick, daring dash that we escaped from the snare in which we found ourselves. . . . Many deeds of daring were done . . . by members of our regiment. . . .

"Captain Walter G. Morrill, of Company B, discovering that the enemy was coming down upon our right flank, marshalled a fragment of his own company and a few men from other commands, formed a little line of battle along the Turnpike, and for some minutes held a large force of the rebels in check. It is doubtful if the brave captain would have retreated at all if a minie ball had not gone crashing through his face and hurled him to the ground. Regaining his feet, he bound a handkerchief around his face and continued to fight until he was blinded and choked with blood, when his brave men assisted him to the rear.

"Three of our men in a clump of bushes saw a dozen rebels close upon them. They called upon them to surrender, and the Johnnies, not mistrusting for a moment how small the Yankee force was, threw down their guns and were brought within our lines.

"Lieutenant Melcher, whose company was the left of our regiment, did not learn that we were flanked, and with a small squad of men continued to advance until he discovered that the firing was all in his rear. Then he went out on the Turnpike and looked [rearward] in the direction of the breastworks, and saw a line of rebel infantry stretched across the road. . . . He went back to his men, told them of the situation, and mustered his force. He found that he had fifteen men. . . . A council of war was held. They must decide [either] to . . . remain where they were and be taken prisoners, or [to] cut their way through the rebel line of battle and rejoin their regiment at the breastworks. Not a single man would listen to the thought of surrender. . . . It was finally decided to cut their way through the enemy's line and escape.

"It was a dangerous undertaking. . . . With loaded rifles and fixed bayonets, they moved with noiseless tread toward the rebel line. . . . With a yell the little band charged. . . . There was a flash and a roar. Melcher's voice was heard calling upon them to surrender. The rebels, of course, were surprised, and their line was broken and divided. The [Union] squad of fifteen lost two or three men in the shock, but swept on to our line of battle, bearing with them thirty prisoners which they had torn from the rebel line in their mad charge."

By this time the entire battle zone was strewn with dead and wounded, and a new and pathetic element was added to the medley of sounds. As had been foreseen by veterans on both sides, the inevitable brush fires crept among numbers of the helpless wounded. The nature of their shrieks told their fate both near and far.

Most of the wounded were luckier. The following story is related by an unidentified Unionist who was shot through the ankle: "It is impossible to describe the sensations experienced by a person when wounded for the first time. The first intimation I had that I was wounded was my falling upon the ground. My leg was numb to my body, and for a moment I fancied that my foot had been carried away. But I soon learned the true condition of my situation. Our regiment was rapidly retreating, and the rebels as rapidly advancing. The forest trees around me were on fire, and bullets were falling thick and fast. If I remained where I was, the most favorable result that I could hope for was captivity. . . .

"I stood up, and, to my joy, found that my leg was not entirely useless. I could step with it, and so long as it remained straight I could bear my weight upon it; but when bent at the knee it refused to bear me up, and I would fall to the ground. Under existing circumstances, I determined to retreat. I threw off all my baggage and equipments, and turned my face toward the line of breastworks. . . . Fear lent wings to my flight, and away I dashed. Frequently my wounded leg would refuse to do good service, and as a result I would tumble headlong upon the

Federals trying to save their wounded from the flames

ground. Then rising, I would rush on again; and I doubt if there has been a champion on the sawdust track . . . who has made such a record of speed as I made on that retreat through the Wilderness.

"In my haste I did not keep so far to my right as I should have done, and consequently was obliged to cross the lower end of [a] field over which we had made [a] charge. It was a sad spectacle, that lonely field in the forest. Here and there a wounded man was limping painfully to the rear; dead men, and others wounded too severely to move, were scattered thickly upon the ground.

"As I was crossing the lower corner of the field, to my surprise and horror [a] rebel line of battle came out on its upper edge, some quarter of a mile from where I was running. . . . A Union officer [of high rank] . . . also came out into the field, not twenty rods from the rebel line. He was on horseback; not a staff officer was with him; his uniform was torn and bloody; blood was trickling from several wounds in his face and head. He had evidently been up to discover why our line of battle had not connected with the Sixth Corps.

"The rebels saw him the moment he emerged from the forest, and called upon him to surrender, while a wild yell rang along their line as they saw their fancied prize. But they did not know the man with whom they had to deal. Shaking his fist at them in defiance, he put spurs to his horse and dashed away. He was a target for every rifle in the rebel line. . . . It was a brilliant ride for life, with all the odds against the daring rider. Bravely he rode in the midst of that storm, as if death had no terror for him. His steed was a noble animal, and, at a three-minute gait, bore his master from his pursuers. Each seemed to bear a charmed life. Over one-half the distance across that field had been passed, and yet the rider sat erect upon the steed that was bearing him onward with such tremendous speed.

"A deep ditch must be crossed before they could gain the cover of the forest—a ditch dug many years before, five or six feet deep, and ten or twelve in width. The rebels knew the ditch was there, and sent up a wild yell of delight, as they fancied the officer would be delayed in crossing, and so fall into their hands. The horse and rider evidently saw the obstacle at the same moment and prepared to meet it. Firmly the rider sat in his saddle and gathered the reins of his horse with a firm hand.

"I never beheld a nobler spectacle than that presented by the gallant steed—his nostrils dilated, his ears pointed forward, his eyes seeming to flash with the fire of conscious strength as he made the fearful leap. For a moment I thought they were safe, but rebel bullets pierced the horse, and, turning a complete somersault, he fell stone dead, burying his rider beneath him as he fell. Again the rebels cheered and rushed on; but to my surprise the officer, with the assistance of a few wounded soldiers, extricated himself from his dead horse, ran across the edge of the field, and made his escape.

"I also entered the woods and continued to run at the top of my speed until I reached the breastworks. . . . I passed beyond these and went back a mile or more to our division hospital in the rear. Many wounded men had already arrived. The surgeons were busily at work. Rough tables had been erected under the trees around the house where the hospital had been established. Wounds were dressed and limbs amputated with a fearful rapidity. Only the most serious cases were attended to. Groans and shrieks filled the air as the fearful work went on. . . . Of course, my wound would receive no attention where there were so many others of a dangerous character. Under a tree, without a blanket, I lay and listened. . . .

"The conflict was raging in all its horror. How can I describe it? For a few moments, perhaps, all would be quiet. Then, upon the right, where the Sixth Corps was [at last] in line, there would be a yell, followed by a terrific musketry fire lasting for ten minutes, while all along the remainder of the line there would be silence. Then, suddenly, a volley on the left; then all along the entire line—until it seemed as if the Wilderness itself throbbed under the terrible concussions."

The failure of Warren's attack was nearly complete when Sedgwick's Sixth Corps went in on the right, and the new attack accomplished little. In the words of George Stevens, the surgeon with the 77th New York: "As our line advanced, it would suddenly come upon a line of gray-coated rebels, lying upon the ground, covered with dried leaves and concealed by the chapparal, when the rebels would rise, deliver a murderous fire, and retire. We thus advanced through this interminable forest more than a mile and a half, driving the rebel skirmishers before us, when we came upon their line of battle, which refused to retire. . . .

"The enemy now charged upon our lines, making a desperate effort to turn our right flank, but without avail. Again and again the rebels in columns rushed with the greatest fury upon the brigades in front without being able to move them from their position. At half-past three o'clock our sufferings had been so great that General Sedgwick sent a messenger to General Burnside, who had now crossed [the bulk of] his corps at Germanna Ford, with a request that he would send a division to our assistance. The assistance . . . [did not arrive], and what remained of the noble old Sixth Corps was left to hold its position alone.

"At four, or a little later, the rebels retired, leaving many of their dead upon the ground. . . . The opposing lines were upon the two slopes of a ravine, through which ran a strip of level marshy ground, densely wooded like the rest of the Wilderness. The Confederates now commenced to strengthen the position on their side of the ravine, felling timber and covering it with earth. The woods resounded with the strokes of their axes as the busy workmen plied their labor within three hundred yards, and in some places less than one hundred yards of our line, yet so dense was the thicket that they were entirely concealed from our view."

Having raged from noon until four o'clock, with the accruement of casualties in the thousands, the fighting along the entire Turnpike sector now subsided without definite result. Aside from its trail of blood, Warren's retreat had cost him only the ground he had gained at the outset. Sedgwick maintained his advanced position on the right.

Union newsman-historian William Swinton assumes the narrative: "The opening act of the drama had been concluded. . . . The air was stifling, and the sun sent down his rays like spears. I went to Warren's headquarters at the Lacy House to rest and await further developments, and found the house had one historic event of interest associated with it, for it was [in a hospital tent in this vicinity] that Stonewall Jackson lay after he was borne, mortally hurt, from the battlefield of Chancellorsville. . . .

"Picking up a copy of Horace, which I found lying on the littered floor, I opened it mechanically and happened to light on where the poet, in the Ode to Mecaenas, speaks of war [and its effect on the mothers of men] . . . which set me a-musing, for to how many mothers whose sons then lay in the dark woods of the Wilderness must wars be 'detestata.'

"But such thoughts were quickly interrupted; for from the far-off left [from the Plank Road sector to the south] there came a guttural, oceanic roar of musketry; and, riding thither, I found that it was Hancock, who had at length come up, had joined the faithful Getty, guardian of the precious junction of roads . . . and was now attacking the enemy."

10

Encounter on the Plank Road

A review of the situation in the southern sector is given by Hancock's assistant adjutant general, Francis A. Walker: "Getty, with his division of the Sixth Corps, had been sent south from the Turnpike to the Plank Road, on a report that the enemy were pushing up this road. . . . Arriving about eleven o'clock, he had encountered the advance of Hill's Corps. . . . No serious engagement had taken place, for General Lee was well disposed to put off the impending battle until Longstreet's Corps could come up. . . . General Hancock found General Getty anxious to make an early attack, in consequence of repeated instructions from General Meade, who addressed similar urgent representations to Hancock himself upon his arrival on the ground; but the latter was strongly desirous of getting his whole corps up and in hand before beginning the fight.

"It is no small matter to bring up twenty-five to thirty thousand men by a single road and form them for battle. . . . The greatest efforts of the staff were put forth to hasten the work; to get the artillery out of the way and to push the infantry forward. At 4:15 P.M., however, General Getty, feeling himself constrained by General Meade's orders, moved forward to undertake to drive the enemy down the Plank Road. . . . Although the Second Corps formation still lacked much of completeness, Hancock had no resource but to throw [David B.] Birney forward, with his own and [Gershom] Mott's division. Birney advanced on both Getty's right and left, [a] section of [R. Bruce] Ricketts' battery on the Plank Road moving forward with the troops."

The artillery section was led by Captain Charles B. Brockway, who

assumes the narrative: "I never expected to come out of the engagement alive, nor to bring any of my men out. The infantry right and left
were to a great extent shielded by the wilderness, but I had to take the
open road, and formed a good mark for the enemy. The road was
narrow—a ditch on each side—with no chance to limber up and retreat
in case of accidents. I had my caissons follow some distance in the rear,
and put my [two] guns *en echelon* [one on either half of the road, but
not abreast] to enable me to open with both at once. I took the precaution to have several shells prepared, as I knew the attack would be
sudden. Our skirmishers were only fifty yards in front of our first line
of battle, the two [supporting] lines following at close distance. We
could not see what was in the woods, but several rebels leisurely paced
the road four hundred yards in our front, and we knew 'by the pricking
of our thumbs, something wicked this way comes.'

"As the minute of the watch pointed to 4:30 P.M. [a Union] advance
was made. A few steps forward and the silence changed to a deafening
roar of musketry. We advanced about two hundred yards, when the
infantry began to waver, and I deemed it proper to perform my share
in the tragedy. The guns were unlimbered and a few percussion shells
sent into the enemy's ranks, now only a few hundred yards beyond.
They immediately placed a section of Napoleon twelve-pounders in the
road, and a couple of solid shot whizzed by our ears. [Belonging to
Colonel William T. Poague's battalion, this section was one of the very
few brought into action on the Confederate side.] Here was a tangible
enemy, and we all breathed freer in seeing something to fire at.

"At this time the whole line was engaged. The line of battle advanced and receded, and the yells of either party rose above the rattle
of musketry and the roar of artillery. By a fortunate shot we exploded
one of the enemy's limber chests, and soon had disabled most of their
men and horses. They then threw rounds of double-shotted canister,
which bounded like hailstones, tearing up splinters in the Plank Road,
and here and there knocked over men and horses. But our percussion
shell was superior, and their artillery was soon withdrawn.

"For a moment there was a lull, and then the rebel line charged.
Slowly they pressed our men back, yelling like demons incarnate. At
first I threw solid shot at the column as it advanced, until they commenced double-quicking. At this time an officer of the 93rd Pennsylvania [infantry] hallooed, 'Stick to it, Charlie. I've got a thirty days'
furlough,' showing me at the same time a gaping wound in his thigh.

"The time had now arrived to use canister, and terrible execution did it do along that narrow Plank Road. The enemy struggled bravely against it. If the line broke, they steadily reformed. If the colors fell, they were seized by another hand. The wounded crawled into the ditches, and the dead formed a barrier to the second line.

"General Hancock was now on the ground, and promptly sent in fresh troops to support us."

Fresh troops were also provided on the Southern side, where Henry Heth's division of Hill's Corps had been first to fight. The reinforcements included a battalion of sharpshooters temporarily detached from its parent brigade for an independent mission. As related by one of the battalion's officers, Captain John D. Young: "The sharpshooters were . . . sent to the left of the Plank Road to protect the flank of the troops ordered to Heth's support. . . . Moving forward, they passed long lines of artillery going into bivouac, well-knowing from the nature of the country that their services would not be needed; while riding about in a restless and eager manner, Colonel William Johnson Pegram was to be seen, asking through many a courier dispatched one after another, if he could not get in a battery, or at least a section, and highly disquieted that his pieces should be silent at such a time. . . .

"Colonel Pegram was invited to go in with us, and would probably have accepted—for battle had a powerful fascination for the calm, spectacled, studious, devout boy-colonel—but that he had been peremptorily ordered to remain with his guns and await developments.

"The sharpshooters, moving on, found that the left of the road was clear [they had entered the gap between Hill's left and Ewell's right, where nothing was happening] . . . leaving them free to rejoin their command, which was actively engaged on the right-hand side of the road. The battalion . . . principally guided by the fire from the front . . . [advanced] through wounded men falling to the rear, through mounted men moving in haste and excitement, and through straggling parties who never failed to have urgent business somewhere in the rear as soon as the business of these bloody days became critical.

"One little thing may be noted. The road was literally strewed with packs of playing cards, thrown away by superstitious soldiers as they went into the fiery focus. It was a noticeable fact among the Confederate soldiers that many who were regular gamblers, who would play poker or anything else all night if permitted, and who would carefully deposit the cards in their haversacks when the game was over, were very careful to throw them away as soon as firing began—after which they would load their guns and be ready to go in coolly.

Confederates awaiting orders during Wilderness fighting

"One figure that the command passed on its way forward . . . [was] the calm courteous, unselfish, gallant, patriotic A. P. Hill. Surrounded by his staff, this beloved general, whose custom it ever was to feel in person the pulse of battle, and who always stationed himself just behind his men in action, sat, a stately presence, anxiously awaiting the issue of events and sending up troops to support General Heth, who was sorely pressed. 'Face the fire and go in where it is hottest!' were the brief words in which the lieutenant general assigned the sharpshooters to their place in battle. They were obeyed with a will. . . ."

Among the regular Confederate infantry units ordered from the rear to support Heth was Samuel McGowan's brigade of Cadmus Wilcox's division. This was the brigade to which J. F. J. Caldwell belonged, and he relates: "We filed to the left and passed through an open field. There were several pieces of artillery here, and near them General Lee and General [Jeb] Stuart, on foot. The battle was evidently not distant, but we flattered ourselves that it was rather late in the day for much to be done towards a general engagement. We were carried nearly a mile farther, through a body of woods, and halted on a clear, commanding ridge. . . . Ewell's Corps was engaged [in a minor way, as flare-ups occurred] at some distance on our left.

"Rev. Mr. Mullaly, chaplain of Orr's Regiment of Rifles, held prayers with his regiment. It was one of the most impressive scenes I ever witnessed. On the left thundered the dull battle. On the right the sharp crack of rifles gradually swelled. . . . Above was the blue, placid heavens; around us a varied landscape of forests and fields, green with the earliest foliage of spring. And here knelt hirsute and browned veterans shriving for another struggle with death.

"In the midst of the prayer, a harsh, rapid fire broke out right on the Plank Road. . . . The order was issued to face about and forward. And then we went, sometimes in quick-time, sometimes at the double-quick, towards the constantly increasing battle. The roar of muskets became continuous, augmented occasionally by the report of cannon, and always by the ringing rebel cheer. . . .

"Just as we reached the Plank Road, two or three shell fell among us, but I believe no one was struck in the brigade. The road was crowded with noncombatants, artillery, and ordnance wagons. Here and there lay a dead man. The firing in front waxed fiercer, if possible, than ever. The 1st Regiment led the march. They, with the Rifles, were filed across the road and fronted. The three remaining regiments were formed with their right resting on the road. . . .

"[The brigade] entered the conflict alone. . . . Balls fired at Heth's division, in front of us, fell among us at the beginning of our advance. We pressed on, guide left, through the thick undergrowth, until we reached Heth's line, now much thinned and exhausted. We had very imprudently begun to cheer before this. We passed over this line cheering. There was no use of this. We should have charged without uttering a word until within a few yards of the Federal line. As it was, we drew upon ourselves a terrific volley of musketry.

"The advance was greatly impeded by the matted growth of saplings and bushes, and in the delay a scattering fire commenced along our line. The fighting of the brigade cannot be described, as a whole, from this time. . . . We did remarkably well. I could not see anything distinctly, on account of the bushes, the smoke of our line and that of the Federal; but other men professed to see the enemy constantly relieving."

Actually, the time at the front was of lengthy duration for many of the Federal regiments, among them the 102nd Pennsylvania Volunteers. According to the unit's chaplain, A. M. Stewart (a stern-faced and rigidly moral man who was nevertheless sensitive and perceptive): "Our regiment was in the front line for three long, *long* hours; during which time our colonel and Captain [Jacob] Drum, with a sorrowful number from the ranks, were instantly killed; while six of the officers and over a hundred privates were wounded, with all manner of mutilations. What awful, what sickening scenes! No, we have ceased to get sick at such sights.

"Here a dear friend struck dead by a ball through the head or heart; another fallen with leg or thigh broken, and looking resignedly yet wistfully to you for help away from the carnage; another dropping his gun, quickly clapping his hand upon his breast, stomach, or bowels, through which a Minnie has passed, and walking slowly to the rear to lie down and die; still another—yea, many more—with bullet holes through various fleshy parts of the body from which the blood is freely flowing, walking back and remarking, with a laugh somewhat distorted with pain, 'See, the rascals have hit me.'

"All this beneath a canopy of sulphur and a bedlam of sounds, like confusion confounded."

A sidelight to the afternoon's events is given by a junior officer in the Confederate lines, J. M. Waddill, who had seen his immediate superiors eliminated by Federal fire and had been raised to the role of company commander: "The flood-tide of battle was at its height. . . . The roar of

Federals throwing up breastworks at Wilderness front

musketry ebbed and flowed all along the line, and . . . my company, lying or kneeling, the better to see the enemy through the dense thicket, as well as for protection, were firing as rapidly as their unfavorable positions would allow. . . . There was little for me to do, every man of the company doing his duty, as I passed along the line, crouching from the rain of bullets, and speaking words of cheer here and there— few, if any, of which were heard in the din and roar of the conflict.

"Pausing for a moment, the shrubbery was parted, and little Johnny Julian, courier for the colonel, came through the bushes . . . and yelled in my ear, 'The colonel's orders are that you take your company at once to the rear and report to Colonel White. . . .' [This was William P. White, a regimental commander in the Confederate cavalry corps, who believed that a unit of Federal cavalry was circling toward his position in A. P. Hill's rear, and had requested infantry support.]

"Within a few seconds we were double-quicking [to the rear], stooping as we went, the better to escape the shower of balls which whistled through the brush on every side. Soon we came upon the Third Corps ordnance train standing in the road. . . . Half a mile further on we met Colonel White. 'Lieutenant, take your company a quarter of a mile further on . . . with guns loaded, ready to repel cavalry,' he ordered. . . .

"Obeying his orders, we reached our position and [with no Federal horsemen appearing] threw ourselves by the roadside to rest. A little later I heard from the thicket nearby what seemed a groan of someone in pain. A second time the sound reached my ears, and I determined to learn the cause. Thirty or forty steps from the road, in a perfect tangle of brush and vines, I espied a blue uniform on the ground. Approaching nearer, I discovered a Federal soldier lying face downwards, apparently dead. [The man was a victim of skirmishing that had occurred on the Plank Road before the battle, while A. P. Hill's van was making its approach.]

"Pulling aside the brush, I knelt and turned the body over as gently as I could, to ascertain if life was extinct. With a groan and a shudder, his eyes opened, while his lips moved as if to speak, but no sound came from them. Raising his head slightly, I placed my canteen to his lips, and in a few moments he seemed much revived. 'What regiment?' I asked. In a weak voice, he replied, 'Fifth New York Cavalry,' which was confirmed by the brass letters on his forage cap lying near.

"Hardened as I was by scenes of blood and suffering, my sympathies were deeply aroused as I looked in the face of the young soldier, for he seemed not more than twenty years of age—a mere boy, though taking a man's place under man's most trying circumstances; a fair, frank, blue-eyed boy, dying, perhaps, far from home or friends. 'How are you hurt,' I asked. Pointing to his hip, a slight rent [in his trousers] and a blood spot or two told the story.

"Placed in as easy a posture as possible, and his thirst again satisfied, he gave a brief account of himself, his name, where from, etc., after which I left him for a short time to [check on] my company. Finding everything quiet, I called one of the men, and together we returned to the wounded youth.

"With our pocket knives we cut away the brush and tangle for some twenty feet around him, and carefully swept up the leaves and rubbish, as fire was raging in the woods not far away. We then built a slight shelter of green branches above his head for protection from the sun, filled his canteen from the creek nearby, and divided our rations of bacon and bread with him.

"He seemed very grateful; offered his watch in return for our services, which I placed in his pocket again; and, bidding him good-bye, promising to [try to] see him again, went back to my company.

"The expected cavalry raid proved a false alarm, and within an hour or two the several companies along the road, mine among others, were hurried back to the battle line, and I saw no more of my Fifth Cavalry man. . . ."

On the Union side, General Grant was at his headquarters, trying to keep abreast of events at the front. At one time during the afternoon, Grant sent Horace Porter to get a report from Hancock. "The fighting," says Porter, "had become exceedingly severe. . . . General Alexander Hays, one of the most gallant officers in the service, commanding one of Hancock's brigades, finding that his line had broken, rushed forward to encourage his troops, and was instantly killed. . . .

"After remaining for some time with Hancock's men, I returned to headquarters to report the situation to the general-in-chief, and carried to him the sad intelligence of Hays's death. General Grant was by no means a demonstrative man, but, upon learning the intelligence I had brought, he was visibly affected. He was seated upon the ground with his back against a tree, still whittling pine sticks.

"He sat for a time without uttering a word, and then, speaking in a low voice and pausing between sentences, said, 'Hays and I were [West Point] cadets together for three years. We served for a time in the same regiment in the Mexican War. He was a noble man and a gallant officer. I am not surprised that he met his death at the head of his troops. It was just like him. He was a man who would never follow, but would always lead in battle.' "

Among the newsmen behind the Union lines that afternoon was twenty-five-year-old Charles A. Page, a representative of Horace Greeley's *New York Tribune.* Being a good writer who was prompt with his submissions, Page was popular with Greeley, but the famous editor once complained to the young correspondent that his expense account in the field was shockingly high. Page explained that he was obliged to operate in a costly way, that he got his earliest and most reliable intelligence from groups of officers whom he regaled with watermelons and whiskey as they came out of battle. Since watermelons were not in season during the Wilderness fighting, it seems safe to assume that Page had come to this field with whiskey in extra supply. The following information, however, was gained largely through personal observation:

"The work was at close range. No room in that jungle for maneuvering; no possibility of a bayonet charge; no help from artillery; no help from cavalry; nothing but close, square, severe, face-to-face volleys of fatal musketry. The wounded stream out, and fresh troops pour in. Stretchers pass out with ghastly burdens, and go back reeking with blood for more. Word is brought that the ammunition is failing. Sixty rounds [per man] fired in one steady, stand-up fight, and that fight not fought [to a decision]. Boxes of cartridges are placed on the returning stretchers, and the struggle shall not cease for want of ball and powder.

"Do the volleys grow nearer, or do our fears make them seem so? It must be so, for a second line is rapidly formed just where we stand, and the bullets slip singing by as they have not done before, while now and then a limb drops from the tree-tops. The bullets are flying high. General Hancock rides along the new line, is recognized by the men, and cheered with a will and a tiger. . . . We hold them, and the fresh men going in will drive them."

Sunset approached, and the fighting on all parts of the southern field remained indecisive. In the words of Union Private Warren Goss: "The underbrush and briars scratched our faces, tore our clothing, and tripped our feet from under us. . . . Two, three, and four times we rushed upon the enemy, but were met by a murderous fire and with heavy loss from concealed enemies. As often as we rushed forward we were compelled to get back. . . .

"The uproar of battle continued through the twilight hours. It was eight o'clock before the deadly crackle of musketry died gradually away, and the sad shadows of the night, like a pall, fell over the dead in these ensanguined thickets. The groans and cries for water or for help from the wounded [replaced] the sounds of the conflict."

According to Hancock's assistant adjutant general, Francis Walker: "The utmost exertions of the medical staff and the ambulance corps could not avail to bring off [many of] the sufferers. The undergrowth was so dense that it was almost impossible to find the victims of the afternoon's battle; and the hostile lines were so close that any movement over the intervening ground quickly brought down a heavy fire."

On both sides, the men in the lines realized that the contest in the Wilderness was far from over. Unionist John W. Urban, who belonged to the Pennsylvania Reserve Infantry, explains that "the desperate nature of the fighting and indecisive results arising from it were enough to convince us that terrible would be the carnage before the great battle was decided. . . . Only those who have been in like situations can fully appreciate the feelings of a soldier on the night after an indecisive battle. Many of his comrades have fallen, and he knows that before the setting of another sun many more will be added to the 'bivouac of the dead.' He cannot avoid thinking that the chances are many that he, too, may be among the number; and how lovingly he thinks of the dear ones at home, and hopes and prays that he may meet them again."

The Union and Confederate fronts of the Turnpike and the Plank Road had developed into combinations that faced each other on an irregular northwest-southeast course extending for five miles. The deployments were not yet complete. On the Union side, Burnside's corps, still north of the field, was preparing for a predawn move to a position between Warren and Hancock. On the Confederate side, Ewell and Hill were still awaiting Longstreet's arrival from the southwest. Lee had sent orders for Longstreet to continue his march through the darkness.

Few of the troops of either front got a full measure of rest that night. Regiments stumbled around in the brush as they sought newly assigned points in the line. Spans of breastworks had to be thrown up, and thousands of men labored with axes, picks, and shovels. There was firing between the lines, some of it minor and some of it building to a heavy roll and to extensive sheets of flickering flame. There was another kind of flame, too, that of the scattered brush fires that glowed toward the dark sky and continued to menace some of the helpless wounded. Their cries, and the cries of the wounded in other spots, could be heard throughout the night, and the sounds were especially painful to men who knew they were coming from bosom comrades or, at least in a few cases, from close relatives. Numbers of the listeners were driven to making rescue attempts, some of which were successful. Behind the lines on both sides, in tents illumined by lanterns, surgeons bent over pale figures on bloodstained tables, and the ghastly harvest of limbs kept growing.

Many individual adventures were experienced by the men in the lines, and Confederate soldier John Worsham found this one unforgettable: "I was aroused about midnight to take a verbal order to the officer in our front on the skirmish line. . . . I was instructed to leave my arms, etc., take my time, and make as little noise as possible. . . . Moving carefully, and thinking that I was getting on splendidly in perfect silence, I was thrown down with such a rattling noise as to awaken everybody in the neighborhood!

"Shooting commenced from the Yankees at once. They fired hundreds of shots in the thicket, and I lay perfectly still until quiet was restored. When I sat up and felt around to see what caused me to fall, my hand came into contact with a saber which I found belted to a dead man. This saber, caught between my legs, threw me. It rattling against the man's canteen, as well as my falling amongst the pine twigs, was the big noise in the night.

"Fully reassured, I proceeded, found the officer, and delivered the order. He was an old friend, and inquired what I made so much noise for. My explanation [brought] a laugh [and] a caution to me not to repeat it.

"A good night [was said], and I started to our line, shaping my course as well as I could, so as to find my dead man again. Fortune favored me. I found him, took his sword, and then felt in his pockets for what he had. I found a knife, a pipe, and a piece of string—and in every pocket, even to the one in his shirt, he had smoking tobacco. . . . He was a Yankee lieutenant."

Miles to the southwest, with little prospect of reaching the battlefield before daylight, Longstreet's corps was on the move. As recalled by D. Augustus Dickert, of Kershaw's division: "Such a march, and under such conditions, was never before experienced by the troops. Along blind roads overgrown by underbrush, through fields that had lain fallow for years, now studded with bushes and briars, and the night being exceedingly dark, the men floundered and fell as they marched. But the needs were too urgent to be slack in the march now, so the men struggled with nature in their endeavor to keep in ranks. Sometimes the head of the column would lose its way, and during the time it was hunting its way back to the lost bridle path [we drew up, and this] was about the only rest we got. The men were already worn out by their forced march of the day before, and now they had to exert all their strength to its utmost to keep up."

One of the nocturnal marches made on the battlefield itself requires special mention. This was a Confederate shift, and it involved John Gordon's brigade, Jubal Early's division, Ewell's corps, which constituted Lee's northern wing, or his left. After making its timely approach and its smashing attack during Ewell's crisis, Gordon's brigade had assumed a position as Early's right-hand unit. During the night the brigade was ordered to swing around the rear and come in on the division's left, which would put the brigade on the extreme left of Lee's army.

Gordon relates: "The night of May 5 was far spent when my command reached its destination. . . . The men were directed to sleep on their arms during the remaining hours of darkness. Scouts were at once sent to the front to feel their way through the thickets and ascertain, if possible, where the extreme right [or northern flank] of Grant's line rested. At early dawn these trusted men reported that they had found it: that it rested in the woods only a short distance in our front, that it was wholly unprotected, and that the Confederate lines stretched a considerable distance beyond the Union right, overlapping it."

Gordon was elated at this information, and he envisioned making an early attack on the exposed flank, believing he could set the stage for Grant's destruction. But Gordon could not move without permission from his superiors. And it would be many hours, during which a lot would happen elsewhere, before the nod was given.

11

A New Storm at Daybreak

The morning of May 6 found both Grant and Lee stirring from their cots while it was still dark. Lee's camp lay close behind his southern wing, commanded by A. P. Hill, and the Confederate chief arose to the disturbing knowledge that Longstreet's corps, which he planned to use against Hancock at Hill's front, was still a few miles from the field. Grant, who was quartered just north of his center, was luckier with his own reserves. As explained by Horace Porter:

"At four o'clock ... we were awakened ... by the sound of Burnside's men moving along the Germanna Road. They had been marching since 1 A.M., hurrying on to reach the left of Warren. The members of the headquarters mess soon after assembled to partake of a hasty breakfast. The general made rather a singular meal preparatory to so exhausting a day as that which was to follow. He took a cucumber, sliced it, poured some vinegar over it, and partook of nothing else except a cup of strong coffee. The first thing he did after rising from the table was to call for a fresh supply of cigars. His colored servant 'Bill' brought him two dozen. After lighting one of them, he filled his pockets with the rest. He then went over to the knoll and began to walk back and forth slowly upon the cleared portion of the ridge."

The sky was graying now, a light mist bore the fragrance of wild-flowers, birds were singing in the brushwood, and thousands of men on both sides were preparing themselves for a renewal of the fighting. An exception was Frank Wilkeson, the Union artillery private who, the day before, had slipped away from his idle gun in the rear in order to come forward and serve with Warren's infantry. At the day's end Wilkeson had wandered southward and, wrapped in blankets taken from one of the dead, had slept at Hancock's front.

"Long before sunrise," Wilkeson recounts, "I had my breakfast; and having seen sufficient of the fighting done by infantry, and strongly impressed with the truth that a light-artilleryman had better stay close to his guns, I bade my acquaintances good-by and walked off, intent on getting to my gun and comparative comfort and safety. But I hung on to my rifle and belt. They were to be trophies of the battle, and I meant to excite the envy of my comrades by displaying them.

"Stepping into the road, I walked along briskly, and saw many other unwounded men rearward bound. A sentinel, with rifle at the carry, halted me and demanded to see blood. I could show none. I assured him that I belonged to the light artillery, and that I had gone to the front the previous day just to see the battle.

"He said, 'You have a rifle; you have a belt and a cartridge box. Your mouth is powder-blackened. You have been fighting as an infantryman, and you shall so continue to fight. You go back, or I will arrest you, and then you will be sent back.'

"To say that I was amazed and disgusted would but faintly express my feelings. There stood the provost guard, who would not let me go home to my battery. I longed to kill him . . . but I was afraid to . . . for fear that his comrades might see me do it. So I turned and hastened back to the front. I determined to fight that day, and go home to the battery the succeeding night. I did not believe that the line of guards extended far. . . . And even if they did I knew that I could pass through the lines in the night.

"Before I rejoined the infantry . . . on the battle line, I equipped myself with a plug of tobacco and two canteens filled with water. Never mind where I got them.

"Away off to the right, toward the Rapidan, the battle rose with the sun."

This was the opening round between the field's northern opponents, who would play a secondary role in the day's events. The main battle would be fought in the south. Dawn found Hancock poised to make an all-out attack on Hill. Hill's two-division front was in disarray after the first day's contest. His reserve division, like Longstreet's entire corps, was still en route to the field. Little had been done to reorganize Hill's two battered divisions (those of Cadmus Wilcox and Henry Heth), since Longstreet had been expected to take over the front before hostilities were resumed. Now Wilcox and Heth could only hope that the foe would be slow to move.

Wilcox narrates: "The tree-tops were already tinged with the early rays of the rising sun, but the enemy lay quiet. At length the sun itself was seen between the boughs and foliage of the heavy forest; and [we] on the Plank Road . . . eager to catch at straws in [our] unprepared state, began to have hopes that the Federals would not advance. But these were soon dispelled."

One of Union General Hancock's men, Color Sergeant D. G. Crotty, tells what happened: "The order comes . . . and we go in, thinking to surprise the Johnnies, but they are up and waiting for us in the thick chaparral. They pour a volley into our ranks, and the ball has commenced once more. Both sides stand and take the fearful fire, and the whole line seems to be one vast sheet of flame in the early morn. The number that fall on both sides is fearful, for we are fighting at very close range. We charge on their lines with great odds, but they stand their ground like a solid wall of masonry.

"The roar of musketry, the dying groans of the wounded, the hellish yells of the rebels, and the shouts and cheers of the Union men mingle together, all making a noise and confusion that is hard to describe. Nothing is thought of but load and fire. The wounded must take care of themselves, and every man must stand and fight till either killed or wounded. The rebels fall in their line, but those who fall have their places filled. . . . We don't like this kind of fighting much, and [go] forward on the charge in four or five lines deep. The rebels now give way, and we chase them through the dense forest."

Union Private Frank Wilkeson was a part of the pursuit. "I saw many dead Confederates. . . . They were poorly clad. Their blankets were in rolls, hanging diagonally from the left shoulder to the right side, where the ends were tied with a string or a strap. Their canvas haversacks contained plenty of corn-meal and some bacon. I saw no coffee, no sugar, no hard bread in any of the Confederate haversacks I looked into. But there was tobacco in plugs on almost all the dead Confederates. Their arms were not as good as ours. They were poorly shod. The direful poverty of the Confederacy was plainly indicated by its dead soldiers. But they fought! Yes, like men of purely American blood.

"We had charged, and charged, and charged again, and had gone wild with battle fever. . . . We were doing splendidly. I cast my eyes upward to see the sun, so as to judge of the time, as I was hungry and wanted to eat, and I saw that it was still low above the trees."

Second day in the Wilderness, viewed from the Union side

As on the previous day, Wilkinson was in the peculiar position of being a stranger on the line. "I knew but few of the men in the regiment in whose ranks I stood, but I learned the Christian names of some of them. The man who stood next to me on my right was called Will. He was cool, brave, and intelligent. . . . When the Second Corps was advancing and driving Hill's soldiers . . . I was flurried. He noticed it, and steadied my nerves by saying, kindly, 'Don't fire so fast. This fight will last all day. Don't hurry. Cover your man before you pull your trigger. Take it easy, my boy, take it easy, and your cartridges will last the longer.' "

At the Confederate front, only Wilcox's division was still in action. Heth's entire line was retiring to reorganize, with some of the units on the run. Wilcox could do little against the pressing Federals. He rode rapidly rearward—making his way past retreating ambulances, supply wagons, and camp followers on foot—and soon found General Lee. "[I] reported the condition of my command. His response was, 'Longstreet must be here. Go bring him up!' Galloping to the road, the head of his corps, Kershaw's division, was met and ordered to file at once to the right and get into line as quickly as possible, for fear [my] division would be forced back on it while forming. Less than a brigade had left the road when Longstreet in person arrived."

Longstreet gives this picture: "As the line deployed, the divisions of Heth and Wilcox came back upon us in disorder, more and more confused as their steps hurried under Hancock's musketry. As my ranks formed, the men broke files to give free passage for their comrades to the rear."

According to one of Longstreet's subordinate commanders, Colonel W. F. Perry, the fugitives included many wounded. "They came in streams, some borne on litters, some supported by comrades, and others making their way alone." Masses of the unwounded seemed to be close to panic as they poured to the right and left of mounted officers who were struggling to breast their flight. These troops were taunted by some of Longstreet's men with such shouts as "Is this Lee's army?"

Again in Longstreet's words: "The advancing fire was getting brisk, but not a shot was fired in return by my troops until the divisions were ready. . . . General Lee, appalled at the condition of affairs, thought to lead the Texas brigade alone into desperate charge. . . . Colonel [Charles] Venable, of his staff, reported to me General Lee's efforts to lead the brigade, and suggested that I should try to call him from it. I asked that he would say, with my compliments, that his line would be recovered in an hour if he would permit me to handle the troops, but if my services were not needed, I would like to ride to some place of safety, as it was not quite comfortable where we were."

Lee had already been stopped by vociferous protests from the Texans themselves, but he remained on his horse near the front, his eyes ablaze with martial ardor and his head bare as he used his hat to make sweeps that hastened the steps of the approaching regiments.

One of the men who passed close to Lee was Colonel William C. Oates, commander of a regiment from Alabama. "I thought him at that moment the grandest specimen of manhood I ever beheld. He looked as though he ought to have been and was monarch of the world. He glanced his eye down on the 'ragged rebels' as they filed around him in quick-time to their place in the line, and inquired, 'What troops are these?' And was answered by some private in the Fifteenth, 'Law's Alabama Brigade.' He exclaimed in a strong voice, 'God bless the Alabamians!' The men cheered and went into line with a whoop."

These troops of Charles Field's division were forming to the left of the Plank Road. Kershaw's division was forming on the right, but with one regiment, the Second South Carolina, astride the road and extending leftward. D. Augustus Dickert, himself with the main body of troops on the right, was inspired when the revered Kershaw, ignoring the bullets that were flying everywhere, dashed about on his horse issuing orders and asking the men to do their duty. Dickert relates: "The columns were not yet in proper order, but the needs so pressing to check the advance of the enemy that a forward movement was ordered, and the lines formed as the troops marched. The Second [South Carolina] moved forward on the left of the Plank Road, in support of a battery stationed there. . . . "

These guns were part of the artillery battalion commanded by Colonel William Poague, who had been supporting Heth's division and had held his ground. Served with canister, Poague's guns were in roaring action. The battalion played an important role in slowing the Federal advance and saving Lee's army from a critical penetration.

Returning to Dickert: "Down the gentle slope the brigade marched, over and under the tangled shrubbery and dwarfed saplings, while a withering fire was being poured into them by, as yet, an unseen enemy. Men fell here and there, officers urging on their commands and ordering them to hold their fire.

"When near the lower end of the declivity, the shock came. Just in front of us, and not forty yards away, lay the enemy. The long line of

Frontline troops urging Lee to go to the rear

blue could be seen under the ascending smoke of thousands of rifles. The red flashes of their guns seemed to blaze in our very faces. Now the battle was on in earnest. The roar of Kershaw's guns mingled with those of the enemy. Longstreet had met his old antagonist . . . Hancock, the Northern hero of Gettysburg. . . . New troops were being put rapidly in action to the right and left of us. Men rolled and writhed in their last death struggle. Wounded men groped their way to the rear, being blinded by the stifling smoke. . . . Regiments were left without commanders, companies without officers. . . . Still the battle rolled on."

On the Union side, Frank Wilkeson "heard the peculiar cry a stricken man utters as the bullet tears through his flesh. I turned my head as I loaded my rifle to see who was hit. I saw a bearded Irishman pull up his shirt. He had been wounded in the left side just below the floating ribs. His face was gray with fear. The wound looked as though it were mortal. He looked at it for an instant, then poked it gently with his index finger. He . . . smiled with satisfaction. He tucked his shirt into his trousers, and was fighting in the ranks again before I had capped my rifle. The ball had cut a groove in his skin only. The play of this Irishman's face was so expressive, his emotions changed so quickly, that I could not keep from laughing."

Wilkeson's light mood was momentary. "Our men fell by scores. Great gaps were struck in our lines. . . . There was great confusion. . . . The men wavered badly. They fired wildly. They hesitated. I feared the line would break, feared that we were whipped. The line was fed with troops from the reserve. The regimental officers held their men as well as they could. We could hear them close behind us, or in line with us, saying, 'Steady, men, steady, steady, steady!' as one speaks to frightened and excited horses. The Confederate fire resembled the fury of hell in intensity, and was deadly accurate. Their bullets swished by in swarms. It seems to me that I could have caught a pot full of them if I had had a strong iron vessel rigged on a pole as a butterfly net. . . . The Confederates [had] got a couple of batteries into action, and they added to the deafening din. The shot and shell from these guns cut great limbs off of the trees . . . and several men were knocked down by them."

A singular thing happened to a corporal from New Jersey, Joseph R. Stewart, while he was in a reserve position, waiting to go on the line. Stewart was squatting in front of a tree, his back against it, his rifle, with its butt on the ground, jutting up between his knees. A solid shot from a Confederate gun snapped off the upper part of the corporal's rifle, passed just above his head, and smashed through the tree. Stewart sustained minor damage to the hand that held the rifle, while his back was wrenched and he was knocked senseless by the tree's violent shudder. He was through fighting for the day, but would soon be back in action.

Again in Frank Wilkeson's words: "Our line strengthened [by reserves], we, in our turn, pushed ahead, and Longstreet's men gave ground slowly before us, fighting savagely for every foot. The wounded lay together. I saw, in the heat of this fight, wounded men of the opposing forces aiding each other to reach the protective shelter of trees and logs, and, as we advanced, I saw a Confederate and a Union soldier drinking in turn out of a Union canteen as they lay behind a tree."

It was about this time that Grant sent Horace Porter to confer with Hancock on matters concerning the continuance of the offensive. Porter relates: "I met Hancock on the Orange Plank Road, not far from its junction with the Brock Road, actively engaged in directing his troops. . . . His face was flushed with the excitement of victory. . . . His right arm was extended to its full length in pointing out certain positions as he gave his orders, and his commanding form towered still higher as he rose in his stirrups to peer through the opening in the woods. . . . He had been well dubbed 'Hancock the Superb.' . . .

"Along the line of Hancock's advance the enemy dead were everywhere visible; his wounded strewed the roads; prisoners had been captured, and battle flags had been taken: but Hancock was now compelled to halt and restore the contact between his commands. . . .

"Sheridan had become engaged in a spirited contest with Stuart's cavalry on the left [i.e., to the south] at Todd's Tavern. . . . The sound of this conflict was mistaken for a time for an attack by Longstreet from that direction, and made Hancock anxious to strengthen his exposed left flank. His embarrassments were increased by one of those singular accidents which, though trivial in themselves, often turn the tide of battle. A body of infantry was reported to be advancing up the Brock Road and moving upon Hancock's left and rear. A brigade which could ill be spared was at once thrown out in that direction to resist the threatened attack. It soon appeared that the body of infantry consisted of about seven hundred of our convalescents [from Chancellorsville] who were returning to join their commands. The incident, however, had caused the loss of valuable time. These occurrences prevented Hancock from further taking the offensive."

Turning to the Confederate side and to Longstreet's subordinate

W. F. Perry: "It was now nearly 9 o'clock in the morning. The great struggle was still to come. The Federal lines were some distance in front of the Brock Road, the most direct route to Spotsylvania and to Richmond. . . . The success of General Grant would have opened an unobstructed road to Richmond and might have been decisive of the campaign."

Lee's army was stronger now. The broken divisions of Heth and Wilcox had reformed, and Hill's reserve division had reached the field. Longstreet was enabled to widen his front. He extended it to his right, or around the southern flank that Hancock was worried about. But the first Federals to yield under the increased pressure were those of a division on Hancock's right, a part of Warren's Fifth Corps that had accompanied the morning's advance and had been fighting well. This division was headed by General James Wadsworth, an elderly New Yorker of great wealth.

As his division was thrown back, Wadsworth rode forward to rally his men, and he was tumbled from his horse by a bullet through the head. He was left behind in the rush. As explained by Confederate General Charles Field, commander of the troops who downed Wadsworth and overran the spot where he fell: "Though mortally wounded and unable to articulate, he was apparently conscious, and . . . myself and associates did all in our power to alleviate his sufferings. He was tenderly propped against a tree and provided with water, and every attention and respect shown him which kindness could suggest."

At Union headquarters near Wilderness Tavern, Grant and his staff became aware, through the sounds they heard, that some of Wadsworth's troops were falling back on a northerly oblique, toward headquarters itself. Grant was urged by his staff to move eastward out of danger, but he chose instead to order the spot defended.

A short distance forward, atop a knoll on the Lacy property, were some Union batteries, and one of the gunners was Augustus Buell, who assumes the narrative: "The sounds of musketry and the dense volumes of smoke rolling up above the scrubby woods began to approach our position. . . . Before long the first rush of stragglers began to emerge from the woods in our front, and we could distinctly hear the Rebel yell through the brush. The musketry in the meantime [that of the entire Hancock-Longstreet front] beat anything ever heard. . . . It was one solid, savage crash, crash, without the slightest lull or intermission, extending along a line over two miles in length. . . .

"We could do nothing, because no horses could have pulled a gun

James S. Wadsworth, mortally wounded May 6

through the brush in which the infantry were fighting. As for the roads, there were only two, the Plank and the Pike, and they were . . . simply wide paths through the thickets. Our artillery had but one chance of work, and that was if our infantry should fall back into the Lacy clearing and the Rebels should attempt to force the position at and about the Wilderness Tavern.

"At about 10 o'clock in the morning it seemed as if we would get that chance. The crash and the yells had kept coming our way for half an hour, when suddenly our infantry . . . came pell-mell out of the woods a little to the left of our front in some confusion. . . . Then came rapid commands [for us] to change front with the left and center sections; to 'fire to the left; load canister—ready.' But the narrow clearing was full of . . . disordered infantry, so we stood at a ready, pieces sighted and lanyards in hand, for several minutes. . . . Meantime [our] infantry had sagged to the left . . . and in a few minutes they cleared a path for our canister.

"But the Johnnies, when they came to the edge of the brush and saw 18 guns looking at them from the Lacy House knoll, hesitated, and, instead of charging as we expected them to do, lay down in the edge of the brush and began sharpshooting at us and our then-rallying infantry. To this we instantly replied with canister, which, after a few ineffectual rounds, was changed to case. Of course, they had no artillery, as they had come through brush that men with muskets could hardly penetrate, let alone teams and gun carriages. No one knows what we did to them with our canister and case, but they hit four or five of us in the three batteries with their sharpshooting, though it was tolerably long musket range. But they did not seriously follow our broken infantry beyond the edge of the brush."

The retreating Federals had brought in a few Confederate prisoners. Cannoneer Buell tells of one, a man of mature years. "He belonged to the Fifth Texas. . . . He had been hit in the shin by a bullet which had temporarily paralyzed his leg without breaking the bone. . . . Some of the boys asked him what he thought of the battle. He was a comical old cuss, and his reply was, 'Battle be ———! It ain't no battle! It's a worse riot than Chickamauga was!' (He had been with Longstreet at Chickamauga the Fall before.) 'You Yanks don't call this a battle, do you? At Chickamauga there was at least a rear, but here there ain't neither front nor rear. It's all a ——— mess! And our two armies ain't nothin' but howlin' mobs!'

"The *sangfroid* of this grizzly old Texan was superb. While he sat there sopping his game leg with a wet rag and gnawing at a hardtack and piece of pork we had given him, a pretty fresh youngster from one of the batteries came along and stopped to chaff with him a little. 'Say, Uncle Johnny,' inquired the youngster, 'Haven't you fellows about made up your minds that one Southerner can't whip five Yankees?' The venerable Rebel looked at him solemnly and responded, 'Son, did you ever hear any Southern man say he could whip five Yankees?'

"'N— no, I don't know that I ever did.'

"'Well, then, whar did you git that notion?'

"'Oh, some of the men who went round up home making speeches to raise companies told us that the Johnnies bragged that one Southerner could whip five Yankees. Maybe they told us that to get our dander up.'

"'I expected as much,' replied Uncle Johnny. 'Now, let me tell you, Sonny, that that story, like a good many other things which helped to bring on this war, wasn't nothin' but a ——— Abolition lie!'

"You couldn't phase that old rooster much. He won our hearts by telling us that he had been in the Second Kentucky [a United States Army regiment] in the Mexican War, and had helped support [our] old battery at Buena Vista."

12

Red Stains in Every Thicket

The late-morning proceedings in front of Grant's headquarters occurred simultaneously with another flare-up in the battlefield's
secondary zone to the north. It was here that Union Generals Warren
and Sedgwick (minus the divisions they had contributed to Hancock's
fight) faced the Confederates under Ewell. One of the Union newsmen
on the scene was Charles Page, of Greeley's *Tribune*, who said in his
report: "The enemy press close upon Warren and Sedgwick, and train
a number of guns exactly upon the latter's headquarters. A man and
three horses are killed within twenty feet of the general. . . . Finding
the enemy disposed to renew the engagement of the early morning,
Sedgwick accepts the challenge and advances his whole line. The men
go in with more dash and hold on more sturdily than in the morning.
Ewell is driven back to his second line, where his guns are in position,
and there makes a stand.

"At this juncture, Warren, who connects with Sedgwick's left, is
extremely anxious to go in with all his might, but the enemy's position
in his front seems too formidable. I see a troop of horsemen riding
rapidly up to the perilous edge of battle, and recognize Warren and his
white horse. . . . With him are [several other officers]. Halting at the first
line, they dismount and walk more than half a mile in front of the men,
who are flat upon their breasts. . . . We hold the woods on one side of
an open space, perhaps one-fourth of a mile across, and the Rebels lie
along the trend of the woods upon the other side. Their intrenchments
are plainly visible, and the open mouths of their artillery peer over.

"No, it will not do to charge across. It were stark madness. The sharpshooters may continue to reply to this [threat], but no man shall start across the plain and live."

It was about noon when this stalemate occurred. At the extreme northern end of Confederate General Ewell's position, where things had been relatively quiet since dawn, John Gordon remained in a fret. Ewell and Jubal Early continued to withhold their permission for Gordon to make an attack around Sedgwick's exposed right flank. They considered such a move to be too dangerous. Meanwhile, General Lee, busy with things in the south, hoped that Ewell would soon do *something* of a bold nature to help strengthen the overall Confederate effort.

Lee's effort in the south was presently going very well. Hancock's entire line, its left flank turned, was in retreat. As depicted by Unionist Frank Wilkeson: "We fired and fired and fired, and fell back fighting stubbornly. We tore cartridges until our teeth ached. But we could not check the Confederate advance, and they forced us back and back and back."

Wilkeson was still in the company of his new friend Will. "During the day I had learned to look up to this excellent soldier, and lean on him. . . . As we were being slowly driven back to the Brock Road by Longstreet's men, we made a stand. I was behind a tree firing, with my rifle barrel resting on the stub of a limb. Will was standing by my side, but in the open. He, with a groan, doubled up and dropped on the ground at my feet. He looked up at me. His face was pale. He gasped for breath a few times, and then said faintly, 'That ends me. I am shot through the bowels.' I said, 'Crawl to the rear. We are not far from the intrenchments along the Brock Road.' . . . He looked at me and said impatiently, 'I tell you that I am as good as dead. There is no use in fooling with me. I shall stay here.' Then he pitched forward dead, shot again and through the head. We fell back before Longstreet's soldiers, and left Will lying in a windrow of dead men."

The narrative is assumed by Union newsman William Swinton: "Hancock, flaming out with the fire of battle, rode hither and thither, directing and animating; but the disruption of the left flank [had] spread calamity through the line . . . and he had to content himself with rallying and reforming his troops behind the breastworks on the Brock Road. . . . It seemed indeed that irretrievable disaster was upon us."

Turning to the Confederate side and to General Charles Field, who had been directing the left wing of Longstreet's attack from a position on the Plank Road: "We all thought . . . the battle was won. . . . As Generals Lee and Longstreet joined me at the front, the latter seized

Lee interrogating Federals captured in the Wilderness

my hand and congratulated me on the brilliant work just done. As we rode chatting down the road, General Lee and myself stopped a moment to have a log and rail obstruction removed from it, Longstreet and Brigadier General [Micah] Jenkins, with their staffs, continuing on."

Micah Jenkins, a South Carolinian in his middle twenties who was devoted to the Confederacy and had a fine war record, now turned to Longstreet and said, "I am happy. I have felt despair for the cause for some months, but am relieved and feel assured that we will put the enemy back across the Rapidan before night."

At that instant the party of officers became the target of a volley of musketry from the woods to the right. "This fire," explains General Field, "came from our own troops . . . which had been employed in the flank movement, and, approaching the Plank Road on a perpendicular line, had in the underbrush mistaken Longstreet for the retiring Federals." Several of the officers were hit, with Micah Jenkins falling mortally hurt even as he finished his optimistic pronouncement.

Longstreet takes up: "At the moment that Jenkins fell, I received a severe shock from a minie ball passing through my throat and right shoulder. The blow lifted me from the saddle, and my right arm dropped to my side, but I settled back to my seat and started to ride on, when in a minute the flow of blood admonished me that my work for the day was done. As I turned to ride back, members of the staff, seeing me about to fall, dismounted and lifted me to the ground."

Sitting against a tree with red foam on his lips, Longstreet ordered the attack continued. But his units were now disorganized, and Union General Burnside had come into position to threaten his left. Moreover, the news of his fall caused dismay as it spread.

For Southerner Robert Stiles, the contemplative artillery officer, the dreadful moment was productive of new insights into Longstreet's character. "It is a little singular that, though nominally attached to his command longer than any other, yet I probably had less acquaintance and association with General Longstreet than with any other of the more prominent generals of the Confederate army in Virginia. Indeed, I do not recall ever having spoken to him, or having heard him utter so much as one word. . . . I could not but feel that there must be something in the nature of the man himself to account for the fact that I knew so little of him. . . . In this Wilderness fight I was suddenly brought in contact with a scene which greatly affected my conception of the man under the regalia of the general.

"It may not have been generally observed that [Stonewall] Jackson and Longstreet were both struck down in the Wilderness [Jackson during the Battle of Chancellorsville], just one year apart, each at the crisis of the most brilliant and, up to the moment of his fall, the most successful movement of his career as a soldier, and each by the fire of his own men.

"I had been sent forward, perhaps to look for some place where we might get into the fight [with our artillery pieces], when I observed an excited gathering some distance back of the lines; and, pressing toward it, I heard that General Longstreet had just been shot down and was being put into an ambulance. I could not learn anything definite as to the character of his wound, but only that it was serious—some said he was dead. When the ambulance moved off, I followed it a little way, being anxious for trustworthy news of the general.

"The members of his staff surrounded the vehicle, some riding in front, some on one side and some on the other, and some behind. One . . . stood upon the rear step of the ambulance, seeming to desire to be as near him as possible. I never on any occasion . . . saw a group of officers and gentlemen more deeply distressed. They were literally bowed down with grief. All of them were in tears. One, by whose side I rode for some distance, was himself severely hurt, but he made no allusion to his wound, and I do not believe he felt it. It was not alone the general they *admired* who had been shot down—it was, rather, the man they *loved*.

"I rode up to the ambulance and looked in. They had taken off Longstreet's hat and coat and boots. The blood had paled out of his face, and its somewhat gross aspect was gone. I noticed how white and dome-like his great forehead looked, and, with scarcely less reverent admiration, how spotless white his socks and his fine gauze undervest, save where the black-red gore from his breast and shoulder had stained it.

"While I gazed at his massive form, lying so still, except when it rocked inertly with the lurch of the vehicle, his eyelids frayed apart till I could see a delicate line of blue between them; and then he very quietly moved his unwounded arm, and, with his thumb and two fingers, carefully lifted the saturated undershirt from his chest, holding it up a moment, and heaved a deep sigh. He is not dead, I said to myself, and he is calm and entirely master of the situation—he is both greater and more attractive than I have heretofore thought him."

It was now well past two o'clock in the afternoon. General Lee had taken personal command at the front, which had fallen relatively quiet, and was reorganizing the troops for a resumption of the attack. Among the badly battered units relieved of further duty for the day was the brigade to which D. Augustus Dickert belonged. He says that some of the men threw themselves on the ground to rest, while others wandered back over the ground covered during the attack. "Friends were hunting out friends among the dead and wounded. The litter-bearers were looking after those too badly wounded to make their way to the rear. Dr. Salmond had established his brigade hospital near where the battle had begun in the morning, and to this haven of the wounded those who were able to walk were making their way.

"In the rear of a battlefield are scenes too sickening for sensitive eyes. . . . [That afternoon] I saw one of the saddest sights I almost ever witnessed. A soldier from Company C, Third South Carolina, a young soldier just verging into manhood, had been shot in the first advance, the bullet severing the great artery of the thigh. The young man, seeing his danger of bleeding to death before succor could possibly reach him, had struggled behind a small sapling. Bracing himself against it, he undertook deliberative measures for saving his life. Tying a handkerchief above the wound, placing a small stone underneath and just over the artery, and putting a stick between the handkerchief and his leg, he began to tighten by twisting the stick around. But too late. Life had fled, leaving both hands clasping the stick, his eyes glassy and fixed."

While Lee and his generals were preparing their new effort, the commanders on the Union side were plotting a move of their own. Horace Porter tells of the plan—and of its disruption: "Generals Meade and Grant . . . decided to have Hancock and Burnside make a simultaneous attack at 6 P.M. . . . I started for Hancock's front to confer with him regarding this movement, and just as I joined the troops the enemy . . . made a desperate assault upon our line. It began at 4:15 P.M."

The brush between the lines was now afire, and numbers of the Union wounded lying out in front of Hancock's breastworks, unreachable in the storm of musketry, were burned to death. Union Private Frank Wilkeson was aghast as he watched from his position inside the works, but he decided that these men did not suffer to the extent that everyone supposed. "The smoke rolled heavily and slowly before the fire. It enveloped the wounded, and I think that by far the larger portion of the men who were roasted were suffocated before the flames curled round them."

Returning to Union staff officer Horace Porter: "The flames were

Confederate hospital in a Wilderness clearing

Lee's men assaulting Hancock's burning breastworks

communicated to [Hancock's] log breastworks and abatis of slashed timber. The wind was, unfortunately, blowing in our direction, and the blinding smoke was driven in the faces of our men, while the fire itself swept down upon them. For a time they battled heroically to maintain their position, fighting both the conflagration and the enemy's advancing columns. At last, however, the breastworks became untenable, and some of the troops . . . now fell back in confusion. The enemy took advantage of the disorder, and, rushing forward with cheers, succeeded in planting some of his battle flags upon our front line of breastworks."

As interjected by Union newsman Charles Page: "Stragglers for the first time in all this fighting streamed to the rear in large numbers, choking the roads and causing a panic by their stampede and incoherent tales of frightful disaster. It was even reported at general headquarters that the enemy had burst entirely through. . . . Grant and Meade, seated with their backs against the same tree, quietly listened to the officer who brought the report, and consulted a moment in low tones. . . . At length Grant says, with laconic emphasis, 'I don't believe it.' He was right."

Horace Porter resumes: "Hancock and all the staff officers present made strenuous exertions to rally the men, and many of them were soon brought back to the front. General [Samuel S.] Carroll's brigade was now ordered to form and retake the line of intrenchments which had been lost. These gallant troops, led by the intrepid Carroll in person, dashing forward at a run and cheering as they went, swept everything before them, and in a few minutes were in possession of the works. . . . Some of Hancock's artillery was served with great efficiency in this engagement, and added much to the result. At five o'clock the enemy had been completely repulsed and fell back, leaving a large number of his dead and wounded on the field.

"Burnside made an attack at half-past five, but with no important results. The nature of the ground was a more formidable obstruction than the enemy. [In the north] Warren and Sedgwick . . . had prevented the enemy in front of them from withdrawing any troops [to send to the southern arena], but notwithstanding their gallant fighting they had substantially gained no ground."

General Lee was very unhappy with his northern wing. He had expected Ewell to make a useful contribution to the fight. Lee rode northward about 5 P.M. (He was unaware that Burnside was about to attack his southern wing, but, as it turned out, the defense did not require his personal attention.) Lee felt an urgent need to talk with Ewell.

As recalled by John Gordon, the brigadier who wanted to launch an attack down upon Grant's northern flank but could not get the permission he needed: "Both General Early and I were at Ewell's headquarters when, at about 5:30 in the afternoon, General Lee rode up and asked. 'Cannot something be done on this flank to relieve the pressure upon our right?' After listening for some time to the conference which followed this pointed inquiry, I felt it my duty to acquaint General Lee with the facts as to Sedgwick's exposed flank, and with the plan of battle which had been submitted and urged in the early hours of the morning and during the day.

"General Early . . . maintained that Burnside's corps was in the woods behind Sedgwick's right; that the movement was too hazardous and must result in disaster to us. With as much earnestness as was consistent with the position of junior officer, I recounted the facts to General Lee, and assured him that General Early was mistaken; that I had ridden for several miles in Sedgwick's rear, and that neither Burnside's corps nor any other Union troops were concealed in those woods. [Burnside's corps, as a matter of fact, was at this time beginning to make a flurry of noise in the south.]

"The details of the whole plan were laid before him. There was no doubt with him as to its feasibility. His words were few, but his silence and grim looks while the reasons for that long delay were being given, and his prompt order to me to move at once to the attack, revealed his thoughts almost as plainly as words could have done. Late as it was, he agreed in the opinion that we could bring havoc to as much of the Union line as we could reach before darkness should check us."

The fighting instigated by Burnside died off while Gordon was starting to move, and the entire field fell silent. As related by Union newsman Charles Page: "It was now nearly sunset. From one end of the line to the other, not a shot could be heard. The day's work seemed over. Our line of tonight would be that of last night. . . . Our assaults had been futile, but the enemy's had been equally so. . . . Men [who had] separated in the heat of the day, now chancing to meet, congratulated each other. The Rebels can't endure another such day, and we can, was the expressed conviction. . . .

"The sun went down red. The smoke of the battle of more than 200,000 men [it was actually less than this number, perhaps about 175,000] destroying each other with villainous saltpetre through all the long hours of a long day filled the valleys and rested upon the hills of all this Wilderness, hung in lurid haze all around the horizon, and built a dense canopy overhead, beneath which this grand Army of Freedom was preparing to rest against the morrow. Generals Grant and Meade had retired to their tents. Quiet reigned. . . .

"Darkness and smoke were mingling in grim twilight, and fast deepening into thick gloom, when we were startled out of repose back into fierce excitement. . . . A wild Rebel yell away to the right. We knew they had massed and were charging. . . . We thought it but a night attack to ascertain if we had changed our position. We were mistaken—it was more. . . .

"The enemy came down like a torrent rolling and dashing in living waves, and flooding up against the [flank of the] Sixth Corps. The main line stood like a rock, but not so the extreme right. That flank was instantly and utterly turned. The Rebel line . . . surged around [Truman] Seymour's brigade, tided over it and through it, beat against Shaler [i.e., Alexander Shaler's brigade], and bore away his right regiments. . . . Seymour's men, seeing their pickets running back and hearing the shouts of the Rebels, who charged with all their chivalry, were smitten with panic . . . and in an incredibly short time made their way through a mile and a half of woods to the [Turnpike] in the rear. They reported, in the frantic manner usual with stampeded men, the entire corps broken. Grant, as in Hancock's case, didn't believe it."

The general knew that Lee's heaviest concentration of troops was in the south facing Hancock. There could be no great horde in the north. Yet the disruption was a major one (with the two brigade commanders having fallen into enemy hands), and Grant took steps to deal with it. Horace Porter explains: "Reinforcements were hurried to the point attacked, and preparations made for Sedgwick's Corps to take up a new line, with the front and right thrown back. General Grant soon . . . seated himself on a stool in front of his tent, lighted a fresh cigar, and there continued to receive further advices from the right.

"A general officer came in from his command at this juncture and said to the general-in-chief, speaking rapidly and laboring under considerable excitement, 'General Grant, this is a crisis that cannot be looked upon too seriously. I know Lee's methods well by past experience. He will throw his whole army between us and the Rapidan, and cut us off completely from our communications.' The general rose to his feet, took his cigar out of his mouth, turned to the officer and replied, with a degree of animation which he seldom manifested, 'Oh, I am heartily tired of hearing about what Lee is going to do. Some of you always seem to think he is suddenly going to turn a double somersault, and land in our rear and on both of our flanks at the same time. Go back to your command and try to think what we are going to do ourselves instead of what Lee is going to do.' The officer retired rather crestfallen, and without saying a word in reply. . . .

"It was soon ascertained that, although Sedgwick's line had been forced back with some loss, and Shaler and Seymour had been made prisoners, only a few hundred men had been captured, and the enemy had been compelled to withdraw. General Grant had great confidence in Sedgwick in such an emergency, and the event showed that it was not misplaced."

On the Confederate side, the two captured generals drew much interest. As noted by Private G. W. Nichols: "General Seymour was a very tall man. I suppose he was six and one-half feet high and would have weighed 150 pounds. The other, General Shaler, was a regular cut-short Dutchman about five feet high, and would have weighed about 250 pounds. There was quite a contrast in them as they were marched out."

In the battlefield's southern zone, things had remained quiet. Says Unionist Frank Wilkeson, who was still at the front and was doubtless the only artilleryman in the army who had spent two days there: "Darkness reigned in the forest where thousands of dead and wounded men lay. The air still smelled of powder smoke. Many soldiers cleaned out their rifles. We ate, and then large details helped to carry their wounded comrades to the road, where we loaded them into ambulances and wagons. I determined to join my battery. I threw away my rifle and belt, and as the first wagons loaded with wounded men moved to the rear I walked by the side of the column and passed the guards—if there were any stationed on that road—without being challenged. When I was well to the rear . . . I cooked and ate a hearty supper, and then rolled myself in the dead soldier's blankets, which I had hung on to."

There was no rest for the people of the ambulance corps Wilkeson had come out with. They and others like them, all up and down the lines, turned every effort to getting the wounded to the rear. The dead were left for burial details that would come later. In the warm weather, some of the corpses of the first day were already bloating and putrefying, their stench mingling with the smell of burnt powder. Some of the work with the wounded at the front was done by feel in the dark, and some by the light of lanterns. The routes to the rear were illumined by the army's myriad campfires.

Among the regimental chaplains who helped with the work of mercy was A. M. Stewart of the 102nd Pennsylvania Volunteers. "I went back about two miles to *one* of the large depots for the wounded. . . . Here about two thousand . . . had been collected. Such multiplied and accumulated suffering is not often seen. Not half the wounded from yesterday had yet been [attended to]. All the surgeons present were exerting themselves to their utmost, the few [male] nurses all busy. The Sanitary and Christian Commissions [civilians from the North] had perhaps a dozen delegates, in all, present. These were unceasing in their distribution of their various comforts to the sufferers, but what were these among so many? . . . When coming in from the field, my strength seemed almost wholly exhausted; but, on seeing such a mass of suffering and need, it revived, and I turned in to help. . . . During the fore part of the night, an order came to have these wounded removed a number of miles towards Fredericksburg, and the work commenced, with all the ambulances which could be procured."

On the Confederate side, the lot of the wounded was somewhat better. Unlike the Yankees, who were on hostile ground, they were among friends. Their medical corps had the aid of many civilian volunteers. Moreover, there were easy train connections with towns that had served as hospital centers all through the war and were well staffed both with medical people and with zealous female citizens.

The Battle of the Wilderness was now over (although this was not clearly evident at the time). Union cannoneer Augustus Buell, like many other participants, would come to believe he had been a part of something unique in military history. "Never before had so great a battle been fought on such ground or under such circumstances. Tactically it did not reflect much credit on any of the generals, Union or Confederate. It was throughout a 'soldier's battle,' and, so long as history endures, it will stand as a marvellous though melancholy evidence of the courage, fortitude, and devotion of the American race embattled."

The two days of indecisive fighting had cost Grant's army 17,666 in killed, wounded, and missing. Confederate losses cannot be given with certainty, but they were probably something like half the Federal number. Because of the scarcity of Confederate reserves, Lee actually suffered the greater damage to his potency.

13

On to Spotsylvania

During the whole of May 5 and 6, while the battle was raging in all its confusion, Washington and Richmond were left guessing as to details. All that was known in either capital was that Grant and Lee had met. As it happened, the people of Richmond regarded this clash, about fifty miles to their north, with only secondary apprehensions. They had a more immediate concern. Union General Benjamin Butler, in cooperation with Grant's overall plan, had transported his army, substantially more than 30,000 men, up the James River from the mouth of the Chesapeake Bay and had set it ashore on the south bank fifteen miles below the city. Worsening matters was that only a few thousand Confederate troops were available for Richmond's defense. The citizens had no way of knowing that Butler would conduct a weak campaign, and that Grant was the city's primary threat.

In Washington President Lincoln and Secretary of War Edwin Stanton had spent the two days of the battle speculating and awaiting some definite news. By the evening of May 6 their suspense was high. They were unaware that Grant was still much too busy to think in terms of reporting to Washington—that, in fact, there was not yet anything clear-cut to report. The two leaders decided to take action through an emissary, and they chose Stanton's assistant, Charles A. Dana, a journalist by profession and a temporary political figure at the special invitation of the Secretary, who liked his views on pursuing the war.

In Dana's words: "I was at a reception when a messenger came with a summons to the War Department. I hurried over to the office in evening dress. The President was there, talking very soberly with Stanton. 'Dana,' said Mr. Lincoln, 'you know we have been in the dark for two days since Grant moved. We are very much troubled, and have concluded to send you down there. How soon can you start?'

" 'In half an hour,' I replied. In about that time I had [wired ahead and had] an engine fired up at Alexandria, and a cavalry escort of a hundred men awaiting me there. I had got into my camp clothes, had borrowed a pistol, and with my own horse was aboard the train at Maryland Avenue that was to take me to Alexandria. My only baggage was a tooth-brush. I was just starting when an orderly galloped up with word that the President wished to see me. I rode back to the Department in hot haste. Mr. Lincoln was sitting in the same place. 'Well, Dana,' said he, looking up, 'since you went away I've been thinking about it. I don't like to send you down there.'

" 'But why not, Mr. President?' I asked, a little surprised.

" 'You can't tell,' continued the President, 'just where Lee is or what he is doing, and Jeb Stuart is rampaging around pretty lively in between the Rappahannock and the Rapidan. It's a considerable risk, and I don't like to expose you to it.'

" 'Mr. President,' I said, 'I have a cavalry guard ready and a good horse myself. If we are attacked, we probably will be strong enough to fight. If we are not strong enough to fight, and it comes to the worst, we are equipped [with horses] to run. It's getting late, and I want to get down to the Rappahannock by daylight. I think I'll start.'

" 'Well now, Dana,' said the President, with a little twinkle in his eyes, 'if you feel that way, I rather wish you would. Good night, and God bless you.'

"By seven o'clock on the morning of May 7th I was at the Rappahannock, where I found a rear guard of the army. I stopped there for breakfast, and then hurried on to Grant's headquarters. . . . There I learned of the crossing of the Rapidan by our army, and of the desperate Battle of the Wilderness on May 5th and 6th."

Dana had instructions not only to send a prompt telegraphic report to Lincoln and Stanton but also to remain with the army for a time. He became a part of Grant's headquarters group.

The general had been up since earliest dawn. As recounted by Horace Porter: "He seated himself at the campfire . . . and looked thoroughly refreshed after the sound sleep he had enjoyed. In fact, a night's rest had greatly reinvigorated everyone. A fog, combined with the smoke from the smoldering forest fires, rendered it difficult for those of us who were sent to make reconnaissances to see any great distance,

Section of Federal breastworks as it looked on the morning of May 7

even where there were openings in the forest. A little after 6 A.M. there was some artillery firing from Warren's batteries, which created an impression for a little while that the enemy might be moving against him; but he soon sent word that he had been firing at some skirmishers who had pushed down to a point near his intrenchments and discharged a few shots. At 6:30 A.M. the general [Grant] issued his orders to prepare for a night march of the entire army toward Spotsylvania Court-house [about ten miles to the southeast] on the direct road to Richmond."

Union newsman William Swinton injects this comment: "The Wilderness . . . was a mere collision of brute masses. . . . It might have been fought by any other commander. But the difference in the result was this: that while any other commander we had thus far seen would have fought the Battle of the Wilderness and gone backward, Grant fought the Battle of the Wilderness and went—*forward.* . . . The time had come for this manner of procedure. The North, fatigued with three years of seemingly fruitless warfare in Virginia, chagrined at the constant advances followed by constant retreats, demanded a captain who, without too chary a regard for human life, should *go on:* and the people were perfectly willing that he should use the resources lavishly, provided only he produced results. If the time had come, the Battle of the Wilderness showed that the man also had come."

Switching to the Confederate side and to General John Gordon: "On the morning of May 7, I was invited by the commanding general [Lee] to ride with him through that portion of the sombre woodland where the movement of my troops upon the Union right had occurred on the previous evening. . . . It would be a matter of profound interest if all that General Lee said [about the Battle of the Wilderness] on this ride could be placed upon record. . . . His comments upon the situation were full and free. He discussed the dominant characteristics of his great antagonist: his indomitable will and untiring persistency; his direct method of waging war by delivering constant and heavy blows upon the enemy's front rather than by seeking advantage through strategical maneuver.

"General Lee also said that General Grant held so completely and firmly the confidence of the Government that he could command to any extent its limitless resources in men and materials, while the Confederacy was already practically exhausted in both. He, however, hoped—perhaps I may say he was almost convinced—that if we could keep the Confederate army between General Grant and Richmond, checking him for a few months longer as we had in the past two days, some crisis in public affairs or change in public opinion at the North might induce the authorities at Washington to let the Southern States go, rather than force their retention in the Union at so heavy a cost.

"I endeavored to learn from General Lee what movements he had in contemplation, or what he next expected from General Grant. . . . Reports had reached me to the effect that General Grant's army was retreating, or preparing to retreat; and I called General Lee's attention to these rumors. He had heard them, but they had not made the slightest impression upon his mind. . . . Indeed, he said in so many words, 'General Grant is not going to retreat. He will move his army to Spotsylvania.' I asked him if he had information of such contemplated change by General Grant, or if there were special evidences of such purpose. 'Not at all,' said Lee, 'not at all; but that is the next point at which the armies will meet. Spotsylvania is now General Grant's best strategic point. I am so sure of his next move that I have already made arrangements to march by the shortest practicable route, that we may meet him there.' "

Lee's preparations, like Grant's, looked toward the end of the day as the time for getting the troops into full motion. Occurring simultaneously with the preparations on both sides were the continuing problems of caring for the wounded and burying the dead. Says Southern Private John Casler: "There was one of the Federals lying beside the road who . . . had lain there nearly three days. I had noticed him the first. I and another soldier started to bury him, when the other fellow said, 'Hold on until I search him.' I said that was no use, as he had been lying there so long, and thousands of troops had passed by him, and that he had probably been searched before he got cold. But he kept on searching, and finally found forty dollars in greenbacks. I then wanted him to divide, but he refused to do so. After that I searched everyone I helped to bury, but found nothing but a few pocket-knives.

"We [had] got out of rations during this battle, and could not get to our wagons, but the Yankees had four or five days' rations of hard-tack and bacon in their haversacks, and we would get them from the dead. (I have been so hungry that I have cut the blood off from crackers and eaten them.)"

Southerner D. Augustus Dickert, having sustained a light wound in the fighting of the 6th, spent the 7th in one of the field hospitals in Lee's rear. "The surgeons and assistant surgeons never get their meed of praise in summing up the 'news of the battle.' . . . Not a moment of rest or sleep do these faithful servants of the army get until every wound is dressed and the hundreds of arms and legs amputated with . . . skill and caution. . . . With the same dispatch are those, who are able to be moved, bundled off to some city hospital in the rear.

"In a large fly-tent near the roadside lay dying the Northern millionaire, General Wadsworth. The Confederates had been as careful of his wants and respectful to his station as if he had been one of their own generals. I went in to look at the general who could command more ready gold than the Confederate States had in its treasury. His hat had been placed over his face, and, as I raised it, his heavy breathing, his eyes closed, his cold, clammy face showed that the end was near. There lay dying the multi-millionaire in an enemy's country, not a friend near to hear his last farewell or soothe his last moments by a friendly touch on the pallid brow. Still he, like all soldiers on either side, died for what he thought was right. . . .

"Hospital trains had been run up to the nearest railroad station in the rear, bringing those ministering angels of mercy, the Citizens' Relief Corps, composed of the best matrons and maidens of Richmond, led by the old men of the city. They brought crutches by the hundreds and bandages by the bolt. Every delicacy that the South afforded . . . [was placed] at the disposal of the wounded soldiers."

Because of the day's relative calm, the war correspondents of both armies were able to circulate with a freedom that broadened their perspective. At five o'clock in the afternoon Unionist Charles Page sat down and wrote: "Up to this hour there has been but little fighting today. . . . I have ridden along several miles of front over the ground most stubbornly contested yesterday—how stubbornly is attested by the trees hewed and trimmed and perforated by bullets, and by the thick-strewn dead. . . . Nearly all the wounded had been removed. . . .

"Far down the Plank Road where Hancock fought, beyond the thickest Rebel dead, lay a boy severely wounded. . . . He had fallen the day before when we were farthest advanced, and had remained unmolested within the Rebel lines. They had not removed him, and he was alone with the dead when I rode up. The poor fellow was crawling about gathering violets. Faint with loss of blood, unable to stand, he could not resist the tempting flowers, and had already made a beautiful bouquet. Having caused a stretcher to be sent for, I saw him taken up tenderly and borne away, wearing a brave, sweet, touching smile.

"About two o'clock the Rebels made a demonstration upon our right flank . . . threatening communication with Germanna [where the army

had crossed the Rapidan]. However, we had cleared the road of everything valuable, had removed the pontoons, and probably did not care
to prevent the Rebels from occupying [it]. . . .

"It is a remarkable circumstance that during the three days of battles the artillery reserve has remained quietly parked three miles to the
rear. The artillery attached to the [army] has been ten times more than
could be brought into action.

"The cavalry has had considerable fighting, and has done important
service. It has hung upon our left, has kept Stuart at bay, has attacked
him when it has been possible to reach him. Sheridan's business was to
protect our immense stores, which were mainly in the rear toward
Chancellorsville—to prevent Stuart from raiding around us toward
Fredericksburg; in short, to take care of that enterprising rider, and
thrash him if he could be brought to an encounter. . . .

"Sheridan seems to have taken the cavalry reins with a master's
hand, and to be fast gaining the confidence of the Cavalry Corps. I
suspect a general cavalry fight may be contested far down on the
enemy's right before many days, for I know the destruction of Stuart's
power for mischief is considered important to the carrying out of the
campaign in the shape contemplated. . . .

"It is now nearly sunset. . . . There is quite vigorous firing, and some
artillery, at different points on the line, induced by an advance on our
part. I think it will not assume the proportions of a general engagement.
It is proposed, doubtless, to learn something of the Rebel position, and
it may be for another object. Perhaps the main one is to inform the
enemy that we are here in full force as night sets in. I doubt if we shall
be when the sun rises. . . . "

Most of Grant's troops knew that the advance was only a feint and
that the army was about to leave the area. Not generally known, however, was the movement's destination. Many soldiers feared that Grant
was planning a retreat. Speculation about this buzzed up and down the
lines, and it extended to the reserve artillery parked in the rear, or to
the east. Frank Wilkeson was back there now, having rejoined his battery early that morning. Wilkeson, however, was not in a mood to
speculate about anything; he was hopping mad. Far from gaining approval for his two days of heroic service with the infantry, he had been
punished for deserting his battery, being made to spend part of the
morning walking about the camp with a log across his shoulders, followed by a guard who pricked him with the point of a sword when he
lagged. Wilkeson had been fuming about his pain and humiliation ever

since. "[It] soured my usually sweet temper." The developments of the evening, however, drove the umbrage from the artillerist's mind.

"The troops began to pour out of the woods in columns. The infantry soldiers marched soberly past the artillery. There were no exultant songs in those columns. The men seemed aged. They were very tired. . . . They seemed to be greatly depressed. I sat by the roadside, in front of the battery, waiting for it to move, and attentively watched the infantry march past. Many of the soldiers spoke to me, asking if there was authentic news as to where they were going. Some of these men were slightly wounded. I noticed that the wounded men . . . had the stride and bearing of veterans.

"There was a gap in the column, and my battery moved on to the road, and other batteries followed us. We marched rapidly [eastward] . . . without halting, until we reached a point whither another road [from the battlefield] . . . joined the road we were on. Here we met a heavy column of troops marching to the rear, as we were. The enlisted men were grave and rather low in spirits and decidedly rough in temper. Marching by my side was a Vermont Yankee sergeant whose right cheek had been slightly burnt by a rifle ball, not enough to send him to the rear, but sufficient to make him irritable and ill-tempered. He talked bitterly of the fight. His men talked worse. They one and all asserted that the army was not whipped, that they had not been properly handled. . . .

" 'Here we go,' said a Yankee private; 'here we go, marching for the Rapidan and the protection afforded by that river. Now, when we get to the Chancellorsville House, if we turn to the left we are whipped—at least so [think] Grant and Meade. . . . '

" 'Suppose we turn to the right; what then?' I asked.

" 'That will mean fighting, and fighting on the line the Confederates have selected and intrenched. But it will indicate the purpose of Grant to fight,' he replied.

"Then he told me that the news in his Sixth Corps brigade was that Meade had strongly advised Grant to turn back and re-cross the Rapidan, and that this advice was inspired by the loss of Shaler's and Seymour's Brigades on the evening of the previous day. This was the first time I heard this rumor [it was actually a falsehood], but I heard it fifty times before I slept that night. The enlisted men, one and all, believed it. . . . None . . . had any confidence in Meade as a tenacious, aggressive fighter. They had seen him allow the Confederates to escape destruction after Gettysburg, and many of them openly ridiculed him and his alleged military ability.

"Grant's military standing with the enlisted men this day hung on the direction we turned at the Chancellorsville House. If to the left, he was to be rated with Meade and Hooker and Burnside and Pope—the generals who preceded him.

"At the Chancellorsville House we turned to the right. Instantly all of us [breathed] a sigh of relief. Our spirits rose. We marched free. The men began to sing. The enlisted men understood the flanking movement. That night we were happy."

Only Sedgwick and Burnside went roundabout by the east toward Spotsylvania. Warren's corps, accompanied by Grant himself, started down the Brock Road, still held by Hancock, who had instructions to follow in Warren's rear. It was dark, except for some starlight, and the movement was wrapped in shadows. Grant relates: "Warren's march carried him immediately behind the works where Hancock's command lay. . . . With my staff and a small escort of cavalry, I preceded the troops. Meade with his staff accompanied me. The greatest enthusiasm was manifested by Hancock's men as we passed by. No doubt it was inspired by the fact that the movement was south. It indicated to them that they had passed through the 'beginning of the end' in the battle just fought. The cheering was so lusty that the enemy must have taken it for a night attack. At all events it drew from him a furious fusilade of artillery and musketry, plainly heard but not felt by us.

"Meade and I rode in advance. We had passed but a little way beyond our left [i.e., beyond the southern flank of Hancock's lines] when the road forked. We looked to see, if we could, which road Sheridan had taken with his cavalry during the day. It seemed to be the right-hand one, and accordingly we took it. We had not gone far, however, when Colonel C. B. Comstock, of my staff—with the instinct of the engineer, suspecting that we were on a road that would lead us into the lines of the enemy, if he, too, should be moving—dashed by at a rapid gallop and all alone. In a few minutes he returned and reported that Lee was moving, and that the road we were on would bring us into his lines in a short distance. We returned to the forks of the road, left a man to indicate the right road to the head of Warren's column when it should come up, and continued our journey. . . .

"My object in moving to Spotsylvania was two-fold. First, I did not want Lee to get back to Richmond in time to attempt to crush Butler before I could get there; second, I wanted to get between his army and

Richmond, if possible; and, if not, to draw him into the open field."

The Confederate troops that Grant and his advance party had nearly encountered in the dark were elements of Longstreet's corps, now under Richard H. Anderson, a South Carolinian of winning appearance but of a personality not suggestive of force. In general, he was a better secondary leader than one of initiative. He and Longstreet had been classmates at West Point.

The outcome of the race for the new arena is given by another Confederate, Lee's closest and most trusted staff officer, twenty-six-year-old Colonel Walter H. Taylor: "The van of the opposing forces, each making for the same goal, arrived almost simultaneously on the morning of the 8th. . . . The Federals, a little in advance, drove back the Confederate cavalry, but were in turn quickly dispossessed of the strategic point by the opportune arrival of Anderson's infantry. [The cavalry's fighting retreat, which slowed the Federals, was critical to Anderson's success.] The two armies then swung round, each forming on its advanced guard as a nucleus, and on the 9th confronted each other in line of battle. General Lee was still between his adversary and Richmond."

14

Sabers at Yellow Tavern

During the maneuvering and skirmishing that led to the new formations at Spotsylvania, Union Generals George Meade and Phil Sheridan fell into disagreement over the performance of Sheridan's cavalry. The fact of the matter was that the troopers got some of their orders through Sheridan and others through Meade, and confusion had resulted. The two commanders argued hotly as to who was at fault, with Sheridan insisting he could work better if he was given more latitude. Grant sided with Sheridan, and the trooper won permission to strike out on his own, conducting a raid around the Confederate army's right flank toward Richmond, his main object to draw Stuart after him and try to force him into a showdown fight.

This was a move of considerable daring. But, as it turned out, Sheridan had an advantage. His corps numbered more than 10,000 men, all well mounted and well equipped, while Stuart had available for pursuit less than 5,000 men, many with mounts in poor condition from overwork and with gear that was barely serviceable. Stuart himself, however, was still the same bold and skillful cavalier. Perhaps his spirits were a shade less buoyant now, but he clung to his hopes for the Southern cause and remained proud to be one of its celebrated champions. There was no doubt he would make the most of what power he had.

The story of the operation that became known as the "Richmond Raid" is begun by a Union participant, Theophilus F. Rodenbough, one of Sheridan's junior officers: "A few hours were spent in preparation. The command was stripped of all impedimenta, such as unserviceable ani-

mals, wagons, and tents. The necessary ammunition train, two ambulances to a division, a few pack-mules for baggage, three days' rations
and a half-day's forage carried on the saddle, comprised the outfit. . . .

"On the 9th of May, 1864, at 6 A.M., this magnificent body of 10,000
horsemen [accompanied by seven batteries of horse artillery] moved
out on the Telegraph Road leading from Fredericksburg to Richmond.
. . . It took four hours at a brisk pace to pass a given point. To those who
viewed it from behind barred windows and doors it was like the rush
of a mighty torrent. The column . . . was thirteen miles long. It had been
moving . . . for two hours before the enemy caught up, and [Williams
C.] Wickham's Brigade began to harass Sheridan's rear. It made no
difference to the progress of the Union column, although numerous
little brushes occurred.

"In one of these [a Confederate regiment] charged our rear guard,
consisting of the Sixth Ohio Cavalry and a section of the Sixth New York
Battery. In the melee a Confederate officer cut his way through the
column to the rear piece. Placing his hand on the gun, he exclaimed,
'This is my piece.' 'Not by a damned sight,' replied a cannoneer, as with
a well-planted blow of his fist he knocked the would-be captor off his
horse and took him prisoner."

A little later, the Union column's rear guard, now reinforced, drew
up to receive another attack. For a description of the outcome we'll
turn to one of Jeb Stuart's staff officers, Henry B. McClellan, who needs
a special introduction. Born and bred a Yankee, his family a distinguished one, Henry had become a private tutor in Virginia in 1858 and
soon renounced his Northern heritage in favor of the Southern point of
view. When war came, he enlisted in a Virginia cavalry regiment. Four
of Henry's brothers were in the Union armies, and he was a first cousin
to George B. McClellan, the Army of the Potomac's early commander,
soon to become Abraham Lincoln's rival for the Union presidency.
Henry says of the rear-guard action:

"Wickham attacked promptly, but made no impression. One or two
of his regiments had recoiled from the charge, when he called for
Matthews' squadron of the Third Virginia, with the remark, 'I know he
will go through.' Matthews led his column-of-fours down the narrow
lane and pierced the enemy's lines, but he did not return. The heavy
force of the enemy closed upon the head of his column, killed five,
wounded three, and captured ten men of his company. Matthews' horse
was killed. While fighting on foot with his saber, he was shot from
behind and mortally wounded. His gallantry excited the admiration of

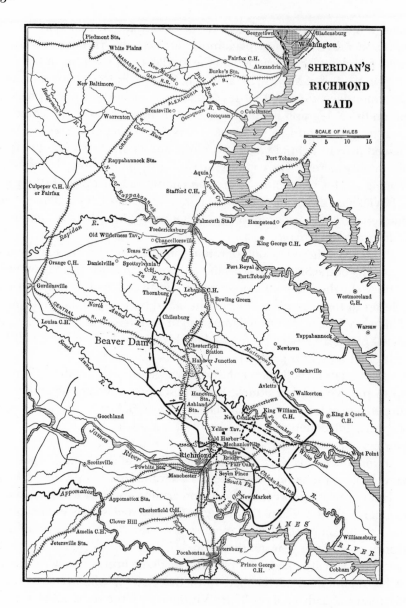

SHERIDAN'S
RICHMOND
RAID

his enemies, who carefully carried him to a neighboring farmhouse, leaving with him one of his company who had been captured in the charge."

At the head of the Union column, the brigade led by the energetic and aggressive George Armstrong Custer was pressing toward Beaver Dam Station on the Virginia Central Railroad. By a curious turn of events, Custer and his men were not the first Yankees to use the Beaver Dam road that day. The troopers happened to be following several miles behind about 400 Union soldiers who had been captured during the Wilderness fighting. A Confederate cavalry guard was herding the group toward Beaver Dam for delivery by train to Richmond. One of the prisoners was John Urban of the Pennsylvania Reserves, who tells what happened:

"The weather was very warm, and, as we were tired out with marching, and received no food, we suffered very much during the day. Some of the men gave out entirely. What became of them I could never ascertain. As we marched along, we were quite an object of curiosity to the natives, who gathered along the road to see the 'Yankees.' Some of them must have formed strange ideas about our appearance and looks, as one good woman exclaimed, 'Why, they look just like our men.' . . . I did not care much about the opinion of most of them, but I could not help wishing that the few really pretty girls we passed would not despise us.

"When within a few miles of Beaver Dam Station, we passed the house of a fellow who was terribly indignant, and had a great deal to say about what should be done with us for coming 'down here and taking our niggers from us,' as he expressed it. . . .

"We . . . were within a short distance of the station when a strange rumbling sound in our rear attracted our attention. The hope had impressed itself on every mind during the day that we might be recaptured; and when I first heard the noise, I made the remark to one of my comrades that I believed our cavalry was coming. One of the [Confederate] guards who was riding close to me overheard the remark, when, turning his horse, he rode to the other side and commenced talking to one of his officers. The officer put spurs to his horse and rode rapidly back to the top of the hill we had just crossed. The noise could be heard coming nearer and nearer, and I suppose from the top of the hill the officer could see the approaching column. . . . He did not stay long to view the sight, as he came back as fast as his horse could carry him, shouting, 'The Yankees are coming! The Yankees are coming!'

George A. Custer

"We were now within a few hundred feet of the station, and the train that was to convey us to Richmond was standing on the track with steam up and ready for starting. The rebel officer who had charge of our guards ordered us to double-quick for the station; but, instead of obeying, we came to a sudden halt. The rebels threatened by saying that if we did not move they would fire into us; but we stubbornly refused to move a step. Finding they could not compel us to move, they turned their attention to the approaching cavalry and formed line of battle across the road, placing us in the rear. They had just about accomplished this when the advance of the cavalry column burst over the hill. . . .

"As the road was narrow, with fence on one side and wood on the other, but a small portion of the advance could charge on our guards. . . . Some of the prisoners fled into the woods, others jumped over the fence, and a few of us got on it, where we could have a better view. . . . The fight was soon over. A few of our guards who had fleet horses succeeded in escaping, but the most of them were cut down or captured. . . . The rebel guards . . . were a brave set of fellows, and fought with a desperation worthy of a better cause. Among the number killed was one who had been very kind to us on the march, and I could not help but pity the fate of him who had been so brave and generous. Several times during the day he dismounted and let some poor fellow, who had given out, ride his horse, he himself walking.

"Among the number captured was a young fellow of about sixteen or seventeen years of age, who [had taken] great delight in teasing us about our unfortunate condition. He had a peculiarly . . . squeaking voice, very much like an old woman's. Annoying as it was to us, it must, however, have been the sweetest music to himself, as he kept his tongue going all the time. One of his frequent expressions, and one that appeared to give him great delight, was, 'Well, boys, Daddy Lee has got you!' And then he would laugh as if he considered it an immense joke. Several of his comrades during the day told him to shut up; but he paid no attention to them. . . . One of our boys, jokingly—and without the least idea that anything of the kind might happen—reminded him that the cards might be turned before the day was over. . . . Little did he [the Union prisoner] think that in a few hours his prediction would come true.

"After the fight was over, we found our tormentor in the hands of the cavalry, and he was the most frightened man I ever saw. Some of our boys could not help but tease him about the change of affairs. One of them exclaimed, 'Well, my lad, Daddy Grant has got you!' at the same time imitating his voice and manner so perfectly as to raise a shout of laughter from the rest. The poor fellow begged piteously that his life might be spared. This was too much for the boys, who told him to rest easy, as he was entirely too innocent to be killed.

"Immediately after the fight, General Custer took possession of the station, where we found an immense amount of rebel supplies, consisting of flour, pork, cornmeal, fish, sugar, rum, and other rations. Two large trains of cars, one loaded with flour, and the other which was to take us to Richmond, were captured and destroyed. Fire was immediately applied to the station and buildings around it. . . .

"The men, in helping themselves around the station, had found several barrels of whisky, and were going to fill their canteens, when General Sheridan, who had come on the ground, ordered the heads of the barrels to be knocked in. It was amusing to see the thirsty fellows run after the dirty stuff, and dip it up as fast as it flowed along the ground. Some of them succeeded in getting too much of it.

"General Sheridan's arrival was greeted with three hearty cheers by the recaptured prisoners. He made us a short speech, in which he advised us to stick to his command, as we might be captured again by the rebels if we did not. He also told us to arm ourselves, but if we found the arms a burden, to throw them away, but by all means try to keep up with his command. He said, also, we should take any horse or mule we could find on the way. Some of the cavalry had lost their horses, and, as they were on the hunt, we did not stand much of a chance of finding any.

"The rebels had quite a number of colored men employed at the station. They did not imitate the example of the whites by fleeing, but hid themselves about the station until they felt sure their masters were out of sight—which, by the way, did not take very long. Then they commenced to pop their heads out of every conceivable hiding place in the vicinity. They appeared to understand perfectly well from the first that we were friends, and they were very demonstrative in their welcome. One big fellow knocked in the top of a sugar barrel, and, taking a tin cup for a scoop, commenced to share out the sugar to all who would accept. He would frequently call out, 'Fall in here, you Yanks, for your rations!' And his broad face would beam with pleasure when someone would accept a dip."

During the night, with the burning buildings lighting the sky, working parties from Sheridan's column destroyed nearly ten miles of railroad track and tore down the paralleling telegraph lines. The column's encampments were just north of Beaver Dam. A part of Jeb Stuart's corps was bivouacked a few miles farther above. Stuart in person spent the night leading his remaining horsemen on a westerly circuit toward the station. It was well into the next morning, May 10, when he arrived, and Sheridan had already resumed his march toward Richmond, thirty miles distant. Only the rear of his column was still in the area. Here the Confederate forces merged. Stuart was pained by the sight of the damage Sheridan had wrought. The loss of the depot and its stores would make Lee's work in the field more difficult. It was a humiliation to Stuart that he had been unable to prevent the blow.

The general had another concern that day. As explained by his aide Henry McClellan (the turnaway Yankee): "While his troops were at Beaver Dam, Stuart snatched a few minutes to visit the residence of Colonel Edmund Fontaine, in the immediate vicinity, to ascertain the safety of his wife [Flora] and children, who were visiting there at that time." In his haste to be off, Stuart talked with Flora from his horse in front of the house, even taking his farewell kiss without dismounting. Stuart had always been duty conscious. In November 1862 he received word that he must come home, that his five-year-old daughter (also Flora) was fatally ill. Stuart was deeply attached to little Flora, but he responded: "I must leave my child in the hands of God. My country needs me here." He cried at the news of the child's death but did not regret his decision.

Returning to narrator Henry McClellan: "Having satisfied himself that his family had escaped the danger to which they had been exposed . . . Stuart divided his command, sending [James B.] Gordon's brigade to follow the rear of the enemy, while he himself, with Fitz Lee's two brigades, marched [on an easterly circuit] to Hanover Junction, [a point] on his way to interpose between the enemy and Richmond. He reached the Junction some hours after dark." The pace had been slow because both men and mounts were overtired. Stuart was unable to push on at once, as he wished. He was obliged to allow his column a few hours of rest.

In Richmond this night of May 10–11 was one of great commotion. The citizens had already experienced several days of worry over Union General Butler's invasion from the south, finding relief only in that their southern defense force, now under the veteran Pierre Beauregard, seemed to be keeping Butler at bay. Phil Sheridan's threat from the north was something else again.

Richmond diarist Judith McGuire (who had a son in the War Department, giving her access to special information) tells of the night and its developments: "We knew that the attachés of the War Department had received orders to spend the night there, and our son had promised us that if anything exciting occurred he would come up and let us know. We were first aroused by hearing a number of soldiers pass up Broad Street. I sprang up, and saw at least a brigade passing by. As we were composing ourselves to sleep, I heard several pebbles come against the window. On looking out, I saw J. [the son] standing below. In a moment the door was opened and he was in our room, with the information, brought by a courier, that 7,000 raiders [actually an underestimate] were within sixteen miles of us, making their way to the city. He also said that 3,000 infantry had marched to meet them. [These troops from south of Richmond were on their way to man the city's northern earthworks, and the emergency force would soon be joined by groups of irregulars that included War Department clerks, old men, green youths, soldiers home on furlough, and even some of the city's convalescing wounded.]

"Every lady in the house dressed immediately, and some of us went down to the porch. There we saw ladies in every porch, and walking on the pavements, as if it were evening. We saw but one person who seemed really alarmed. Everyone else seemed to expect something to occur to stop the raiders. Our city had too often been saved as if by a miracle. About two o'clock a telegram came from General Stuart that he was in pursuit of the enemy. J. came up [from the War Department] to bring us the information, and we felt that all was right. In a very short time families had retired to their chambers, and quiet reigned in this hitherto perturbed street. For ourselves, we were soon asleep."

It was true that Jeb Stuart was in pursuit of the enemy, but it wasn't true that all was right. Ahead of Stuart a detachment from Sheridan's column made a predawn raid at Ashland Station, on the railroad between Richmond and Fredericksburg, doing extensive damage before retreating under the fire of the Confederate van. Now that his men and their mounts were rested, however, Stuart was able to proceed on his easterly circuit, by which he hoped to get around to Sheridan's front, with greater speed. He was helped by the fact that Sheridan, confident of his strength and wishing to spare his horses, was moving at an easy pace.

Henry McClellan rode by Jeb Stuart's side in the early morning. "We conversed on many matters of personal interest. He was more quiet than usual, softer, and more communicative. . . . He reached the Yellow Tavern at about ten o'clock, and found himself in advance of the enemy's column, and in full time to interpose between it and Richmond."

Stuart had performed well, but his situation was precarious. Phil Sheridan was bearing down upon his two brigades with a numerical advantage of at least three to one. Stuart placed his small command in a good defensive position—one not across Sheridan's front but to the east of his route of march on a parallel with the column's left flank—and awaited attack.

In the words of an unidentified private in the Sixth Virginia Cavalry: "On the morning of the fight at Yellow Tavern . . . I was acting as one of Stuart's couriers. . . . The enemy could be easily seen emerging from a piece of woods and forming for battle. . . . Pretty soon from the enemy came lively volleys whistling through the trees and starting the dust in the road. . . . Stuart, taking out his field-glass, deliberately watched the maneuvers of the enemy, though balls were whizzing past him. Presently, regardless of the increasing fire, which was now accompanied with shouts, Stuart put his glass away, and, taking out paper and pencil, wrote an order. Handing it to [Lieutenant Walter Hullihen], he told him to take it to General [Lunsford] Lomax. That officer replied by pointing to me and suggesting that I should carry it. Stuart assented, and I rode off in search of General Lomax. The firing continued to increase, and many squadrons were in sight. The enemy, awake to their superior numbers, seemed about to make a general advance, while our men were availing themselves of the character of the ground to repel their attack.

"After going a few rods to the rear, my horse, excited by the firing, suddenly stopped and refused to budge. After several vain attempts with the spur and the flat side of my sword to start him, I at last struck him with all my strength right between the ears. This downed him, but he soon rose and ran off at the top of his speed. I soon came to where General Lomax was, and, coming into collision with his horse, gained his immediate attention. After reading the note, he told me to go back and tell General Stuart that the order had been delivered."

Lomax, whose brigade made up the left of Stuart's line, was soon heavily pressed by the Federals. Lomax gave way for a short distance, then held firm. His stubbornness resulted in a lull that extended along the battlefield's entire front. Then the Union brigade under George Custer was sent against Lomax. Custer relates:

"The enemy was strongly posted on a bluff in rear of a thin skirt of woods, his battery being concealed from our view by the woods, while they had obtained perfect range of my position. The edge of the woods nearest to my front was held by the enemy's dismounted men, who poured a heavy fire into my lines, until the Fifth and Sixth Michigan were ordered to dismount and drive the enemy from his position, which they did in the most gallant manner. . . .

"From a personal examination of the ground, I discovered that a successful charge might be made upon the battery of the enemy by keeping well to the right. With this intention I formed the First Michigan Cavalry in column of squadrons under cover of the wood. At the same time I directed . . . the Fifth and Sixth Michigan Cavalry forward [to] occupy the attention of the enemy on the left, [Edward] Heaton's Battery to engage them in front, while the First charged the battery on the flank.

"The bugle sounded the advance, and the three regiments moved forward. As soon as the First Michigan moved from the cover of the woods the enemy divined our intention and opened a brisk fire from his artillery with shell and canister. Before the battery of the enemy could be reached, there were five fences to be opened [for passage] and a bridge to cross, over which it was impossible to pass more than three at one time, the intervening ground being within close range of the enemy's battery. Yet, notwithstanding these obstacles, the First Michigan . . . advanced boldly to the charge, and when within 200 yards of the battery, charged it with a yell. . . . Two pieces of cannon, two limbers filled with ammunition, and a large number of prisoners were among the results of this charge. . . .

"After the enemy was driven across a deep ravine, about a quarter of a mile beyond the position held by his battery, he rallied and re-formed his forces and resisted successfully the farther advance of the First Michigan. The Seventh Michigan, commanded by Major [Henry W.] Granger, was ordered forward at a trot, and, when near the enemy's position, was ordered to charge with drawn sabers. Major Granger, like a true soldier, placed himself at the head of his men and led them bravely up to the very muzzles of the enemy's guns; but, notwithstanding the heroic efforts of this gallant officer, the enemy held their position, and the Seventh Michigan was compelled to retire—but not until the chivalric Granger had fallen, pierced through the head and heart, by the bullets of the enemy."

The setback was temporary. By this time Phil Sheridan had renewed

The cavalry fight at Yellow Tavern

his entire attack (while from off in his background came the sounds of a related action, that of his rear guard holding at bay the troops that had been following his march). His extensive front was an undulating ribbon of blue, its myriad weapons crashing, sparkling, and smoking. Many of the men were on foot, which diminished them as targets and enhanced their marksmanship—altogether the more practical way to fight such a battle.

On the Confederate side, the unidentified courier was back with Jeb Stuart, marking that "he was sitting on his horse, close behind a line of dismounted men who were firing at the advancing Federals. The disparity of numbers between the opposing forces was very great. . . . Our men seemed aware of their inferior strength, but were not dismayed. The enemy confidently pressed forward with exultant shouts, delivering tremendous volleys. The Confederates returned their fire with yells of defiance.

"Stuart, with pistol in hand, shot over the heads of the troops, while with words of cheer he encouraged them. He kept saying, 'Steady, men, steady. Give it to them.' Presently he reeled in the saddle [as a bullet entered his midsection]. His head was bowed and his hat fell off. He turned and said as I drew nearer, 'Go and tell General Lee [i.e., Fitz] and Dr. Fontaine to come here.' I wheeled at once and went as fast as I could to do his bidding. Coming to the part of the line where General Lomax was, I told him Stuart was hurt and that he wanted General Fitz Lee. He pointed to the left and told me to hurry. Soon I found General Lee and delivered the message. He was riding a light gray . . . and instantly upon receipt of the news went like an arrow down the line. When I returned, Stuart had been taken from his horse and was being carried by his men off the field. I saw him put in an ambulance."

The general had turned his command over to Fitz Lee. Even in his badly injured condition, Stuart was aware that Sheridan's men were beginning to best his own. Says Henry McClellan: "As he was being driven from the field he noticed the disorganized ranks of his retreating men, and called out to them, 'Go back! Go back and do your duty as I have done mine, and our country will be safe. Go back! Go back! I had rather die than be whipped.' These were his last words on the battlefield."

The courier followed the ambulance for a time, looking in upon Stuart. "He lay without speaking . . . but kept shaking his head with an expression of the deepest disappointment."

The ambulance headed for Richmond, taking a roundabout route to elude pursuit by the enemy. (There was, in fact, a party of Federals *ahead* on the direct route; Sheridan had sent a reconnaissance toward the city's first line of defenses.) On the battlefield the firing died as all of the Confederates were driven away. One of the Union brigade commanders, Henry Davies, sums things up: "When the engagement was concluded . . . the road to Richmond was clear, and not an enemy was to be seen in front of any portion of our lines. The losses on both sides were heavy. . . . The Confederates . . . left most of their dead and wounded on the field . . . and they also lost many prisoners."

15

Stuart Makes His Exit

Even though the Confederate troopers reorganized almost as soon as they were out of sight, there was no denying they had been dealt a sharp defeat. Phil Sheridan had already achieved his primary goal. But his expedition and its adventures were far from over. He prepared now to move to the rim of Richmond's northern defenses. From that point he expected to make an easterly circuit of the city in order to contact Union General Butler's army in the southern environs. Butler was to resupply him for his trip back to the Army of the Potomac.

It was only a few hours after the battle closed that the Union troopers began moving down the Brook Turnpike. Night had set in, and the weather was rainy. The column included many Confederate captives on foot, among them Luther W. Hopkins, a twenty-year-old Virginian. "The prisoners," says Hopkins, "marched two abreast, with a line of cavalry guard on each side. We had, of course, to keep up with the cavalry. Our guard was very kind to us, and allowed us to take hold of their stirrup straps, which was quite a help to us as we marched along, especially in crossing streams, one of which . . . was up to our waists. . . . As we had no sleep the night before [the battle], but rode all night, and now were walking all night in the rain and mud, and without food, you may know we were in a wretched condition. Every now and then a friendly Yank would hand us a cracker from his haversack, saying, 'Here, Johnnie.' But they were on short rations themselves, and could not help us much in that respect."

Not all of the prisoners got considerate treatment that night. There was a special reason for this, and the explanation is given by Phil Sheridan himself: "The enemy, anticipating that I would march by this route, had planted torpedoes along it, and many of these exploded as the column passed over them. . . . The torpedoes were loaded shells planted on each side of the road, and so connected by wires attached to friction tubes in the shells, that when a horse's hoof struck a wire the shell was exploded by the jerk. . . .

"After the loss of several horses and the wounding of some of the men by these torpedoes, I gave directions to have them removed, if practicable. So about twenty-five of the prisoners were brought up and made to get down on their knees, feel for the wires in the darkness, follow them up, and unearth the shells. The prisoners reported the owner of one of the neighboring houses to be the principal person who had engaged in planting these shells, and I therefore directed that some of them be carried and placed in the cellar of his house, arranged to explode if the enemy's column [of cavalry] came that way, while he and his family were brought off as [temporary] prisoners. . . .

"Meanwhile, the utmost excitement prevailed in Richmond. The Confederates, supposing that their capital was my objective point, were straining every effort to put it in a state of defense, and had collected between four and five thousand irregular troops, under General [Braxton] Bragg, besides bringing up three brigades of infantry from the force confronting Butler south of the James River, the alarm being intensified by the retreat, after the defeat at Yellow Tavern, of Stuart's cavalry, now under General Fitzhugh Lee . . . to Mechanicsville, on the north side of the Chickahominy [and east of the Union march]; for, falling back in that direction, [the Confederate troopers] left me between them and Richmond.

"Our march during the night of the 11th was very tedious, on account of the extreme darkness and frequent showers of rain."

General James Wilson's division was in the lead. As recounted by one of the junior artillery officers in Wilson's command: "We marched all night, virtually. The halts were frequent and exasperating. It was so dark that we [artillerymen] could only follow the cavalry by putting a bugler on a white horse directly in rear of the regiment in front of us, with orders to move on as soon as they did. Finally, whether the bugler fell asleep waiting, or we fell asleep while watching the white horse, it happened that we found a gap of unknown dimensions in front of us, and started at a trot to close it. . . . It was a swampy region; the hoofs and the wheels made little or no sound. Once the deep blackness was pierced by a jet of vivid flame, and a sharp explosion on the road showed that we had sprung one of the torpedoes. . . .

"While in doubt as to the road, we came upon a man wrapped in a blue overcoat standing near a gate, who told us that General Sheridan had left him to show us the way. Of course, we followed his directions and entered the gate. It was evident that we were very near the city, as we could see the lights and hear the dogs barking. The road became less plainly marked and seemed to lead into extensive pleasure grounds [i.e., a public park], and finally we brought up on the edge of a large fish-pond. At that moment half a dozen flashes came from what seemed to be an embankment, and we found that we were in a regular trap and immediately under the fire of one of the outworks of the city.

"The guide who had given us the direction was either a deserter or a rebel in our uniform, and had deliberately misled us. He received the reward of his treachery, for Colonel [John B.] McIntosh, who had from the first suspected him, kept near him, and, when their guns opened, blew out his brains with a pistol."

With the coming of daylight, the gathering Federals advanced upon the Confederate defenses but were repelled. In the city the people awoke to a strange combination of gunfire and storm noises. John B. Jones, a clerk in the War Department, said in his diary: "I shall never forget the conformation of the clouds this morning. . . . There were different strata running in various directions. . . . The meeting of these was followed by tremendous clashes of lightning and thunder; and between the pauses of the artillery of the elements above, the thunder of artillery on earth could be distinctly heard.

"It is said that preparations have been made for the flight of the President, cabinet, etc., up the Danville Road in the event of the fall of the city."

Such preparations may indeed have been made (since both Sheridan and Butler were at Richmond's gates), but that morning Jefferson Davis, at least, was not thinking in terms of flight. According to his wife, Varina: "Mr. Davis came hurriedly in from the office for his pistols, and rode out to the front. . . . At the Executive Mansion, the small-arms could be distinctly heard like the popping of fire-crackers. I summoned the children to prayer, and as my boy Jefferson knelt, he raised his little chubby face to me and said, 'You had better have my pony saddled and let me go out to help father. We can pray afterward.' "

Prayer was in the minds and hearts of many that morning. Judith McGuire made an early entry in her diary: "The cannon is now roaring

in our ears. . . . The Lord reigneth. In that is our trust. . . . General
J. E. B. Stuart . . . was brought to the city last night. One of his aides,
our relative, Lieutenant T. S. Garnett, has told us with what difficulty
they got him here in an ambulance, going out of the way, hither and
thither, to avoid the enemy—of course, every jolt inflicting intense
agony. He is now at the house of his brother-in-law, Dr. [Charles]
Brewer, surrounded by the most efficient surgeons and devoted friends.
The prayers of the community are with him."

In his bed at Dr. Brewer's, Stuart himself heard the gunfire to the
north, and he asked what it meant. Told that Confederate forces were
fighting Sheridan, he responded, "God grant that they may be successful." Then he turned his head aside and said with a sigh, "But I must
be prepared for another world."

By this time Phil Sheridan was involved not only with the extensive
line of infantry in the Richmond defenses, but also with the Confederate troopers from Yellow Tavern. It began to seem as though he had led
his command into a bad spot. Sheridan describes the problem and his
attitude toward it: "With the troops from Richmond . . . on my front and
right flank, with Gordon's cavalry in the rear, and Fitzhugh Lee's cavalry [i.e., his original division command] on my left flank, holding the
Chickahominy and Meadow Bridge [the desired crossing for an easterly
march around Richmond to Butler's army], I was apparently hemmed
in on every side; but, relying on the celerity with which mounted troops
could be moved, I felt perfectly confident that the seemingly perilous
situation could be relieved under circumstances even worse than those
surrounding us. . . . I concluded that there would be little difficulty in
withdrawing, even should I be beaten."

Not all of Sheridan's men shared his point of view. Quite a few, in
fact, saw their plight as desperate. The Confederate captives from Yellow Tavern were openly jubilant. "Sheridan was in close quarters," says
Luther Hopkins, "and we prisoners had made up our minds that he
would have to surrender his army. We got so bold and impudent that
we hailed Yankee officers as they passed us, and said, 'Hey there, Mr.
Yank, I speak for that horse.' Among these officers so hailed was a
red-headed major who was in command of our guard. Prior to this he
had been very surly and exceedingly gruff and harsh. So disagreeable
was he that the prisoners whispered among themselves that if we did
get him in our hands we'd make him sweat; and when it became evident not only to us, but to the enemy, that they were in danger of
capture, this particular officer changed his attitude toward us very per-

ceptibly. He took our jeers and taunts without a word."

The narrative is assumed by John Urban of the Pennsylvania Reserves, who had remained with Sheridan's column after his rescue from Confederate captivity by George Custer at Beaver Dam Station: "The forts and redoubts bristled with bayonets, and . . . we were in range of the heavy guns of some of the forts. . . . The rebel cavalry had succeeded in . . . destroying part of the bridge on our line of retreat, and had a strong force . . . in position on the other side to oppose our crossing. At the same time, we could see heavy columns of troops marching from the fortifications for the purpose of attacking. . . . Fortunately for the Union cause, the Federal force was in command of an officer who was known to be very fertile in resources. . . . He immediately formed the plan of repairing the bridge . . . and escaping by way of Mechanicsville. . . .

"I was at headquarters during this time, and was perfectly astonished at the unshrinking bravery and self-possession of General Sheridan. . . . Where the fighting was severest and the danger the greatest, there was Sheridan, encouraging his men."

The general sent Wesley Merritt's division to the river to confront Fitz Lee in his position on the far side of the bridge. Two dismounted regiments were crossed on a railroad span a short way downstream (to the east), and they came in on Lee's left flank. The Union regiments were repelled, but the distraction, coupled with fire from Merritt's main body across the river, weakened Lee's hold on the bridge.

This turn of events surprised Confederate prisoner Luther Hopkins. "Oh, the irony of Fate. On a hill fronting the river—not far from the bridge—was an old Virginia mansion. The prisoners were led to this house and ordered to tear it down and carry the timbers to the river and rebuild the bridge. . . . Of course, we had to obey, but we made loud complaints; and while we were carrying this timber and rebuilding the bridge, our enemy was protecting us . . . by keeping back the Confederates, who were pouring shot and shell into their ranks."

Returning to Union soldier John Urban: "To repel the rebel assaults from the direction of Richmond, Sheridan had formed a line of all his artillery, supported by a [line] of cavalry dismounted and fighting as infantry. . . . The rebels in strong column advanced to the assault, cheering loudly and evidently expecting an easy victory. [Their confidence was bolstered when Sheridan's left fell back before them.] The Union troops [on the right] reserved their fire until the enemy was in short range of their guns, when they received them with a terrible discharge of grape and canister, which tore terrible gashes through their ranks.

"The line reeled and commenced to give way; but the rebel officers succeeded in getting their line re-formed and again advanced to the assault. Again and again the artillery poured volleys of double-shotted grape and canister into their ranks; but they pressed forward until they came within range of the carbines in the hands of the cavalry, when they received a storm of bullets that [together with an equally punishing fire from the Union left, which had rallied] shattered their ranks and drove the entire line in the utmost confusion back towards Richmond. . . .

"I was watching the flight of the demoralized enemy . . . when loud cheering in the direction of the bridge announced the fact that our men . . . were forcing the enemy from their position on the opposite side. The enemy, however, fell back but a short distance when they made the most determined resistance to the further advance . . . of our forces. The bridge, however, had been [fully] gained."

Soon the Federals crossed in strong numbers, and Fitz Lee's men were driven from the area. Meanwhile, the Confederate troopers on the Brook Turnpike, in Sheridan's rear, made an attack down the roadway but were easily repulsed. All of the fighting was over by noon, and for the next few hours the Federals remained on the field undisturbed.

"Our time," says Phil Sheridan, "was spent in collecting the wounded, burying the dead, grazing the horses, and reading the Richmond journals, two small newsboys with commendable enterprise having come within our lines from the Confederate capital to sell their papers. They were sharp youngsters, and, having come well supplied, they did a thrifty business. When their stock in trade was all disposed of, they wished to return, but they were so intelligent and observant that I thought their mission involved other purposes than the mere sale of newspapers, so they were held till we crossed the Chickahominy [in the late afternoon] and then turned loose. . . .

"The main purposes of the expedition had now been executed. They were 'to break up General Lee's railroad communications, destroy such depots of supplies as could be found in his rear, and to defeat General Stuart's cavalry.' Many miles of the Virginia Central and of the Richmond and Fredericksburg Railroads were broken up, and several of the bridges on each burnt. At Beaver Dam, Ashland, and other places, about two millions of rations had been captured and destroyed.

"The most important of all, however, was the defeat of Stuart. Since the beginning of the war this general had distinguished himself by his management of the Confederate mounted force. Under him the cavalry of Lee's army had been nurtured and had acquired such prestige that it thought itself well-nigh invincible; indeed, in the early years of the war it had proved to be so. This was now dispelled by the successful march we had made in Lee's rear; and the discomfiture of Stuart at Yellow Tavern had inflicted a blow from which entire recovery was impossible."

During Sheridan's quiet afternoon before Richmond and his ensuing march across the river, Stuart was spending his last hours on earth. As reported in a Richmond newspaper: "Occasional delirium attacked him, and, in his moments of mental wandering, his faculties were busy with the past. His campaigns . . . and . . . engagements were subjects that quickly chased themselves through his brain. Fresh orders were given as if still on the battlefield, and injunctions to his couriers to 'make haste.' Then he would wander to his wife and children. . . . Then his mind would again carry him onto the battlefield. . . . Occasionally his intellect was clear, and he was then calm and resigned, though at times suffering the most acute agony. He would even, with his own hand, apply the ice that was intended to relieve the pain of his wound.

"As evening wore on, mortification set in rapidly. In answer to his inquiry, he was told that death was fast approaching. He then said, 'I am resigned, if it be God's will, but I would like to see my wife. . . . ' Several times he roused up and asked if she had come. Unfortunately, she was in the country at the time, and did not arrive until too late.

"As the last moments approached, the dying man . . . turned to the Rev. Dr. [G. W.] Peterkin, of the Episcopal Church, of which he was a strict member, and asked him to sing the hymn commencing,

'Rock of Ages, cleft for me,
Let me hide myself in thee.'

"In this he joined with all the strength of voice his failing powers permitted. He then prayed with the minister and friends around him; and with the words, 'I am going fast now; I am resigned; God's will be done,' yielded his fleeting spirit to Him who gave it."

On May 13 Judith McGuire wrote in her diary: "General Stuart died of his wounds last night, twenty-four hours after he was shot. . . . Thus passed away our great cavalry general, just one year after the immortal Jackson. This seems darkly mysterious to us, but God's will be done. The

Jeb Stuart

funeral took place this evening. . . . My duty to the living prevented my attending it, for which I am very sorry; but I was in the hospital from three o'clock until eight, soothing the sufferers [from the battlefields around the city] in the only way I could, by fanning them, bathing their wounds, and giving them a word of comfort. . . . Others of our household were at the funeral. They represent the scene as being very imposing."

Stuart was interred in Richmond's Hollywood Cemetery, near the still-fresh mound covering the remains of his beloved little daughter Flora. During the graveside ceremonies, the earth trembled with an exchange of cannon fire between elements of Beauregard's and Butler's forces south of the city.

The sounds of this fire reached the ears of Phil Sheridan and his troopers as they circled east of Richmond on their way toward Butler's base on the James River. The march was continued unaltered. Sheridan relates: "We got to the James on the 14th with all our wounded and a large number of prisoners. . . . The prisoners, as well as the captured guns, were turned over to General Butler's provost-marshal, and our wounded were quickly and kindly cared for by his surgeons. Ample supplies, also, in the way of forage and rations, were furnished us by General Butler, and the work of refitting for our return to the Army of the Potomac was vigorously pushed. By the 17th all was ready, and having learned by scouting parties . . . that the enemy's cavalry was returning to Lee's army I started that evening on my return march."

16
Prelude on a New Field

Much had happened at Spotsylvania since Sheridan and Stuart left their respective armies on May 9. Grant and Lee spent the 9th establishing their lines. Lee's took the shape of a caret (^), with the apex pointing northward. Each wing was about two miles in length, and both were heavily laced with breastworks of earth and logs. The apex became known as the "Angle," or, since it was actually rounded, the "Mule Shoe." Such a salient was the natural result of the general deployment, which made the best use of the available terrain, but the projection was a recognized weak spot, for it was exposed to attack from three directions, north, east, and west. Grant's units, facing generally southward, formed a several-mile arc about the salient.

"Aside from the movements to take up positions," says Union newsman-historian William Swinton, "the day was passed in [relative] quiet. The Confederate sharpshooters were, however, very active, and early in the day their deadly aim brought down an illustrious victim in the person of General Sedgwick, the beloved chief of the Sixth Corps, who was shot while standing in the breastworks along his line, and almost instantly expired. The loss of this lion-hearted soldier caused the profoundest grief among his comrades, and throughout the army, which felt it could better have afforded to sacrifice the best division. General [Horatio] Wright succeeded to the command."

During the preparations for fighting in this new arena, the wounded of the previous battlefield were still a monstrous problem, particularly for the alien Federals. May 9 was the day their ambulance wagon trains began arriving at Fredericksburg, which had been chosen as the first

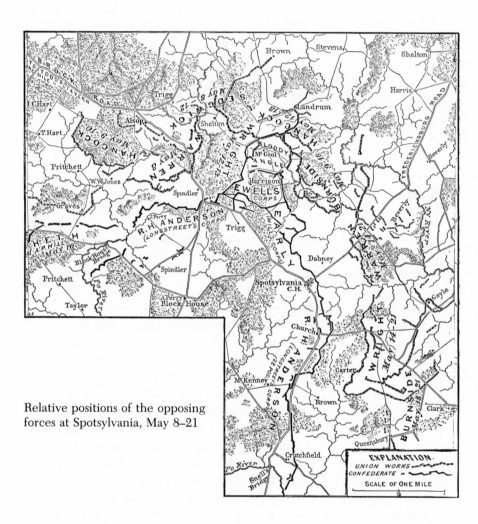

Relative positions of the opposing
forces at Spotsylvania, May 8–21

stop along a route designed to relay the wounded to Northern hospitals. Among the surgeons with the earliest train, one composed of a great many wagons, was the Sixth Corps's George Stevens:

"Over a rough road, nearly fifteen miles, these unfortunate men, with shattered or amputated limbs, with shots through the lungs or head or abdomen, suffering the most excruciating pain from every jar or jolt of the ambulance or wagon, crowded as closely as they could be packed, [had been] transported. . . . They were worn out with fatigue and suffering. . . .

"The train had been preceded by some three hundred men who were wounded but able to walk. Mayor [Montgomery] Slaughter and other rebel citizens surrounded these unarmed men, made them prisoners, and delivered them to some rebel cavalry, who took them to Richmond.

"The process of unloading the wounded at once commenced. All the churches and other public buildings were first seized and filled. Negroes who could be found in town were pressed into the work; yet, with all the help that could be obtained, it was a slow process. . . . The churches were filled first, then warehouses and stores, and then private houses, until the town was literally one immense hospital.

"The surgeons were too much engaged in transferring the men from the wagons to the houses to find time that day to dress many wounds, and many an unfortunate soldier whose stump of an arm or leg had not been dressed since the first day of the fighting became the victim of gangrene, which set in as the result of this unavoidable want of care. . . . To relieve the wants of all these thousands of suffering men, not more than forty surgeons had been sent from the field. . . .

"It was [at first] almost impossible to obtain sufficient supplies either of food or dressings. Everything that could be spared from the field had been sent, but . . . there was little to spare. Food was obtained in very limited quantities in town, and men went to the houses of citizens and demanded sheets, which were torn into bandages. . . .

"Many of the people of Fredericksburg exhibited the most malignant spite against the Yankee wounded; but others, while they claimed no sympathy with our cause, showed themselves friends of humanity and rendered us all the assistance in their power. No men, except Negroes and white men unfit for military duty, were left in town, but the women were bitter rebels. Some of them made fierce opposition to the use of their houses as hospitals, but they were occupied notwithstanding their remonstrances.

"At one fine mansion a surgeon rang the doorbell, and in a moment saw the door open just enough to show the nose and a pair of small twinkling eyes of what was evidently a portly woman. 'What do you want?' snarled out the female defender of the premises. 'We want to come and see if we can place a few wounded officers in this house.' 'You can't come in here!' shouted the woman, slamming the door. . . .

"A few knocks induced her again to open the door two or three inches. 'Madam, we must come in here. We shall do you no harm.' 'You can't come in here. I am a lone widow.' 'But I assure you no harm is intended you.' Again the door was closed, and again at the summons was opened. 'Madam, it will be much better for you to allow us to enter than for me to direct these men to force the door; but we must enter.'

"The woman now threw the door wide open, and, rushing into the yard with as much alacrity as her enormous proportions would admit, threw her arms out and whirled about like a reversed spinning top, shouting for help. She was again assured that no harm was intended her, but that unless she chose to show us the house we should be obliged to go alone. Concluding that wisdom was the better part of valor, she proceeded to show us the rooms.

"At another mansion, one of the finest in Fredericksburg, a red-haired woman thrust her head out of the side window, in answer to the ring of the doorbell. 'What do you want here?' 'We wish to place some wounded officers in this house.' 'You can't bring any officers nor anybody else to this house. I'm all alone. I hope you have more honor than to come and disturb defenseless, unprotected women.' 'Have you no husband?' 'Yes, thank God. He's a colonel in the Confederate service.' 'Well, if your husband was at home, where he ought to be, you would not be a defenseless woman.'

"The woman refused to unbolt the door, in spite of all persuasion, but while she railed at the 'detestable Yankees' a soldier climbed in at a window in the rear and unbolted the door. Her splendid rooms and fine mattresses furnished lodgings for twenty wounded officers."

As for Lee's wounded, many were being sent southwestward by rail. On the morning of May 9 a female citizen of Charlottesville (about fifty miles from the battle zone) wrote a letter in which she stated: "Charlottesville is in a whirl of excitement, and the ladies go in crowds to the depot to assist the wounded, who come in train after train. We are all going this afternoon laden with ice water, buttermilk, etc., to see what we can do. Dr. C. is going with us, and I hope we will do some good. It was urged by Mr. Meade in church yesterday that the ladies should render their assistance, as upwards of four or five thousand are expected this afternoon. . . . Gen. Longstreet passed through here yesterday, painfully, but not seriously, wounded in the shoulder." (The wound, actually, was serious enough to keep Longstreet out of action for the next five months.)

Back at Spotsylvania, the following morning—that of May 10— found Grant, in his lines north of Lee's, preparing for a general attack in the afternoon. The greater part of his army was to strike Lee's western wing, while Burnside reconnoitered the eastern wing with a view to attacking if conditions proved favorable. As it happened, Burnside restricted himself to probing, but the western zone was the scene of several furious actions.

Even before Grant got his attack under way, there was a clash on his extreme western flank, or his right, where Hancock's Second Corps was located. (See map on p. 184, "Hancock's Flank Movement.") On the previous day, Hancock had crossed the easterly flowing Po River, using three improvised bridges, to take this position in order to threaten Lee's extreme left. The move had isolated the Second Corps from the rest of Grant's army. And the Po was again in Hancock's front, for it swung south past his left flank and turned briefly westward before continuing toward the south and east.

During the night Lee had buttressed the threatened spot with Heth's division, Hill's corps, and there was now a set of defenses on the heights south of the Po's Block House Bridge. In the morning Grant decided to cancel Hancock's flank effort and bring the Second Corps, except for one division, back across the northern segment of the Po to join in the planned attack farther up Lee's left wing. As Hancock made his withdrawal, Heth's troops came down from their heights, crossed the Po's southern segment, and moved toward the tarrying division, that of Francis Barlow, whose four brigades were commanded by Nelson Miles, Thomas Smyth, John Brooke, and Hiram Brown. Miles and Smyth were hurried northward to cover the approaches to the improvised crossings, while Brooke and Brown faced the enemy's advance. Hancock himself was on the scene, and he tells what happened:

"In a few minutes [Miles and Smyth] were prepared to resist the enemy should he overpower Brooke and Brown and attempt to carry the bridges. I directed that all the batteries on the south side of the river, save [William] Arnold's . . . First Rhode Island, should cross to the north bank and take position commanding the bridges. These dispositions had scarcely been completed when the enemy, having driven in

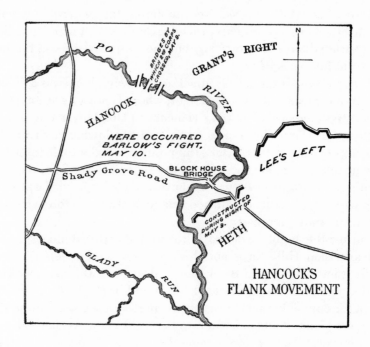

the skirmishers of Brooke's and Brown's brigades, pressed forward.
. . . Advancing in line of battle supported by columns, they attacked
with great vigor and determination, but were met by a heavy and
destructive fire, which compelled them to fall back at once in confusion
with severe losses in killed and wounded.

"Encouraged, doubtless, by the withdrawal of Miles' and Smyth's
brigades from our front line, which it is supposed they mistook for a
forced retreat, they reformed their troops and again assailed Brooke's
and Brown's brigades. The combat now became close and bloody. The
enemy . . . appeared to be determined to crush the small force opposing
them, and, pressing forward with loud yells, forced their way close up
to our line, delivering a terrible musketry fire as they advanced. Our
brave troops again resisted their onset with undaunted resolution.
[Our] fire along the whole line was so continuous and deadly that the
enemy found it impossible to withstand it, but broke again and retreated in the wildest disorder, leaving the ground in our front strewed
with their dead and wounded.

"During the heat of this contest the woods on the right and in rear
of our troops took fire. The flames had now approached close to our line,
rendering it almost impossible to retain the position longer. The last
bloody repulse of the enemy had quieted him for a time, and during this
lull in the fight General Barlow directed Brooke and Brown to abandon
their position and retire to the north bank of the Po. Their right and
rear enveloped in the burning wood, their front assailed by overwhelming numbers of the enemy, the withdrawal of the troops was attended
with extreme difficulty and peril; but the movement was commenced
at once, the men displaying such coolness and steadiness as are rarely
exhibited in the presence of dangers so appalling. . . .

"The enemy, perceiving that our line was retiring, again advanced,
but were again promptly checked by our troops, who fell back through
the burning forest with admirable order and deliberation, though in
doing so many of them were killed and wounded, numbers of the latter
perishing in the flames.

"One section of Arnold's Battery had been pushed forward by Captain Arnold during the fight to within a short distance of Brooke's line,
where it had done effective service. When ordered to retire, the horses
attached to one of the pieces, becoming terrified by the fire and unmanageable, dragged the gun between two trees, where it became so firmly
wedged that it could not be moved. . . . This was the first gun ever lost
by the Second Corps.

"Brooke's Brigade, after emerging from the wood, had [an] open plain to travel. . . . This plain was swept by the enemy's musketry in front, and by their artillery on the heights above the Block House Bridge on the south side of the river. Brown's Brigade, in retiring, was compelled to pass through the entire wood in its rear, which was then burning furiously. Although under a heavy fire, it extricated itself from the forest, losing very heavily in killed and wounded. . . .

"As soon as Brooke's and Brown's Brigades had crossed the Po, General Barlow directed Colonel Smyth . . . to march his command across the pontoon bridge and take position immediately on the north side, where his fire would sweep the bridges in case the enemy designed forcing a passage. Miles' Brigade was thus left to cross last and tear up the bridges at that point. I had sent a detachment to destroy the upper bridge. . . .

"The enemy, now seeing but a few regiments remaining on the south bank, attempted to cross the open plain in their front, but were at once driven back by . . . Miles' troops and our artillery on the heights. A furious artillery fire was also opened by the enemy's batteries on the heights above the wooden bridge over the Po. Our batteries replied with a well-directed fire, which speedily silenced them, exploding one of their caissons and forcing them to withdraw their guns. Miles' Brigade now crossed to the north bank, taking up the pontoon bridge and thoroughly destroying the other. The enemy made no attempt to cross the stream."

Grant's efforts against Lee's left wing involved several spots between the Po River and the apex of the salient, ground occupied by Confederate Generals Anderson (Longstreet's successor) and Ewell. Anderson was in the south, his left on the Po, and Ewell was holding the salient. The Union work required a good deal of artillery preparation, with its attendant roar; and there was a lot of marching and counter-marching through brushy woodlands and across meadows and furrowed fields as the various units found their positions. Each advance upon the Confederate breastworks resulted in a withdrawal marked by a trail of fallen men. Says Southern artillery officer Robert Stiles: "For frequency and pertinacity of attack, and repetition and constancy of repulse, I question if [the action on] the left of General Lee's lines on the 10th of May, 1864, has ever been surpassed. I cannot pretend to identify the separate attacks or to distinguish between them, but should think there must have been at least a dozen of them. [These were components of several major advances.] One marked feature was that,

Confederate breastworks at Spotsylvania

while fresh troops poured to almost every charge, the same muskets in the hands of the same men met the first attack . . . and the last."

Some of the defenders, actually, came to be supplied with more than one musket. Obtained during a lull in the fighting, the weapons were of Northern manufacture. As explained by Confederate brigade commander E. M. Law: "Anticipating a renewal of the assaults, many of our men went out in front of their breastworks, and, gathering up the muskets and cartridge boxes of the dead and wounded, brought them in and distributed them along the line. If they did not have repeating-rifles, they had a very good substitute—several loaded ones to each man."

Grant's troops had been taking the higher casualties, and their field hospitals became busy places. Boston newsman Charles Carleton Coffin paid a visit to one of these. "The air was thick with smoke from cannon and musket, and the cloud hung low. . . . Upon the ground lay hundreds of wounded. I beheld men with bandaged heads and limbs; those who had lost an arm or foot; those with ghastly wounds from which their life-blood was flowing. . . . I had been so long with the army that the soldiers recognized me as a correspondent, and were eager for news. 'How is the battle going? Are they driving us? Will the boys hold them?' Such the questions. Natural questions they were . . . for if the Confederates were to sweep back their comrades the hundreds of wounded would become prisoners of war.

" 'I do not think that the enemy can drive us; our position is a strong one,' was my reply. It was a cheery word spoken for their comfort. A soldier who had just lost his left arm, who was weak and faint from the amputation, with his heart all aglow for the old flag, broke into the song which, through the war, had been sung by the bivouac fire and on the march:

> 'We are marching to the field, boys; we're going to
>   the fight,
> Shouting the Battle Cry of Freedom;
> And we bear the glorious Stars for the Union and
>   the Right,
> Shouting the Battle Cry of Freedom.'

"It was like the quaffing of wine to weak and fainting men who heard it, and all around I saw them lift themselves—some to stand erect, others half reclining, swinging their caps as they joined in the chorus:

A Union field hospital: Fifth Corps, Spotsylvania

'The Union forever; hurrah, boys, hurrah!
Down with the traitor; up with the Stars,
While we rally round the flag, boys, rally once again,
Shouting the Battle Cry of Freedom!' "

It was late in the day when Grant made his final effort, one against
Ewell and aimed at a point just west of the salient's apex. Chosen to take
in twelve picked regiments was a young colonel named Emory Upton,
the product of a New York farm family who had graduated from West
Point just before the outbreak of the war and had become an ardent
supporter of the Union cause. Upton tells the story of his attack, beginning with its formation a half mile west of the Confederate works:

"All the officers were instructed to repeat the command 'Forward'
constantly from the commencement of the charge till the works were
carried. At ten minutes before 6 P.M., Captain [Henry] Dalton brought
me the order to attack as soon as the column was formed, and stated
that the artillery would cease firing at 6 P.M. Twenty minutes elapsed
before all the preparations were completed, when, at command, the
lines rose, moved noiselessly to the edge of the wood, and then, with
a wild cheer and faces averted [in anticipation of the enemy's response],
rushed for the works.

"Through a terrible front and flank fire the column advanced,
quickly gaining the parapet. Here occurred a deadly hand-to-hand conflict. The enemy sitting in their pits with pieces upright, loaded, and
with bayonets fixed, ready to impale the first who should leap over,
absolutely refused to yield the ground. The first of our men who tried
to surmount the works fell pierced through the head by musket balls.
Others [still outside the works], seeing the fate of their comrades, held
their pieces at arm's length and fired downward, while others, poising
their pieces vertically, hurled them [as spears] down upon their enemy,
pinning them to the ground.

"Lieutenant [James] Johnston, of the One Hundred and Twenty-first
New York, received a bayonet wound through the thigh. Private
[James] O'Donnell, Ninety-sixth Pennsylvania Volunteers, was pinned
to the parapet but was rescued by his comrades. A private of the Fifth
Maine, having bayoneted a rebel, was fired at by [a Confederate] cap-
tain, who, missing his aim, in turn shared the same fate [by the bayonet].
The brave man [from Maine] fell by a shot from [a] rebel lieutenant.

"The struggle lasted but a few seconds. Numbers prevailed, and, like
a resistless wave, the column poured over the works, quickly putting

hors de combat those who resisted, and sending to the rear those who surrendered. Pressing forward and expanding to the right and left, the second line of intrenchments, its line of battle, and the battery fell into our hands.

"The column of assault had accomplished its task. The enemy's lines were completely broken, and an opening had been made for the division which was to have supported on our left, but it did not arrive.

"Re-enforcements arriving to the enemy, our front and both flanks were assailed. The impulsion of the charge being lost, nothing remained but to hold the ground. I accordingly directed the officers to form their men outside the works and open fire."

Grant now sent in a supporting attack at a point to the south, or the right, that he felt might be vulnerable. The moment is depicted by Confederate officer E. M. Law: "Near sunset our skirmishers were driven in, and the heavy, dark lines of attack came into view, one after another, first in quick-time, then in a trot, and then with a rush toward the works. The front lines [of the attacking troops] dissolved before the pitiless storm that met them, but those in the rear pressed forward, and over their dead and dying comrades reached that portion of the works held by the Texas Brigade. These gallant fellows, now reduced to a mere handful by their losses in the Wilderness, stood manfully to their work. Their line was bent backward by the pressure, but they continued the fight in rear of the works with bayonets and clubbed muskets. Fortunately for them . . . a portion of [another brigade] turned upon the flank of their assailants, who were driven out, leaving many dead and wounded inside the works."

In the north there was a lull in the fire fight between Union Colonel Emory Upton's troops and the Confederates in the works Upton had been forced to abandon.

Turning to Southern officer Robert Stiles, whose howitzer unit was a part of the scene: "When it became evident that the attack had failed, I suggested to the chaplain, who happened to be with the howitzer guns, perhaps for [a] sundown prayer meeting . . . that there might be some demand for his ministrations where the enemy had broken over; so we walked up there and found their dead and dying piled higher than the works themselves. It was almost dark, but as we drew near we saw a wounded Federal soldier clutch the pantaloons of [a] Captain Hunter, who at that moment was passing by . . . and heard him ask, with intense eagerness, 'Can you pray, sir? Can you pray?' The old captain looked down at him . . . and pulled away, saying, 'No, my friend. I don't wish you any harm now, but praying's not exactly my trade.'

"I said to the chaplain, 'Let's go to that man.' As we came up he caught my pants in the same way and uttered the same words, 'Can you pray, sir? Can you pray?' I bent over the poor fellow, turned back his blouse, and saw that a large canister shot had passed through his chest at such a point that the wound must necessarily prove mortal, and that soon.

"We both knelt down by him, and I took his hand in mine and said, 'My friend, you haven't much time left for prayer, but if you will say after me just these simple words, with heart as well as lips, all will be well with you: 'God have mercy on me, a sinner, for Jesus Christ's sake.'

"I never saw such intensity in human gaze, nor ever heard such intensity in human voice, as in the gaze and voice of that dying man as he held my hand and looked into my face, repeating the simple, awful, yet reassuring words I had dictated. He uttered them again and again, with the death rattle in his throat and the death tremor in his frame, until someone shouted, 'They are coming again!' and we broke away and ran down to the guns.

"It proved to be a false alarm, and we returned immediately—but he was dead; yes, dead and half-stripped. But I managed to get my hand upon his blouse a moment and looked at the buttons. He was from the far-off State of Maine."

There was some renewed firing between the Confederates in the works and Emory Upton's ousted Federals, but the fight was about over. "Night had arrived," says Upton. "Our position was three-quarters of a mile in advance of the army, and, without prospect of support, was untenable. . . . Under cover of darkness . . . the regiments [returned] to their former camps.

"Our loss in this assault was about 1,000 in killed, wounded, and missing. The enemy lost at least 100 in killed at the first intrenchments, while a much heavier loss was sustained in his effort to regain them. We captured between 1,000 and 1,200 prisoners and several stand of colors. . . . Many rebel prisoners were shot by their own men in passing to the rear [with us] over the open field.

"Our officers and men accomplished all that could be expected of brave men."

The vast arena now saw the smoke of battle replaced by the smoke of campfires. In both armies, those men not busy with work details reveled in the comforts of the fireside. They savored their simple rations and found a balm in their smoking or chewing tobacco. They talked of the day's events and speculated about the morrow. They wrote letters, engaged in group prayer, and sang some of the era's hauntingly sad songs. A favorite, of course, was "Home, Sweet Home." As usual after such a day, the hospital facilities were greatly overtaxed, and many of the wounded lay unattended in the deep darkness between the lines, some within hearing of the campfire songs. On both sides, news correspondents wandered about the camps gathering data for their dispatches. Relates the Union's Charles Carleton Coffin:

"It was nearly eleven o'clock in the evening when I dismounted from my horse at the headquarters of General Grant. He was sitting on a camp chair smoking a cigar. The only person present was Hon. E. B. Washburne, a member of Congress, his most intimate friend from Galena, his old home in Illinois, who had been instrumental in bringing about General Grant's appointment as lieutenant-general. [Washburne had been visiting with the army and planned to return to Washington the next day.]

"There were times when the commander-in-chief was reticent upon all subjects. He has been called, like William of the Netherlands, the Silent Commander; but there were times also when General Grant gave free expression to his thoughts. I asked for information in regard to the events of the day, that I might communicate it to readers far away, which was kindly given. And then, not in response to any question, he said, 'We have had hard fighting today, and I am sorry to say we have not accomplished much. We have lost a good many men, and I suppose that I shall be blamed for it.'

"He was silent a moment, and then added: 'I do not know any way to put down this rebellion and restore the authority of the Government except by fighting, and fighting means that men must be killed. If the people of this country expect that the war can be conducted to a successful issue in any other way than by fighting, they must get somebody other than myself to command the army.'"

If Lee had the satisfaction of besting Grant on May 10, he was not too confident about his situation. The security of the salient, or Mule Shoe, was a growing concern. Lee ordered a set of fortifications thrown across its half-mile base, to connect solidly with both his wings. That way, if the salient was shattered his defenses would still be continuous from flank to flank. Without the precaution, his line might be cut in two and the army brought to disaster.

A sidelight to affairs at Spotsylvania during the night of May 10–11 is given by Southern soldier John Casler: "Sam Nunnelly came to me and said we would get over in front of our works that night and plunder the dead, as he knew there were plenty of them there that had never been searched. I told him I would not do it, as we would be in danger of being shot by our own men as well as the enemy. But he said he would go by himself and crawl around and play off wounded. So he went, and was gone all night, coming back at daylight. He got three watches, some money, knives, and other things. He would risk his life any time for plunder."

17

Hancock Breaks Through

A ccording to General Grant's aide, Horace Porter: "The 11th of May gave promise of a little rest for everybody, as the commander expressed his intention to spend the day simply in reconnoitering for the purpose of learning more about the character and strength of the enemy's intrenchments . . . with a view to breaking through. He sat down at the mess table that morning and made his entire breakfast of a cup of coffee and a small piece of beef cooked almost to a crisp; for the cook had by this time learned that the nearer he came to burning the beef the better the general liked it.

"During the short time he was at the table he conversed with [Congressman] Washburne . . . who was now about to return to Washington. After breakfast the general lighted a cigar, seated himself on a camp chair in front of his tent, and was joined there by Mr. Washburne and several members of the staff. At half-past eight o'clock the cavalry escort which was to accompany the congressman was drawn up in the road nearby, and all present rose to bid him good-by. Turning to the chief, he said, 'General, I shall go to see the President and the Secretary of War as soon as I reach Washington. I can imagine their anxiety to know what you think of the prospects of the campaign, and I know they would be greatly gratified if I could carry a message from you giving what encouragement you can as to the situation.'

"The general hesitated a moment, and then replied, 'We are certainly making fair progress, and all the fighting has been in our favor; but the campaign promises to be a long one, and I am particularly anxious not to say anything just now that might hold out false hopes to the people,' and then, after a pause, added, 'However, I will write a letter . . . giving the general situation, and you can take it with you.'

"He stepped into his tent, sat down at his field-table, and, keeping his cigar in his mouth, wrote a despatch of about two hundred words. In the middle of the communication occurred the [soon to become] famous words, *'I propose to fight it out on this line if it takes all summer.'*

"When the letter had been copied [by a clerk], he [the general] folded it and handed it to Mr. Washburne, who thanked him warmly, wished him a continuation of success, shook hands with him and with each of the members of the staff, and at once mounted his horse and rode off. . . .

"It was learned afterward that the President was delighted to read this despatch . . . and that he had said, a few days before, when asked by a member of Congress what Grant was doing, 'Well, I can't tell you much about it. You see, Grant has gone to the Wilderness, crawled in, drawn up the ladder, and pulled in the hole after him, and I guess we'll have to wait till he comes out before we know just what he's up to.' "

Grant's reconnoitering operations on May 11 were unaffected by the fact that the morning saw the beginning of a rainy spell, the campaign's first bad weather. Nor, it seems, was Union morale diminished. In the words of Captain Henry Blake, of the Eleventh Massachusetts, Hancock's corps: "Musicians usually lurk in the rear, but a band that was sheltered by the line of breastworks in the front played martial airs at intervals, and invariably enlivened the soldiers, who loudly cheered. The watchful sharpshooters [on both sides of the battle arena] pierced with their unerring rifles every object that might be a human being; the cannon resounded occasionally; but there was no serious battle during the day."

For General Lee May 11 was a day of uncertainty, since he had no way of fathoming Grant's intentions. His scouts reported a good deal of motion among the various Federal units, and he spent much time pondering its meaning. He rode about his lines urging the men to greater efforts with their entrenchments, and he remained especially concerned about the security of Ewell's corps at the salient.

Ewell's troops themselves were edgy about their position. "Everyone who had to be near the front," says Private Casler, "had a hole to get into. . . . We were exposed to shells from two directions, and shells from one direction would drop in behind the works from the opposite angle. Therefore, on part of the line we had to throw dirt on each side of the ditch.

"While making a ditch of this kind . . . they opened on us with artillery. Most of the [men] ran to another ditch, which was already completed. . . . Several of them, myself included, remained where we were working, and among the number was one great big cowardly fellow named Ayleshire, of the Tenth Virginia, who always carried a big knapsack and wore a number 13 shoe. He was six feet high, and could take half a plug of tobacco at one chew. At the first fire he fell flat to the ground. As the shells passed over, he would attempt to rise to run to the works, but by the time he would get on his hands and knees another shell would pass over, when he would fall flat and stretch out as before. He would then attempt to rise again, but never did get on his feet to run.

"He kept up that motion while the shelling lasted, which was about half an hour. He had nearly pumped himself to death, and had the ground all pawed up with his feet—the balance of us laughing at him and hallooing to him to 'Run, Ayleshire! Run, Ayleshire!'

"If I had known I would be killed for it the next minute I could not have helped laughing at him, it was so ridiculous. I was wishing a shell would take his knapsack off without hurting him. If one had, I believe he would have died right there from fright."

Returning to the Union side and to Horace Porter: "The result of the day's work on our front was to discover more definitely the character of the salient in Lee's defenses. . . . The ground in front sloped down toward our position, and was in most places thickly wooded. There was a clearing, however, about four hundred yards in width immediately in front of the apex. Several of the staff officers were on that part of the field a great portion of the day.

"At three o'clock in the afternoon the general had thoroughly matured his plans, and sent instructions to Meade directing him to move Hancock [who was still on the army's extreme right, or in the west] with all possible secrecy under cover of night to the left . . . and to make a vigorous assault on the Angle at dawn the next morning. Warren and Wright [remaining in place as the army's western wing] were ordered to hold their corps as close to the enemy as possible, and to take advantage of any diversion caused by [Hancock's] attack to push in if an opportunity should present itself. . . . Burnside [in the east] . . . was to attack simultaneously with Hancock. . . .

"The threatening sky was not propitious for the movement, but . . .

the preparations went on regardless of the lowering clouds and falling rain."

Grant's attack plan was favored by a remarkable piece of luck, a mistake on the part of Lee. As explained by Confederate officer Jedediah Hotchkiss, Ewell's topographical engineer: "The shifting about of troops in the Federal lines [during the daylight hours] on the 11th led Lee to the conclusion that Grant was about to draw back from the Spotsylvania Court House field of combat [either in retreat or for the purpose of beginning another flank maneuver to the southeast]; so he made preparations to meet any new movement he might attempt by ordering all the artillery . . . in difficult positions to be withdrawn to where it could be quickly assembled for marching. Obeying this order, General Long [Armistead Long, Ewell's chief of artillery] withdrew the guns from the northern portion of the great salient, so that Edward Johnson's division, at the apex, was left on guard with only muskets and two pieces of artillery."

It was about 10 P.M., with the wet weather continuing, when the units of Union General Hancock's corps began their march eastward from Grant's right flank, their destination the grounds around the Brown house, located about a mile north of the Confederate salient. (See map on p. 199, "The Salient at Spotsylvania.") The muddy trek is described by one of Hancock's aides, Major W. G. Mitchell: "Night exceedingly dark, and roads very rough; men tired and worn out, but kept well closed up and moved along briskly; no accidents save one, when some pack mules laden with intrenching tools ran away and made some confusion, under the supposition that we had marched into the enemy.

"When the troops arrived at the Brown house [around midnight] they were quietly marched in front of our intrenchments [created earlier by other units] near to the enemy's picket line, so as to be ready for the intended assault in the morning. This was accomplished without noise or confusion, and was most happily favored by an exceedingly dark night. The men, too, knowing that we were near the enemy and that we were engaged in a perilous undertaking, kept remarkably quiet during the whole movement."

The Federals, however, did not go undetected. Says Confederate General Johnson: "Scouts and officers on the picket line, and brigade commanders, informed me that the enemy were . . . concentrating in my front, and all concurred in the opinion that my lines would be assaulted in the morning." Johnson ordered his troops to be on the alert,

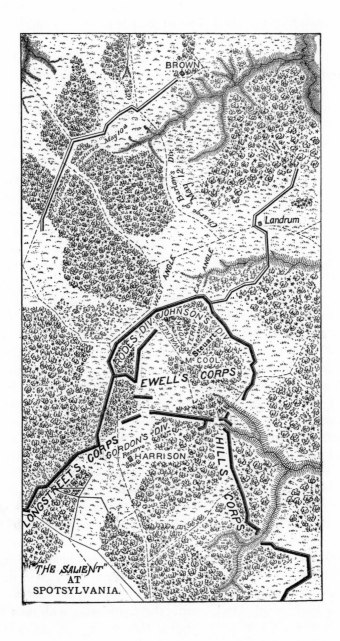

"THE SALIENT"
AT
SPOTSYLVANIA.

and he hastened a request to corps commander Ewell that the missing artillery pieces be returned. The request was acted upon, but, unaccountably, without any special urgency.

Union General Hancock, according to Major Mitchell, had "almost a solid rectangular mass of nearly 20,000 men to hurl upon the enemy's works as soon as it should be sufficiently light for our purpose. A dense fog fell before daylight, and we all stood shivering with cold and wet until 4:30 A.M., when the fog lifted somewhat and the command was given to advance. The whole corps [with the divisions of Francis Barlow and David Birney spanning the front], stepped off at the same moment, and, in about 300 yards, marched over the enemy's pickets, who were so astounded at our appearance, marching on them out of the fog, that they never fired a shot, nor did we, but moved right over them.

"The first fire we received was from the picket-reserve stationed at the Landrum house, about halfway between the point at which we formed for the assault and the enemy's works. Their fire killed Colonel [David L.] Stricker, Second Delaware Volunteers, and a few men. A regiment was sent to disperse them, and our column kept on."

The moment was one of great anxiety for Confederate General Johnson, astride his horse at the front. "I . . . found that the artillery which had withdrawn the night previous had not returned, but looking [toward the rear] I saw it just coming in sight. I dismounted, went into the trenches, collected all the men possible to hold the enemy in check until the artillery could get into position and open upon this column, which came up in large numbers but in great disorder, with a narrow front, but extending back to the rear as far as I could see. I ordered the artillery to drive up at a gallop. . . . I felt confident that a few shots would disperse this force, which offered so fair a mark to artillery."

But there wasn't time for an effective deployment of the pieces. Again in the words of the Union's Major Mitchell: "The ground was open and rolling from the Landrum house to the works, and the troops dashed over it in fine style, not meeting a heavy fire until when within about 300 yards. The Irish Brigade then gave a wild cheer, and immediately the enemy opened a tremendous fire of musketry on us over the parapets, with some artillery, but nothing could now stop our men, who rushed up to the works, and, tearing the abatis away with their hands, poured in like a great wave, driving the enemy out pell-mell with clubbed muskets and bayonets, capturing twenty pieces of artillery and nearly 4,000 prisoners [the number, actually, was probably no more than 3,000]—nearly the whole of the celebrated Stonewall Brigade; also capturing Maj. Gen. Edward Johnson, commanding a division. . . . The prisoners got mixed up among our own men in the works, and were dodging in all directions from the bullets of their friends, who were firing upon us as they fell back.

"In the midst of this confusion and crowd, a soldier attracted my attention by shouting out to me, 'Major Mitchell, here is a rebel general.' I at once rode up to General [George H.] Steuart, who gave me his name and rank [he was one of Johnson's brigadiers], and I directed a captain of the Fifty-third Pennsylvania Volunteers to conduct him to General Hancock [who was headquartered back near the attack's starting point]. When Steuart was taken to the general, the latter, who knew him before the war, held out his hand, saying, 'How are you, Steuart?' The latter replied, 'Under the circumstances, I decline to take your hand.' 'And under any other circumstances I should not have offered it,' said General Hancock."

Hancock had a friendlier meeting with Johnson, who was not belligerent but simply very sad. According to an unnamed Federal observer: "Johnson put his hand to his heart, and, as he gazed upon his fellow prisoners and the earthworks [recently] under his command, heavy tears coursed down his cheeks and his whole frame heaved with emotion. But he took a drink with Hancock, who then sent him on horseback to Grant's headquarters."

Hancock also sent Grant a message explaining that his troops had broken the enemy's first line and were sweeping down through the salient. Grant's staff officers, standing around a campfire that was hissing and steaming in the rain, broke into a round of cheers that rang through the woods about them. The commander himself did not join in. He quietly set about reinforcing Hancock and dispatching orders aimed at improving the support the general was getting from the army's flanks.

For General Lee the flank pressure was not a critical worry, for he believed that both his flanks were strong enough to resist direct attacks—which, indeed, they were. But the piercing of Ewell's line at the salient imperiled his flanks from the rear. To worsen matters, some of the Confederates of the salient who hadn't been captured were running from Hancock like frightened rabbits. Lee, on horseback, was in a rearward region of the salient at this time, and, according to Robert Stiles, "he had only one or two attendants with him. His face was more serious than I had ever seen it, but showed no trace of excitement or alarm. Numbers of demoralized men were streaming past him, and his voice was deep as the growl of a tempest as he said, 'Shame on you, men;

shame on you! Go back to your regiments; go back to your regiments!'

". . . It was the only time I ever knew his faintest wish not to be instantly responded to by his troops; but . . . every soldier of experience knows that when a man has reached a certain point of demoralization, and until he has settled down again past that point, it is absolutely useless to attempt to rouse him to a sense of duty or of honor. I have seen many a man substantially in the condition of the fellow who, as he executed a flying leap over the musket of the guard threatening to shoot him and crying 'Halt!'—called back, '[I'll] give any man fifty dollars to halt me, but can't halt myself!' "

The only positive element in Lee's desperately urgent situation was that Ewell's reserve division, stationed about a half mile south of the salient's apex, was commanded by the alert and aggressive John Gordon. (The brigadier had been elevated to division commander after his outstanding work in the Wilderness.) Gordon lost no time in starting his troops northward. The general relates:

"The mist and fog were so heavy that it was impossible to see farther than a few rods. Throwing out in front a small force to apprise us of our near approach to the enemy, I rode at the head of the main column, and by my side rode General Robert Johnston, who commanded a brigade of North Carolinians. . . . Before we had moved one half the distance to the salient [i.e., to its apex], the head of my column butted squarely against Hancock's line of battle. The men who had been placed in our front to give warning were against that battle line before they knew it. They were shot down or made prisoners.

"The sudden and unexpected blaze from Hancock's rifles made the dark woodland strangely lurid. General Johnston, who rode immediately at my side, was shot from his horse, severely . . . wounded in the head. His brigade was thrown inevitably into great confusion, but did not break to the rear. As quickly as possible I had the next ranking officer in that brigade notified of General Johnston's fall, and directed him at once to assume command. He proved equal to the emergency. . . .

"The Federals were still advancing, and every movement of the North Carolina brigade had to be made under heavy fire. The officer in charge was directed to hastily withdraw his brigade a short distance, to change front so as to face Hancock's lines, and to deploy his whole force in close order as skirmishers, so as to stretch, if possible, across the entire front of Hancock. This done, he was ordered to charge with his line of skirmishers the solid battle lines before him.

"His looks indicated some amazement at the purpose to make an attack which appeared so utterly hopeless, and which would have been the very essence of rashness but for the extremity of the situation. He was, however, full of the fire of battle and too good a soldier not to yield prompt and cheerful obedience.

"That order was given in the hope and belief that, in the fog and mists which concealed our numbers, the sheer audacity of the movement would confuse and check the Union advance long enough for me to change front and form line of battle with the other brigades. The result was not disappointing, except in the fact that Johnston's brigade, even when so deployed, was still too short to reach across Hancock's entire front. . . .

"When the daring charge of the North Carolina brigade had temporarily checked that portion of the Federal forces struck by it, and while my brigades in the rear were being placed in position, I rode with Thomas G. Jones, the youngest member of my staff, into the intervening woods, in order, if possible, to locate Hancock more definitely. Sitting on my horse near the line of the North Carolina brigade, I was endeavoring to get a view of the Union lines through the woods and through the gradually lifting mists.

"It was impossible, however, to see those lines; but . . . the direction from which they sent their bullets soon informed us that they were still moving and had already gone beyond our right. One of those bullets passed through my coat from side to side, just grazing my back. Jones, who was close to me and sitting on his horse in a not very erect posture, anxiously inquired, 'General, didn't that ball hit you?' 'No,' I said. 'But suppose my back had been in a bow like yours? Don't you see that the bullet would have gone straight through my spine? Sit up or you'll be killed!' [With a] sudden jerk . . . he straightened himself. . . .

"I then . . . placed my troops in line for a countercharge, upon the success or failure of which the fate of the Confederate army seemed to hang. General Lee evidently thought so. His army had been cut in twain by Hancock's brilliant *coup de main*. Through that wide breach in the Confederate lines, which was becoming wider with every step, the Union forces were rushing like a swollen torrent through a broken mill dam. General Lee knew, as did everyone else who realized the momentous import of the situation, that the bulk of the Confederate army was in such imminent peril that nothing could rescue it except a counter-movement, quick, impetuous, and decisive.

"Lee resolved to save it, and, if need be, to save it at the sacrifice of his own life. With perfect self-poise, he rode to the margin of that breach and appeared upon the scene just as I had completed the align-ment of my troops and was in the act of moving in that critical counter-charge upon which so much depended. As he rode majestically in front of my line of battle, with uncovered head and mounted on Old Travel-ler, Lee looked a very god of war. Calmly and grandly, he rode to a point near the center of my line and turned his horse's head to the front, evidently resolved to lead in person the desperate charge, and drive Hancock back or perish in the effort.

"I knew what he meant; and, although the passing moments were of priceless value, I resolved to arrest him in his effort, and thus save to the Confederacy the life of its great leader. I was at the center of that line when General Lee rode to it. . . . Instantly I spurred my horse across Old Traveller's front, and, grasping his bridle in my hand, I checked him. Then, in a voice which I hoped might reach the ears of my men and command their attention, I called out, 'General Lee, you shall not lead my men in a charge. No man can do that, sir. Another is here for that purpose. These men behind you are Georgians, Virginians, and Carolinians. They have never failed you on any field. They will not fail you here. Will you, boys?'

"The response came . . . in the monosyllables, 'No, no, no; we'll not fail him!' Yet they were doubtless to him more eloquent because of their simplicity and momentous meaning. But his great heart was destined to be quickly cheered by a still sublimer testimony of their deathless devotion. . . . I shouted to General Lee, 'You must go to the rear!' The echo, 'General Lee to the rear! General Lee to the rear!' rolled back with tremendous emphasis from the throats of my men; and they gath-ered around him, turned his horse in the opposite direction, some clutching his bridle, some his stirrups, while others pressed close to Old Traveller's hips, ready to shove him by main force to the rear. I verily believe that, had it been necessary or possible, they would have carried on their shoulders both horse and rider to a place of safety.

"This entire scene, with all its details of wonderful pathos and deep meaning, had lasted but a few minutes, and yet it . . . had lifted these soldiers to the very highest plane of martial enthusiasm. . . . Fully realizing the value of such inspiration for the accomplishment of the bloody task assigned them, I turned to my men as Lee was forced to the rear, and, reminding them of their pledges to him, and of the fact that the eyes of their great leader were still upon them, I ordered, 'Forward!'

"With the fury of a cyclone, and almost with its resistless power, they rushed upon Hancock's advancing column. With their first terrific onset . . . his leading lines were shivered and hurled back upon their stalwart supports. In the inextricable confusion that followed, and before Hancock's lines could be reformed, every officer on horseback in my division, the brigade and regimental commanders and my own superb staff, were riding among the troops, shouting in unison, 'Forward, men; forward!' But the brave line officers on foot and the enthused privates needed no additional spur to their already rapt spirits. Onward they swept, pouring their rapid volleys into Hancock's confused ranks, and swelling the deafening din of battle with their piercing shouts.

"Like the debris in the track of a storm, the dead and dying of both armies were left in the wake of this Confederate charge. In the meantime, the magnificent troops of [Robert Rodes's division] were rushing upon Hancock's dissolving corps from another point [from their entrenchments along the west face of the salient], and Long's artillery, and other batteries, were pouring a deadly fire into the broken Federal ranks. [Also a part of the counterattack were elements of Cadmus Wilcox's division, of Lee's eastern wing.] Hancock was repulsed and driven out. . . . There was not one Union soldier left with arms in his hands inside of that great crescent."

18

The Bloody Angle

Hancock had been thrown back, but he hadn't been defeated. The greater portion of his troops ended their flight and faced about as soon as they arrived outside the Confederate defenses along the salient's northern rim, with the new Union front stretching for perhaps half a mile and embracing both the "East Angle" and the "West Angle." Some of Hancock's western regiments had failed to stop when they cleared the salient, and that wing was unstable; but elements of Wright's Sixth Corps had begun moving from Grant's original lines to the spot that needed bolstering.

Among the earlier units to make the advance was the brigade under Emory Upton, the New Yorker who had led the temporary breakthrough on May 10. One of the enlisted men with Upton was G. Norton Galloway, who recounts:

"At a brisk pace we crossed a line of [Union] intrenchments a short distance in our front, and, passing through a strip of timber, at once began to realize our nearness to the foe. . . . Our forces were hastily retiring at this point . . . and these, with our wounded, lined the road.

"We pressed forward and soon cleared the woods and reached an insidious fen, covered with dense marsh grass, where we lay down for a few moments awaiting orders. I cannot imagine how any of us survived the sharp fire that swept over us at this point—a fire so keen that it split the blades of grass all about us, the minies moaning in a furious concert as they picked out victims by the score. [This fire was not coming from the salient's rim, but from a secondary line some distance to the rear. The rim defenses had not yet been reoccupied.]

"The rain was still falling in torrents and held the country about in obscurity. The command was soon given to my regiment, the 95th Pennsylvania Volunteers . . . it being the advance of Upton's brigade, to 'rise up,' whereupon with hurrahs we went forward, cheered on by Colonel Upton. . . . It was not long before we reached an angle of works [the West Angle] constructed with great skill. . . . At this moment Lee's strong line of battle . . . appeared through the rain, mist, and smoke [but still some distance behind the Angle]. We received their bolts, losing nearly one hundred of our gallant 95th. Colonel Upton saw at once that this point must be held. . . . The order was . . . given us to lie down and commence firing. . . .

"Under cover of the smoke-laden rain, the enemy was pushing large bodies of troops forward. . . . Could we hold on until the remainder of our brigade should come to our assistance? Regardless of the heavy volleys of the enemy that were thinning our ranks, we stuck to the position and returned the fire until the 5th Maine and the 121st New York of our brigade came to our support, while the 96th Pennsylvania went in on our right. Thus reinforced, we redoubled our exertions.

"The smoke, which was dense at first, was intensified by each discharge of artillery to such an extent that the accuracy of our aim became very uncertain; but nevertheless we kept up the fire in the supposed direction of the enemy. Meanwhile, they were crawling forward under cover of the smoke, until, reaching a certain point and raising their usual yell, they charged gallantly up to the very muzzles of our pieces and reoccupied the Angle.

"Upon [their] reaching the breastwork, the Confederates for a few moments had the advantage of us, and made good use of their rifles. Our men went down by the score. All the artillery horses were down. The gallant Upton was the only mounted officer in sight. Hat in hand, he bravely cheered his men and begged them to 'hold this point.' All of his staff had been either killed, wounded, or dismounted.

"At this moment, and while the open ground in rear of the Confederate works was choked with troops, a section of Battery C, 5th United States Artillery, under Lieutenant Richard Metcalf, was brought into action and increased the carnage by opening at short range with double charges of canister. This staggered the apparently exultant enemy. In the maze of the moment these guns were run up by hand close to the . . . Angle, and fired again and again; and they were only abandoned when all the drivers and cannoneers had fallen.

"The battle was now at white heat. The rain continued to fall, and clouds of smoke hung over the scene. Like leeches we stuck to the work, determined by our fire to keep the enemy from rising up. Captain John D. Fish . . . seemed to court death as he rode back and forth between the caissons and cannoneers with stands of canister under his 'gum' [i.e., his raincoat]. 'Give it to them, boys! I'll bring you the canister,' said he. And, as he [added a cheer] . . . he fell from his horse, mortally wounded. In a few moments the two brass pieces . . . cut and hacked by . . . bullets . . . lay unworked with their muzzles projecting over the enemy's works and their wheels half sunk in the mud. . . . Near at hand lay the horses of these guns, completely riddled. The [Confederate] dead and wounded [had been] torn to pieces by the canister as it swept the ground where they had fallen.

"The mud was halfway to our knees, and by our constant movement [our] fallen were almost buried at our feet. We now backed off from the breastwork a few yards . . . but still keeping up a fusillade. We soon closed up our shattered ranks, and the brigade settled down again to its task. Our fire was now directed at the top of the breastworks, and woe be to the head or hand that appeared above it."

Supports continued coming up behind both sides along the half-mile front. There was also fighting, some of it heavy, along the works on both of Lee's flanks as Union Generals Burnside and Warren closed in, but these clashes never rose to special consequence. The northern rim of the salient remained the critical zone, and the West Angle (to become known as the "Bloody Angle") continued as the point of fiercest contention, chiefly because this is where Lee chose to make his strongest effort.

An explanation of the rim's military significance is offered by Confederate General John Gordon: "Why did the commanders of the two armies put forth such herculean efforts over so short a line? In what respect was this small space of earthworks so essential to either army as to justify the expenditure of tons of lead and barrels of blood? . . . That short reach of works was an integral part of Lee's battle line. The Confederates held the inside of it, the Federals the outside. . . . If Lee could drive Grant's men from the outer slope his entire line would be completely reestablished. If Grant could drive the Confederates from the inner slope he would hold a breach in their lines—narrow, it is true, but still a breach—through which he might again force his way, riving Lee's army a second time, as the rail-splitter's wedge rives the timber as it is driven into the narrow crack. Therefore, the complete possession by the Federals of that disputed section meant to Grant a coveted opportunity. To Lee it meant a serious menace. Neither could afford to surrender so important a point without a desperate struggle."

And a desperate struggle the affair continued to be. Among the supports that came up on the Confederate side was Samuel McGowan's brigade of South Carolinians, to which Lieutenant J. F. J. Caldwell belonged: "About the time we reached the inner [or secondary] line, General McGowan was wounded by a Minie ball in the right arm, and forced to quit the field. Colonel [Benjamin] Brockman, senior colonel present, was also wounded, and Colonel J. N. Brown, of the Fourteenth regiment, assumed command, then or a little later. . . . Soon the order was given to advance to the outer line. We did so, with a cheer and at the double-quick, plunging through mud knee-deep, and getting in as best we could. Here, however, lay [Nathaniel] Harris's Mississippi brigade. We were ordered to close to the right [in order to find a place at the front]. We moved by the flank up the works, under the fatally accurate fire of the enemy, and ranged ourselves along the intrenchment.

"The sight we encountered was not calculated to encourage us. The trenches dug on the inner side were almost filled with water. Dead men lay on the surface of the ground and in the pools of water. The wounded bled and groaned, stretched and huddled in every attitude of pain. The water was crimsoned with blood. Abandoned knapsacks, guns, and accoutrements, with ammunition boxes, were scattered all around. In the rear, disabled caissons stood, and limbers of guns. The rain poured heavily, and an incessant fire was kept upon us. . . . Nor were these foes easily seen. They barely raised their heads above the logs, at the moment of firing. It was plainly a test of bravery and endurance now. We entered upon the task with all our might."

Switching to the Union side and to Hancock's aide, Francis Walker: "The conflict had now become the closest and fiercest of the war. The Confederates were determined to recover their intrenchments at whatever the cost. . . . Amid a cold, drenching rain, the combatants were literally struggling across the breastworks. They fired directly into each other's faces; bayonet thrusts were given over the intrenchments; men even grappled their antagonists across the piles of logs and pulled them over, to be stabbed or carried to the rear as prisoners. . . . Never before, since the discovery of gunpowder, had such a mass of lead been hurled into a space so narrow. . . . On either side, a long ghastly procession of the wounded went limping or crawling to the rear. On either side, fast rose the mounds of the dead, intermingled with those who

Hand to hand at the Bloody Angle

were too severely hurt to extricate themselves from their hideous environment."

Some of these helpless wounded were pressed so heavily by the dead that they themselves died of suffocation. And there were points where the gathering corpses impeded the fighting and had to be flung to the rear.

This day, of course, was another of grueling activity at the various tent hospitals behind the lines on both sides. But, in a few cases at least, the overworked staffs managed to maintain a high degree of efficiency.

Hobbling from the front with a bullet wound in his thigh, Union Captain Henry Blake turned in at the hospital serving Gershom Mott's division of Hancock's corps, and he found himself very favorably impressed with the way things were run:

"The arrangements for the treatment of the disabled were most excellent. A board of experienced surgeons held a consultation upon every case in which amputation took place; and all that medical skill and attention could effect was readily performed. The Government supplies were abundant; nourishment of every description was bestowed; and faithful [male] nurses often brought the cold water, which was Nature's restoring liniment, and saturated the bandages. . . . The sufferers of every rank, and both armies, received the same kind treatment, and reposed upon beds of pine boughs in the capacious hospital tents.

"More than three-fourths of the number were untroubled by pain; and one man who had lost a leg remarked, 'I should think that my foot was on, for I have a queer feeling in the ankle.' Another replied to this as he raised the stump that had once been the right arm, 'I have the same feeling in my wrist which you have in your ankle.'

"The rebels frankly admitted that their wounds were better dressed than they would have been if they had not been taken prisoners; and many amicable conversations ensued between those who had been rendered helpless while engaged in the deadly combat. . . . Those who belonged to Steuart's brigade evinced a deep hatred towards him on account of his tyrannical conduct, and hoped he would be treated in the harshest manner by the Union troops. . . .

"The correspondents of the newspapers eagerly questioned the [wounded] staff officers to ascertain the details of the battle. . . .

"A large number of skulkers [from Union regiments] concealed themselves in the forests, or bivouacked near the hospitals, and feigned wounds by binding up their heads and arms in bloodstained bandages, or limped, with the assistance of a crutch, in apparent pain; and details of the provost guard frequently patrolled the ground to seize these base wretches and escort them to the front.

"The army thieves who lurked in the rear . . . grasped with their remorseless hands the valuables, clothing, and rations of the unwary wounded soldiers, [also] the flattened bullets that had been retained as priceless relics by those from whom they were extracted, and the invaluable swords which officers had borne with honor through scenes of carnage. In the tent to which, with twenty others, I was assigned, a member of the regiment was robbed of everything, including an old knife and a diary, while he was unconscious on account of a ball which entered his head; and another person was plundered in a similar style before he had recovered from the effect of the ether which had been administered when his arm was amputated."

At the front, the brutal contest continued, with Grant failing to make a new break in Lee's line, and with Lee failing to drive Grant away. By this time the Confederate commander had determined to withdraw his troops to the set of defenses he had ordered constructed across the base of the salient and tied in with his eastern and western wings. Eliminating the salient would tighten and strengthen his position. (There were those Confederates who claimed that the creation of the salient had been a mistake in the first place.) The new defense line, however, was not yet ready. A host of men were working back there, sweating in the rain: pioneers with axes, picks, and shovels; and teams from combat units employing such makeshifts as bayonets, sharpened sticks, flattened canteens, and metal cups. But the work was not advancing at a pace adequate to the emergency. With his front under heavy pressure and his retirement line unfinished, Lee was having an anxious time of it.

As the hellish day wore on, its din resounded for miles under the low-hanging clouds. On the Union side, Grant spent much of his time riding back and forth through the dripping woods and muddy fields some distance behind his lines. On one occasion, according to Horace Porter, "the general came to a humble-looking farmhouse, which was within range of the enemy's guns and surrounded by wounded men, sullen-looking prisoners and terror-stricken stragglers. The fences were broken, the ground was furrowed by shells; and the place presented a scene which depicted war in its most repulsive aspect. An old lady and her daughter were standing on the porch.

"When the mother was told that the officer passing was the general-

Grant in the field

in-chief, she ran toward him, and, with tears running down her cheeks, threw up her arms and cried, 'Thank God! Thank God! I again behold the glorious flag of the Union that I have not laid eyes on for three long, terrible years. Thank the Lord that I have at last seen the commander of the Union armies! I am proud to say that my husband and my son went from here to serve in those armies, but I have been cut off from all communication, and can get no tidings of them. Oh, you don't know, sir, what a loyal woman suffers in this land. But the coming of the Union troops makes me feel that deliverance is at last at hand, and that the gates have been opened for my escape from this hell.'

"The general was so touched by this impassioned speech . . . that he dismounted and went into the yard, and sat for a little time on the porch, to learn the details of her story, and to see what he could do to comfort and succor her. She gave an account of her persecutions and sufferings which would have moved the sternest heart. The general, finding that she was without food, ordered a supply of rations to be issued to her and her daughter, and promised to have inquiries set on foot to ascertain the whereabouts of her husband and son. She was profuse in her expressions of gratitude for these acts of kindness."

It was perhaps around this same time there occurred another behind-the-lines incident involving a Union officer and a Southern woman. The officer was a voracious reader (he sometimes even read while he was under fire), and he was always looking for people with whom to discuss his favorite books. "For the last week," Horace Porter recounts, "he had been devouring Victor Hugo's 'Les Misérables.' It was an English translation, for the officer had no knowledge of French. As he was passing a house in rear of the Angle, he saw a young lady seated on the porch, and, stopping his horse, bowed to her . . . and endeavored to engage her in conversation. Before he had gone far he took occasion to remark, 'By the way, have you seen 'Lees Miserables?'', anglicizing the pronunciation. Her black eyes snapped with indignation as she tartly replied, 'Don't talk to me that way. They're a good deal better than Grant's miserables anyhow!' "

Returning to the front lines and to Union enlisted man G. Norton Galloway: "The great difficulty was in the narrow limits of the Angle, around which we were fighting, which precluded the possibility of getting more than a limited number into action at once. At one time our ranks were crowded in some parts four deep by reinforcements. . . . Our losses were frightful. What remained of many different regiments that had come to our support had concentrated at this point and had planted their tattered colors upon a slight rise of ground. . . .

"To keep up the supply of ammunition, pack mules were brought into use, each animal carrying three thousand rounds. The boxes were dropped close behind the troops. . . . [I] fired four hundred rounds . . . and many others as many or more. In this manner, a continuous and rapid fire was maintained. . . .

"Finding that we were not to be driven back, the Confederates began to use more discretion, exposing themselves but little, using the loopholes in their works to fire through, and at times placing the muzzles of their rifles on the top logs, seizing the trigger and small of the stock, and elevating the breech with one hand sufficiently to reach us.

"During the day a section of [Andrew] Cowan's battery took position behind us, sending shell after shell close over our heads, to explode inside the Confederate works. In like manner, Coehorn mortars eight hundred yards in our rear sent their shells with admirable precision gracefully curving over us.

"Sometimes the enemy's fire would slacken, and the moments would become so monotonous [or, more likely, filled with uncertainty over Confederate intentions] that something had to be done to stir them up. Then some resolute fellow would seize a fence rail or piece of abatis, and, creeping close to the breastworks, thrust it over among the enemy, and then drop to the ground to avoid the volley that was sure to follow.

"A daring lieutenant in one of our left companies leaped upon the breastworks, took a rifle that was handed to him, and discharged it among the foe. In like manner he discharged another, and was in the act of firing a third shot when his cap flew up in the air and his body pitched headlong among the enemy.

"On several occasions, squads of disheartened Confederates raised pieces of shelter-tents above the works as a flag of truce. Upon our slacking fire and calling to them to come in, they would immediately jump the breastworks and surrender. One party of twenty or thirty thus signified their willingness to submit; but, owing to the fact that their comrades occasionally took advantage of the cessation [of our fire] to get a volley into us, it was some time before we concluded to give them a chance.

"With leveled pieces, we called to them to come in. Springing upon the breastworks in a body, they stood for an instant panic-stricken at the terrible array before them. That momentary delay was the signal for their destruction. While we . . . shouted to them to jump, their troops,

Union Coehorn mortars

massed in the rear [presumably believing that the silhouettes were those of Union men], poured a volley into them, killing or wounding all but a few, who dropped [on our side of the works] . . . and crawled in under our pieces, while we instantly began firing."

It wasn't only Confederates who sought to end their ordeal by surrendering. As explained by J. F. J. Caldwell, the lieutenant from South Carolina: "Some of the enemy lay against our works in front. I saw several of them jump over and surrender during relaxations of firing. . . .

"This was the place to test individual courage. Some ordinarily good [Confederate] soldiers did next to nothing, others excelled themselves. The question became, pretty plainly, whether one was willing to *meet* death, not merely to run the chances of it.

"Two men, particularly, attracted my attention. The first of these, I believe, belonged to the Fourteenth Regiment. He was a tall, well-formed man, apparently just arrived at maturity. He was a private. He would load his piece with the greatest care, rise to his full height— which exposed at least half of his person—and, after a long, steady aim, deliver his fire. Then he would kneel and reload. Sometimes he would aim, but take down his piece and watch again for his mark, then aim again and fire. The balls flew round him like hail. . . .

"I saw him fire at least a hundred times. . . . Finally, late in the evening, I saw him rise and single out his man, in the grass in front, and draw down upon him. Then, appearing not to be satisfied, he recovered his piece, remaining erect and watching. After perhaps half a minute, he raised his rifle and aimed. Just as his finger touched the trigger, I heard the crash of a ball, and . . . saw a stream of blood gush from his left breast. He fell and died without a struggle.

"Another soldier, of probably not more than eighteen years, interested me. . . . Although scarcely so deliberate as the other, he fired with great perseverance and coolness. . . . He was a handsome boy, tall and slender, with eyes as tender as a woman's, and a smooth, fair cheek, just darkening with the first downy beard. Seeming to be weary, about sunset, he sat down in the cross-trench to rest. He was hardly down when a ball glanced from a tree and struck him just behind the right ear. He struggled up and shook with a brief convulsion. Someone caught him in his arms. He raised his eyes with the sweetest, saddest smile I think I ever saw on earth, and died almost on the instant. It was a strange wound. I could see nothing but a small red blister where the ball struck him. . . .

"We were told that if we would hold the place till dark we should be relieved. Dark came, but no relief. The water became a deeper crimson. The corpses grew more numerous. Every tree about us, for thirty feet from the ground, was barked by balls. Just before sunset, a tree of six or eight inches in diameter, just behind the works, was cut down by the bullets of the enemy. We noticed, at the same time, a large oak hacked and torn in a manner never before seen. Some predicted its fall during the night, but the most of us considered that out of the question. But, about ten o'clock, it did fall forward upon the works, wounding some men and startling a great many more. . . . It was twenty-two inches in diameter! This was entirely the work of rifle balls.

"Midnight came. Still no relief; no cessation of firing. Numbers of the troops sank, overpowered, into the muddy trenches and slept soundly. The rain continued.

"Just before daylight [actually, about 3:30 A.M.] we were ordered, in a whisper which was passed along the line, to retire slowly and noise-lessly from the works. We did so. . . . The enemy . . . did not attempt to pursue us. Day dawned as the evacuation was completed. A second line of works, or rather a third, had been thrown up some 500 yards in our rear, and in this, as we passed over, we found troops of Longstreet's corps, ready for the enemy."

According to General Grant's visitor from Washington, Assistant Secretary of War Charles Dana, who had been keeping an eye on events for President Lincoln: "The first news which passed through the ranks the morning after the battle of Spotsylvania was that Lee had aban-doned his position during the night. Though our army was greatly fatigued from the enormous efforts of the day before, the news of Lee's departure inspired the men with fresh energy, and everybody was eager to be in pursuit. Our skirmishers [engaged in a reconnaissance ordered by Grant] soon found the enemy along the whole line, how-ever, and the conclusion was that their retrograde movement had been made to correct their position after the loss of the key points taken from them the day before, and that they were still with us in a new line as strong as the old one. Of course, we could not determine this point [for certain] without a battle, and nothing was done that day to provoke one. It was necessary to rest the men."

The fighting of May 12–13 had lasted for twenty hours, and it had cost Grant nearly 7,000 in killed, wounded, captured, and missing. Lee probably lost some 4,500 in killed and wounded, and at least 3,000 more in captured and missing. It might be said that the fight achieved nothing. Yet, as in the Wilderness, the advantage went to Grant. He had deprived Lee of another mass of troops that would be hard to replace, whereas Union reserves were in ready supply.

The Battle of the Angle was never to lose its reputation for uniqueness. Years later, Confederate General John Gordon made this assessment: "Looking back to it . . . with the calmer thought and clearer perceptions that come in more advanced age, I am still more deeply impressed with the conviction that . . . this battle . . . has no parallel in the annals of war. Considered merely in their sanguinary character . . . many of the battles of our Civil War surpassed it. . . . But to Spotsylvania history will accord the palm, I am sure, for having furnished an unexampled muzzle-to-muzzle fire; the longest roll of incessant, unbroken musketry; the most splendid exhibition of individual heroism and personal daring by large numbers, who, standing in the freshly spilt blood of their fellows, faced for so long a period, and at so short a range, the flaming rifles as they heralded the decrees of death.

"This heroism was confined to neither side. It was exhibited by both armies. . . . It would be a commonplace truism to say that such examples will not be lost to the Republic."

19

Stalemate on the North Anna

For several days after the Battle of the Angle, as the dismal weather continued, the two armies held their positions—except for a series of tactical shiftings—without another general contest. "We have a kind of rest," says Union Color Sergeant D. G. Crotty. "Only some hard skirmishing going on, which in ordinary campaigns would be called hard fighting." This period saw the burial of many of the dead on both sides, but most of those at the very front were neglected because of the danger involved in their removal.

"During the night of the 13th," relates a Union colonel from New Hampshire, "as officer of the day, I was ordered to take a detail of men from our brigade, and, if possible, find the dead bodies of members of the Ninth Regiment. We went over the intrenchments and into that terrible darkness, under orders 'to strike not a match, nor speak above a whisper.' When near the spot where they fell, we crawled upon our hands and knees, and felt for the dead ones, and in this manner succeeded in finding upwards of twenty, and conveyed them within our lines, where, with a few others, they were buried the next morning in one trench."

The regions of the Angle were presently unoccupied. Hancock and Wright had withdrawn to Grant's original lines, while Lee's salient troops held to their base defenses. Three or four days after the fight, however, Lee sent a reconnaissance to the north side of the salient's rim. The move incurred no violence, but, according to Georgia Private G. W. Nichols, no participant ever forgot it:

"We marched over the ground on which they [the Yankees] had

charged and re-charged . . . so many times on the 12th. In places, the dead Union soldiers . . . were as thick as corn hills. I saw an officer's horse lying on five men, and two or three men were lying against the horse. Here in this death angle there were several acres of ground the worst strewn with dead men I saw during the war. I saw an oak tree, probably eighteen or twenty inches in diameter, that was very nearly cut down with canister shot and minnie balls, and the ground around it was covered with dead men, it being on the lowest ground the enemy had to advance over, and where our batteries and small arms had a full sweep on them. Those who were not very badly mutilated were swollen as long as they could swell. Their faces were nearly black, and their mouths, nose, eyes, hair, and the mutilated parts were full of maggots! This is a horrible picture, but . . . it is not overdrawn. What an awful scent!"

By May 17 the weather had finally cleared. On the 18th Grant sent Hancock and Wright on another attack straight down from the north, their orders to cross Lee's old works and try to carry his base position. Confederate General John Gordon tells what happened:

"In superb style, and evidently with high hopes, the Union army moved to the assault. The Confederates . . . were ready for them; and as Hancock's and Wright's brave men climbed over the old abandoned works and debouched from the intervening bushes, a consuming fire of grape, canister, and Minié balls was poured in incessant volleys upon them. Such a fire was too much for any troops. They first halted before it and staggered. Then they rallied, moved forward, halted again, wavered, bent into irregular zigzag lines, and at last broke in confusion and precipitate retreat. Again and again they renewed the charge, but each assault ended, as the first, in repulse and heavy slaughter."

This was a day of massive discouragement for General Grant. It wasn't only that his attack failed, and that his total casualties for the Wilderness and Spotsylvania were now upwards of 33,000. Word came that things were going badly in other theaters of the war as well. Only Sherman in Georgia was making progress. South of Richmond, Butler had fallen back before Beauregard. In Virginia's Shenandoah Valley, too, the Federals were in retreat. There was also news of a Union defeat in Louisiana. Grant's master plan for ending the war by applying pressure in all theaters at the same time was faltering.

But the general remained fully aware of the primary importance of his personal campaign against Lee, and continued to give it his dogged attention. He intended, of course, to keep moving toward Richmond, and he now enlisted the aid of the U.S. Navy in transferring his base of supplies from Fredericksburg to Port Royal, farther down the Rappahannock. And there were tentative plans for a longer jump, to White House on the Pamunkey, another waterway with Chesapeake connections. By this time, it might be noted, civilian volunteers from the North, both men and women, were beginning to staff Grant's rear-area hospitals.

On May 19 General Lee sent Ewell on a reconnaissance-in-force around Grant's western flank, and this brought on another substantial fight. Then the deadly guns of Spotsylvania fell relatively quiet. In the predawn hours of the 21st, Grant started his fatigued and mud-spattered troops on another move by the left to the southeast, with Lee quickly putting his own battered units on a march that would keep them between Grant and Richmond. The armies headed toward Hanover Junction, below the southeasterly flowing North Anna River, about twenty-five miles from Spotsylvania, with Lee on the shorter route. Grant put Hancock's corps in the lead, while Ewell led for Lee.

In the words of Union soldier Warren Goss: "A cavalry division . . . preceded the marching column and cleared the way. . . . The country over which Hancock's corps now marched was unlike any on which the Union army had previously set foot in Virginia. This region had hitherto escaped the devastating hand of war. . . . It was like a garden blooming in the midst of desert places. The rich bottom-lands . . . were green with grass and sprouting wheat. Herds of cattle grazed in fenced pastures. Sleek, blooded horses shook their manes and galloped over the fields at the unwonted sight of marching men with burnished arms. . . . The perfume of blossoms, the growing corn, the fragrant clover, and the hum of bees gratefully saluted the senses of men long unused to sounds of peace and scenes of comfort. Along the roads . . . broad, spreading, ancestral elms gave grateful shade to the halting columns."

As added by Frank Wilkeson, the Union artillery private: "Many Negro slaves were working in the fields. Some of the slaves did not quit their work to look at us. I saw none drop their tools and hail us with vociferous shouts as liberators and eagerly join us, as I had been led to believe they would. [This, as will be seen, was the calm before the storm.]

"Many of the farm-houses we passed were mansions built of brick, and around which piazzas ran. On these, women and children and old, white-haired men stood in silent groups and looked intently at us. I saw no young men, no white men fit for war, around any of these farm-houses. There were many barns and sheds and groups of Negro quarters.

"We, the ever-hungry, predatory enlisted men quickly discovered that we were marching through a corn and tobacco and stock-raising country, and we raided tobacco barns in a quiet manner, and killed some sheep and many chickens; and much food was stolen from the farm-houses. I paid a pale-faced woman, whose little children clung to her skirts as she stood in her kitchen door appealing to the Union soldiers not to strip her of stores as she had children to feed, two dollars in greenbacks for a piece of sweet bacon, which I had found in a barn where an aged Negro stood solemnly assuring the predatory soldiers that there was not a bite of food on the place. . . .

"Before noon we came to the village of Bowling Green, where many pretty girls stood at cottage windows or doors, and even as close to the despised Yankees as the garden gates, and looked scornfully at us as we marched through the pretty town to kill their fathers and brothers.

"There was one very attractive girl, black-eyed and curly-haired and clad in a scanty calico gown, who stood by a well in a house-yard. She looked so neat, so fresh, so ladylike and pretty, that I ran through the open gate and asked her if I might fill my canteen with water from the well. And she, the haughty Virginia maiden, refused to notice me. She calmly looked *through* me and *over* me, and never by the slightest sign acknowledged my presence. But I filled my canteen and drank her health. I liked her spirit.

"It was a weary march, but a march during which there was no straggling. We could look back from hill tops and see the long steel-tipped column stretching for miles behind us."

The ribbon of men, according to the previous narrator, Warren Goss, "halted late in the afternoon of the 21st at the Mattapony River near Milford Station . . . [and soon] crossed the river and intrenched."

It was probably around this same time that, riding with a Confederate artillery column a few miles to the west, Robert Stiles experienced a moment of special pleasure. "I was sent ahead, upon a road which led through a tract of country which had not been desolated by the encampments or the battles of armies, to select a night's resting place for the battalion. Forests were standing untouched, farm lands were protected by fences, crops were green and untrampled, birds were singing, flowers blooming—Eden everywhere. Even my horse seemed to feel the change from the crowded roads, the deadly lines, the dust, the dirt, the mud, the blood, the horror.

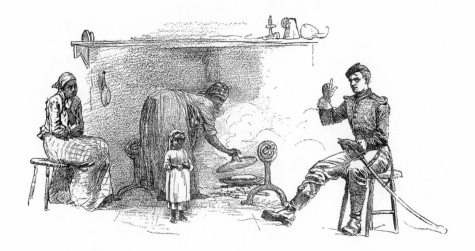

Waiting for breakfast. A Yankee invasion of a Virginia home

Union artillerists fording the Mattapony

"We were passing through a quiet wood at a brisk walk, when suddenly he roused himself and quickened his gait, breaking of his own accord into a long trot, his beautiful, sensitive ears playing back and forth in the unmistakable way which, in a fine horse, indicates that he catches sounds interesting and agreeable to him. It was, perhaps, several hundred yards before we swung around out of the forest into the open land where stood a comfortable farm house, and there, in a sweet and sunny corner, were several chubby little children chatting and singing at their play. Mickey, dear old Mickey, trotted right up to the little people, with low whinnies of recognition and delight, and rubbed his head against them. They did not seem at all afraid, but pulled nice tufts of grass for him, which he ate with evident relish and gratitude."

On both sides the encampments that night represented a rapturous change from the scenes of recent days. Union General Hancock's troops were permitted to remain in their bivouac for an extra twenty-four hours. This was ordered by Grant, both for the purpose of resting the men after their hard fighting at Spotsylvania and to allow for the army's rearward corps to come up.

"Our unpretentious little dog-tents," says Union soldier Warren Goss, "were pitched in a field near the beautiful wood-skirted stream [the Mattapony]. The people at one of the home-like estates claimed to be Union people, and requested a safety guard over their house. I was sergeant of the guard during [the] day around this place, and had a very comfortable time while so engaged.

"While seated near the house, endeavoring to make a sketch of the picturesque homestead, with its background of foliage and Negro shanties, I was interrupted by a shadow falling across my small sketching-board, and, upon turning, was not unpleasantly confronted by a tall, black-eyed miss who had been glancing over my shoulder. 'That's our place!' she exclaimed, evidently in surprise; and then, in apology for the rudeness, said, 'You were so engaged you did not hear me speak, and I looked over your shoulder to see what you were doing. Where did you learn to draw?'

"I told her, when she replied, 'I was at boarding-school near there two years before the war.' I found her more intelligent than most of the Southern girls I had thus far met, and from her inquiries I got the impression that she had a tender attachment for a young gentleman in the North. Her questions were quite searching regarding people whom, as it chanced, I knew by reputation.

"I finished the roughly executed sketch and presented it to her with

Northern soldier and Virginia woman

such compliments as a susceptible young man of twenty-three years might make to a young lady. . . .

"Her father was an elderly, white-haired man with courtly manners and a lurking bitterness of expression towards those who were using his fences for campfires, and his chickens for rations. It was of little use for a small guard to attempt to preserve a large estate from the locust-like swarm of soldiers, all blessed with appetites so disproportioned to their supplies."

Numbers of the plantations along the Union's line of march now began losing more than their fences and food reserves. Their Negroes took to deserting them and to seeking Federal protection. According to Boston newsman Charles Carleton Coffin, the processions included "old men with venerable beards, horny hands crippled with hard work and harder usage; aged women, toothless, almost blind, steadying their steps with sticks; little Negro boys driving a team of skeleton steers— mere bones and tendons covered with hide—or wall-eyed horses, spavined, foundered, and lame, attached to rickety carts and wagons piled with beds, tables, chairs, pots and kettles, hens, turkeys, ducks; women with infants in their arms and a sable cloud of children trotting by their side.

" 'Where are you going?' I said to a short, thick-set, gray-bearded old man shuffling along the road, his toes bulging from his old boots, and a tattered straw hat on his head, his gray [hair] protruding from the crown. 'I do'no, boss, where I's going, but I reckon I'll go where the army goes.' 'And leave your old home, your old master, and the place where you have lived all your days?' 'Yes, boss. Master, he's gone. He went to Richmond. Reckon he went mighty sudden, boss, when he heard you was coming. Thought I'd like to go along with you.'

"His face streamed with perspiration. He had been sorely afflicted with rheumatism, and it was with difficulty that he kept up with the column; but it was not a hard matter to read the emotions of his heart. He was marching towards freedom. . . . He had broken loose from all which he had been accustomed to call his own—his cabin, a mud-chinked structure with the ground for a floor; his garden patch—to go out, in his old age, wholly unprovided for, yet trusting in God that there would be food and raiment on the other side of Jordan. . . .

"It was the Sabbath-day [May 22]—bright, clear, calm, and delightful. There was a crowd of several hundred colored people at a deserted farm house. 'Will it disturb you if we have a little singing? You see, we feel so happy today that we would like to praise the Lord.' It was the

Runaway slaves entering Union lines

request of a middle-aged woman. 'Not in the least. I should like to hear you.'

"In a few moments a crowd had assembled in one of the rooms. A stout young man, black, bright-eyed, thick-[haired], took the center of the room. The women and girls, dressed in their best clothes, which they had put on to make their exodus from bondage in the best possible manner, stood in circles round him. The young man began to dance. He jumped up, clapped his hands, slapped his thighs, whirled round, stamped upon the floor. 'Sisters, let us bless the Lord. Sisters, join in the chorus,' he said, and led off with a kind of recitative, improvised as the excitement gave him utterance. . . . 'We are going to the other side of Jordan. . . . So glad! So glad! Bless the Lord for freedom. So glad! So glad! We are going on our way. So glad! So glad! To the other side of Jordan. So glad! So glad!'

". . . And so it went on for a half-hour, without cessation, all dancing, clapping their hands, tossing their heads. It was the ecstasy of action. . . . The old house . . . rang with their jubilant shouts and shook in all its joints. I stood an interested spectator. One woman, well-dressed, intelligent, refined in her deportment, modest in her manner, said, 'It is one way in which we worship, sir. It is our first day of freedom.'

". . . Apart from the dancers was a woman with light hair, hazel eyes, and fair complexion. She sat upon the broad steps of the piazza and looked out upon the fields, or, rather, into the air, unmindful of the crowd, the dance, or the shouting. Her features were so nearly of the Anglo-Saxon type that it required a second look to assure one that there was African blood in her veins. She alone of all the crowd was sad in spirit. She evidently had no heart to join in the general jubilee.

" 'Where did you come from?' I asked. 'From Caroline County.' Almost everyone else would have said, 'From old Caroline.' There was no trace of the Negro dialect. . . . 'You do not join in the song and dance,' I said. 'No, sir.' Most of them would have said 'master' or 'boss.' 'I should think you should want to dance on your first night of freedom, if ever.' 'I don't dance, sir, in that way.' 'Was your master kind to you?' 'Yes, sir; but he sold my husband and children down South.' The secret of her sadness was out. 'Where are you going? Or where do you expect to go?' 'I don't know, sir, and I don't care where I go.'

". . . It was late at night before the dancers ceased, and then they stopped, not because of a surfeit of joy, but because the time had come for silence in the camp."

The defection of the blacks was naturally a matter of angry concern to the plantation owners. Their ire was not directed at the blacks themselves, but at the Yankees, who they believed were luring the slaves with false promises. As Richmond diarist Judith McGuire put it: "Abolition preachers [with the Union army] were constantly collecting immense crowds, preaching to them the cruelty of the servitude which had been so long imposed upon them, and that Abraham Lincoln was the Moses sent by God to deliver them from the 'land of Egypt and the house of bondage,' and to lead them to the Promised Land. . . . Poor, deluded creatures! I am grieved not so much on account of the loss of their services, though that is excessively inconvenient and annoying, but for their grievous disappointment. Those who have trades, or who are brought up as lady's maids or house servants, may do well, but woe to the masses who have gone with the blissful hope of idleness and free supplies!"

To return to military affairs: While Hancock was bivouacking and the other Union corps were moving up, Lee's army occupied Hanover Junction, about fifteen miles south of Hancock's position. This was the strategic spot below the North Anna River that both Grant and Lee had been eyeing. Says Jed Hotchkiss, the Confederate topographical engineer: "By this timely and well-executed movement, Lee had again . . . anticipated Grant's progressive, but indirect, 'on to Richmond' [march], and placed himself directly across the roads the latter desired to follow to the Confederate capital."

By this time Lee had received about 8,000 reinforcements, some from Richmond and some from the Shenandoah Valley, both of which regions, thanks to the recent Confederate victories they had seen, were free of immediate Union threat. On the morning of May 23, while his troops were digging in along a five-mile stretch of the river bank, and while Grant was making his approach, Lee wrote his wife: "The army is now south of the North Anna. We have the advantage of being nearer our supplies and less liable to have our communications, trains, etc., cut by [Grant's] cavalry, and he is getting farther from his base. Still, I begrudge every step he takes toward Richmond."

On the same morning that Lee wrote this message, the general's bright young aide, Walter Taylor, recorded in his notebook: "No doubt the entire North is this day rejoicing over our retreat to this point; yet the battlefield [of Spotsylvania] was left in our possession, and we marched here without any molestation whatever. This does not look like a retreat. . . . Grant . . . will feel us again before he reaches his prize [i.e., Richmond]. His losses have been already fearfully large. Our list

Confederate entrenchments on the North Anna River

of casualties is a sad one to contemplate, but does not compare with his terrible record of killed and wounded. He . . . seems entirely reckless as regards the lives of his men. This, and his remarkable pertinacity, constitute his sole claim to superiority over his predecessors. He certainly holds on longer than any of them."

Upon his arrival at the North Anna, Grant brought on hostilities by testing Lee's flanks. The Confederate commander soon decided to rearrange his lines, and the result was a defensive masterpiece. (See "North Anna" map.) Keeping his center on the river at Ox Ford, Lee drew back his extremities. His right wing angled toward the southeast and his left wing toward the southwest. As Grant moved to make a corresponding deployment, he was obliged to divide his army and cross the river at two places, which put his eastern wing out of contact with his western. This was a serious disadvantage. Some localized fighting flared, but the Union commander hesitated to make a general attack.

Lee saw the situation as a great opportunity to take the offensive himself, but Fate did not permit this. The general came down with diarrhea, even as he had during a crucial moment at Gettysburg, and this time he was almost completely disabled. And there seemed to be no one who could lead in his place. Longstreet was wounded and out of action, Ewell and Hill were themselves sickly and mentally overtaxed, and Anderson (Longstreet's successor) was not sufficiently aggressive for so great a task.

Sorely missed by Lee at this time was the support, both military and moral, of Jeb Stuart, who was not only his cavalry chief but also a family friend. Lee had been hit hard by Stuart's death, telling an aide, "I can scarcely think of him without weeping."

Profoundly frustrated by his incapacitation, Lee called from his cot, "We must strike them a blow! We must strike them a blow! We must never let them pass us again!" Very soon, the general knew, Grant would be so grave a threat to Richmond that the Confederate army would be compelled to retire to the line of works east of the city, after which its options would be strictly limited. (Lee would put the fear into words a few days later, telling General Jubal Early, "We must destroy this army of Grant's before he gets to James River. If he gets there it will become a siege, and then it will be a mere question of time.")

Lee's illness was the cause of deep concern among his men. Jubal Early said later that "it was then rendered more manifest than ever that he was the head and front, the very life and soul of the army."

One of Lee's soldiers was his own young son, Robert. "I saw my

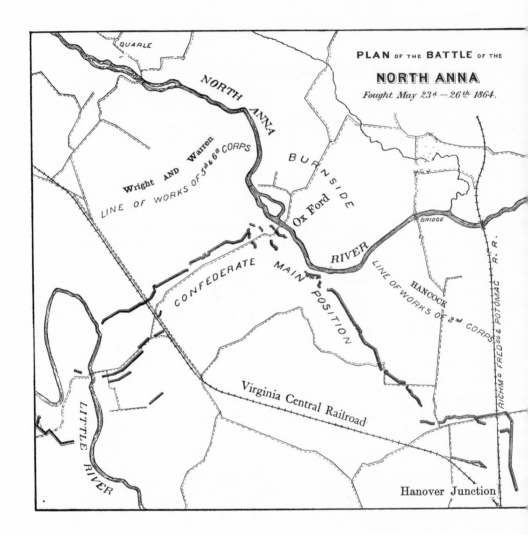

QUARLE

PLAN OF THE BATTLE OF THE

NORTH ANNA

Fought May 23ᵈ — 26ᵗʰ 1864.

NORTH ANNA

BURNSIDE

Wright AND Warren
LINE OF WORKS OF 5ᵗʰ & 6ᵗʰ CORPS

Ox Ford

RIVER

BRIDGE

CONFEDERATE MAIN POSITION

HANCOCK

LINE OF WORKS OF 2ⁿᵈ CORPS

RICHMᵈ FREDᵍᵍ & POTOMAC R. R.

Virginia Central Railroad

LITTLE RIVER

Hanover Junction

father only once or twice, to speak to him, during the [progression of the campaign], but, in common with all his soldiers, I felt that he was ever near, that he could be entirely trusted with the care of us, that he would not fail us, that it would all end well. The feeling of trust that we had in him was simply sublime. When I say 'we,' I mean the men of my age and standing, officers and privates alike. Older heads may have begun to see the 'beginning of the end' when they saw that slaughter and defeat did not deter our enemy but made him the more determined in his 'hammering' process; but it never occurred to me, and to thousands and thousands like me, that there was any occasion for uneasiness. We firmly believed that 'Marse Robert,' as his soldiers lovingly called him, would bring us out of this trouble all right. . . .

"When we learned that General Lee was ill—confined for a day or two to his tent . . . this terrible thought forced itself upon us: suppose disease should disable him, even for a time, or, worse, should take him forever from the front of his men! It could not be! It was too awful to consider! And we banished any such possibility from our minds."

The unproductive confrontation at the North Anna is described as it was experienced by Frank Wilkeson, the Union artillery private: "We saw that Lee's soldiers were skilfully intrenched and that the Army of the Potomac could not dislodge them. The fact was instantly comprehended by the enlisted men. . . . We . . . impatiently waited for our generals to discover that the position could not be forced. . . .

"One day some men of the Fortieth New York Infantry came to my battery to gamble. I took a hand in a game of seven-up for a dollar-a-corner and five-on-the-rubber. We spread a blanket on the ground behind the earthworks and squatted around it. My partner, a Fortieth New York soldier, was a heavy-jawed, light-haired, blue-eyed lad of nineteen, an Albany boy, who played well, and fought well too. He was a wit, and, when in the humor, would make a whole regiment of sick men laugh.

"We were a few dollars winners, and he was graphically and humorously describing [a] brigade of regulars running against a swamp in the Wilderness; and the mythical conversation between the gray-haired commander and the second lieutenant just out of West Point—as the old soldier asked if there was anything in the new books about getting a brigade across a swamp—was delicious.

"As we laughed, the handsome lad fell face down into the blanket and began to vomit blood. We grabbed him, turned him over, tore up his shirt, and saw where a ball had entered his side, cutting a gash instead of a hole. The wounded soldier did not speak. The blood rushed out of his mouth; his eyes glazed, his jaw dropped—he was dead. A chance ball had struck the tire of one of the wheels of the No. 1 gun and glanced forward and killed this delightful comrade. His death ended the game. We put his body alongside a couple of other dead men and buried the three that night.

"The picket-firing and sharpshooting at North Anna was exceedingly severe and murderous. We were greatly annoyed by it; and, as a campaign cannot be decided by killing a few hundred enlisted men—killing them most unfairly and when they were of necessity exposed—it did seem as though the sharpshooting pests should have been suppressed. Our sharpshooters were as bad as the Confederates, and neither of them were of any account as far as decisive results were obtained. They could sneak around trees or lurk behind stumps, or cower in wells or in cellars, and from the safety of their lairs murder a few men. Put the sharpshooters in battle-line, and they were no better, no more effective, than the infantry of the line, and they were not half as decent.

"There was an unwritten code of honor among the infantry that forbade the shooting of men while attending to the imperative calls of nature, and these sharpshooting brutes were constantly violating that rule. I hated sharpshooters, both Confederate and Union . . . and I was always glad to see them killed. . . .

"[At] North Anna I discovered that our infantry were tired of charging earthworks. . . . Here I first heard savage protests against a continuance of the generalship which consisted in launching good troops against intrenched works which the generals had not inspected. Battle-tried privates came into [our] battery and sneeringly inquired if the corps and army commanders had been to see [the] line. Of course, we replied 'No.' 'Well,' said one sergeant of the Pennsylvania Reserves, 'I have fought in this army for three years, and in no other campaign have I seen so many general officers shirk as they have in this one. . . . If Grant or Meade, or Hancock, or Warren, or Wright, or Burnside would inspect those works at close range, they would see the folly of staying here, where we are losing two hundred or three hundred men every day by sharpshooters. We ought to get out of here and try it farther down.'

"He but expressed what we all thought. At North Anna the rank and file of the Potomac army, the men who did the fighting, and who had been under fire for three weeks, began to grow discouraged.

"We lay for three days in the trenches at North Anna. Three days of woe and sorrow and hardship. Three days . . . which had cost us hundreds of men and line officers. How we longed to get away from North Anna, where we had not the slightest chance of success, and how we feared that Grant would keep sending us to the slaughter!

"Joyfully we received the order to march on the night of May 26th. Eagerly the tired troops fell into line behind their foul intrenchments. With pleasure we recrossed the North Anna and [making a rightward swing] resumed the flank movement to the south.

"That night . . . we . . . had a good night's sleep, undisturbed by picket firing. We [of the artillery] awoke the next morning to find the rest of the army gone, and we started after them—being, for the first and last time during the campaign, in the rear. Before us, in the distance, rose the swells of Cold Harbor, and we marched steadily and joyfully to our doom."

20

First Clash at Cold Harbor

Grant was pursuing a southeasterly course through the country north of the Pamunkey River. He planned to cross to the south bank at Hanovertown, some twenty miles from his North Anna works, and then turn southwest toward Richmond. Grant's Confederate counterpart, though still unwell, was alert to the situation. Says Southern officer Jed Hotchkiss: "As soon as apprised of Grant's withdrawal from the North Anna, on the 27th of May Lee ordered the Second Corps, now temporarily under Early [because Ewell was ailing] to march southward . . . and take position covering the roads to Richmond from the Hanovertown crossing of the Pamunkey, which he was confident Grant would now seek." Early was soon followed by the rest of Lee's infantry. Units of cavalry operating out in front of the army began a series of clashes with Phil Sheridan, who was a distance ahead of Grant.

The Union army began crossing the Pamunkey around noon on May 28. Thanks to some vigorous work by Sheridan throughout the day, the infantry movement was uncontested. The Federals were now pouring onto the Virginia "Peninsula," the scene of Union General George McClellan's amphibious campaign against Richmond, conducted from the Chesapeake in 1862. Many of the present troops had served with McClellan. One of these, the chaplain from Pennsylvania, A. M. Stewart, found time during the afternoon to write a letter home, the first he'd written since the days of Spotsylvania.

"As to how we came here from Spotsylvania Court House, a volume would scarcely suffice to tell. What skirmishings and fightings—what long, long, weary marches by day and night—what countermarches,

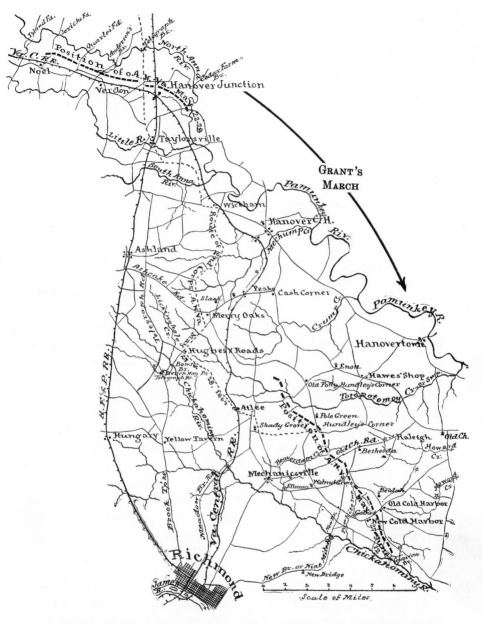

Country traversed by Lee in his march from the North Anna, with his Totopoto-moy–Cold Harbor line shown at lower right. Drawn by Ewell's topographical engineer, Jed Hotchkiss

now far to the right, again away to the left—passing over hot, dusty roads, corduroy bridges and pontoons; through mud, creeks, fields, woods, swamps, and sloughs; amid moonlight and thick darkness, showers, thunderstorms, and sunshine.

"Much of this may never, *can* never be written; and, were it, could not be understood by those not exercised therein. No matter; we are here on the south bank of the Pamunkey River, which we lately crossed on a pontoon bridge. Yes, here again on the *Peninsula,* although from another point than formerly approached. Again on *this Peninsula,* where, two years ago, we endured so much, suffered so terribly, and from whence we retreated so ingloriously. The future will tell whether this latter coming will prove more successful than the first."

Grant himself, in company with his staff, crossed the Pamunkey as a part of the main movement. Among the civilian newsmen who arrived on the south bank with the headquarters group that afternoon was Charles Carleton Coffin, who relates: "We . . . rode a mile or two across the verdant intervale [i.e., the low-lying grassland], and halted beneath the oaks, magnolias, and buttonwoods of an old Virginia mansion. . . . When McClellan was on the Peninsula, the shadow of the war-cloud swept past the place. Some of the Negroes ran away, but . . . the campaign of 1862 left the estate unharmed.

"Sheridan's cavalry, followed by the Sixth Corps, in its march from the North Anna, had suddenly and unexpectedly disturbed the security of the old plantation. There [had been] a rattling of fire from carbines, a fierce fight, men wounded and dead, broken fences, trodden fields of wheat and clover; ransacked stables, corn bins, meat houses; and a swift disappearing of livestock of every description.

"But to go back a little. . . . When the war began, the owner of this magnificent estate enlisted in the army and was made a colonel of cavalry. . . . He fell in an engagement on the Rappahannock in October, 1863, leaving a wife and three young children.

"The advance of [Grant's] army . . . left the widow no time to remove her personal estate, or to send her Negroes to Richmond for safe-keeping. Fitzhugh Lee [and Wade Hampton] disputed Sheridan's advance. The fighting began on this estate. Charges by squadrons and regiments were made through the cornfields. Horses, cattle, hogs, sheep were seized by the cavalrymen. The garden, filled with young vegetables, was spoiled. In an hour there was complete desolation. . . .

"Passing by one of the Negro cabins on the estate, I saw a middle-aged colored woman packing a bundle. 'Are you going to move?' I

Federals laying a corduroy road

asked. 'Yes, I am going to follow the army. . . . I want to go to Washington to find my husband. He ran away a while ago, and is at work in that city.'

". . . Returning to the mansion to see the wounded [gathered there during the cavalry fight], I met the owner of the place in the hall. She evidently did not fully realize the great change which had taken place in her affairs, and the change was not complete at that moment. The colored steward was there, hat in hand; obsequious, bowing politely, and obeying all commands. A half-hour before, I had seen him . . . making arrangements to leave the premises. . . .

" 'I wish I had gone to Richmond,' said the lady. 'This is terrible, terrible! They have taken all my provisions, all my horses and cattle. My servants are going. What shall I do?' She sank upon the sofa, and for a moment gave way to her feelings. 'You are better off here than you would be there, with the city full of wounded, and scant supplies in the market,' I remarked. 'You are right, sir. What could I do with my three little children there? Yet how I am to live here I don't know. When will this terrible war come to an end?'

". . . There were hundreds of Southern homes where the change had been equally great. Secession was not what they who started it thought it would be."

On May 29 Grant sent three columns fanning westward in search of Lee, who was found blocking the way to Richmond, his left on Totopotomoy Creek and his right stretching to the southeast. The two armies now began maneuvering for advantage and involving themselves in some sharp but indecisive fighting.

Lee's troops, according to Private John Casler, did some of their work on empty stomachs. "Our rations of corn bread and bacon would be cooked in the rear and brought up to the front, three days' rations at a time; but as we were moving about so much and changing positions all the time we often missed our grub. We were allowed one pint of corn meal (not sifted) and one-fourth of a pound of bacon for one day's ration. . . . The corn bread would get so hard and moldy that when we broke it it looked like it had cobwebs in it. Numbers of the citizens came into our lines who had been robbed of everything they had, and their houses burned besides, and we often divided our scanty rations with them to keep them from starving."

On the Union side civilian newsman Charles Page made the following comments in a report he filed on May 31: "This is the twenty-ninth day of the campaign. Every day has seen more or less marching, more or less fighting. 30,000 wounded have been sent back on honorable furlough. 5,000 dead have been buried in honorable though obscure graves. . . . The roads are strewn with the carcasses of 6,000 horses. Actual marching has worn out 50,000 pairs of shoes. Two-thirds of the men . . . have not changed a garment since they started. . . .

"The rank and file have a pretty good appreciation of the strategy of the campaign. They understand that it has been a series of splendid flank movements; and 'flanking' has become the current joke with which to account for everything from a night march to the capture of a sheep or a pig. A poor fellow, terribly wounded yesterday, said he saw the shell coming but hadn't time to 'flank it.' And he enjoyed his joke with a smile and a chuckle. . . . The shell had 'flanked' him by taking off an arm."

On the Confederate side during this period, a Sergeant J. Graham took up paper and pencil and composed this message for his sweetheart at home: "My Sainted Love,—If the Yankee cusses will let me alone, I will write you. U. S. Grant is a 'bull-dog,' and Meade a match for the devil. No matter how deep we get into the woods, the Yanks are sure to find us. They fight more fiercely than I have ever seen them before. They build strong works, and then our brave officers order us to charge them. We have done so, and get hell every time. My dear, you will excuse this language, for if you were here you would say hell, too. Do not blame me, my sainted love, but I really wish I was out of this army and joined to you in the holy bond of matrimony. I must close; the Yankees are coming."

Since this letter was found on the field by a Union soldier, there is a strong likelihood that J. Graham never returned to his sainted love.

The narrative is taken up by Southerner William Oates, commander of the Fifteenth Alabama: "Other parts of the army were more or less engaged now every day, but the Fifteenth was not until the 31st of May. On that day I was left with the Fifteenth in what seemed a deserted entrenchment, with instructions to remain and hold it until the enemy disappeared from that locality. I was told that they were then drawing off. . . . A piece of artillery was also left with me. A line of rifle pits in my front were occupied by Union sharpshooters, who kept firing at us, annoying us, wounding one or two men, and seemed to have no disposition to withdraw. No Confederate troops were in sight. All had gone. I fired a few shots at them with the Napoleon gun, but could not dislodge them that way. I became impatient at the delay and annoyance, and ordered Lieut. Pat O'Conner, in command of Company K,

A break in a Union march

to deploy his company and charge, kill, capture, or disperse them.

"He made a dash and succeeded in dispersing them very easily; but Pat—poor, brave fellow—received a mortal wound. His men brought him in and told me . . . that he asked for water. I caused a canteenful from a cold spring nearby to be given him. He drank it, gave me his hand, and bade me farewell. He gave me his new swordbelt and requested me to send his sword to his mother, who lived in Columbus, Georgia, and to tell her that he never disgraced it, but died a brave soldier in the discharge of his duty. . . . Within a minute more the brave and faithful Irishman was dead. I had a grave dug immediately, wrapped him in his blanket, and buried him. I got a shingle, had his initials, company, and regiment lettered on it, stuck it down at the grave, and soon thereafter left the poor brave Pat in the lonely bivouac of the dead.

"About this time a very considerable force of the enemy—at least a brigade—appeared in my front and began to advance on me. Company K, from the rifle pits, and my piece of artillery, opened fire on them, which brought them to a halt. They deployed quite a number of skirmishers preparatory to an assault. I felt that in my isolated position the probabilities of being attacked by at least four times my own force placed me in a dilemma. I could do nothing but make the best possible defense according to my orders.

"Just at this point I heard a noise in my rear. I looked and beheld Gen. John B. Gordon, with his Georgia brigade [i.e., the unit, now a part of his division, that he had commanded before his promotion], coming up in line of battle in splendid style. Gordon was the gamest-looking man in battle I ever saw, and he never looked more so than on this occasion. He saw a prospect of a lively little affair. He ordered his men over the works and forward. He stopped a moment to speak with me and then dashed onward, but before he got within range the enemy were in full retreat."

Gordon took some prisoners, and among them was John Urban, the Pennsylvanian who had been captured in the Wilderness and rescued by Phil Sheridan during his Richmond raid. Actually, this was Urban's third time as a prisoner. He had been taken in 1862 during the Peninsula Campaign, gaining his freedom, after two and a half months, through a prisoner exchange. Urban says of his present predicament:

"The rebels had captured between three and four hundred prisoners, and, as they marched us to the rear, we were cursed and abused to such an extent that some of the prisoners commenced to entertain the thought that we would all be murdered after they got us back into the wood. They certainly were the most enraged set of rebels I had ever met with. . . . I suppose the fact that they had been compelled to fall back day after day had something to do with their ill nature. . . . After being taken to the rear, we were marched into a field close to the road, and given in charge of other guards, who were more friendly. . . .

"During the night a long train of ambulances loaded with wounded passed us, going in the direction of Richmond. . . . We could hear groans from the inmates in almost every wagon. . . .

"In the morning we were taken to Richmond, and, as we marched through the principal part of the city . . . we had a good opportunity of seeing the famous, or, I might say, infamous Capital of the Southern Confederacy. I could not help noticing the difference in regard to the feelings of the people and appearance of the city compared to what it was two years before, when I was marched through its streets as a prisoner of war. Then the people were demonstrative and loud in their boasts of what they would do, and how soon the Northern invaders would be driven from Southern soil. The city then had an animated and lively appearance, but now everything looked gloomy and despondent, and the boastful spirit of the people appeared to be broken.

"The papers still kept up the cry that Grant was accomplishing nothing and getting his men all butchered; but the people evidently realized the fact that, somehow or other, the enemy was getting nearer and nearer to their Capital, and that the prospects of Southern independence were not very bright. While the papers kept up the cry of 'Grant the Butcher,' they no doubt wished the butcher a good deal farther off.

"In the afternoon we were lodged in the notorious Libby Prison."

By this time Grant and Lee were thinning their fronts by extending their lines southeastward toward Cold Harbor, a drowsing crossroads about five miles from the Totopotomoy and less than ten miles from Richmond. Essential reinforcements were being provided to both armies, and all of these were from the Butler-Beauregard theater south of Richmond, where little was happening, since Beauregard had the inept Union commander pinned in his lines at Bermuda Hundred, his back to the James. The reserves from Beauregard—Robert Hoke's division of 7,000 men—began assembling at Cold Harbor while those from Butler—the 16,000 men of W. F. "Baldy" Smith's Eighteenth Corps— were still en route. These were coming by naval transport to White House on the Pamunkey, fifteen miles in Grant's rear, and from there by foot.

Cold Harbor was the next point that offered Grant an opportunity to swing around Lee's right, and the place also beckoned to Lee, for it was a possible gateway for a move around Grant's left to strike at his line of supply and reinforcement, and also to block his way to the James. Fitz Lee's cavalrymen, supported by one of Hoke's brigades, took Cold Harbor first, but Phil Sheridan quickly drove them out. Upon the approach of Hoke's other brigades from the south, Sheridan prepared to retreat, but word came from Grant that he must hold until the Union infantry arrived. Though apprehensive, Sheridan dismounted his troopers and had them dig in.

Along with the earliest Confederate infantry to reach the scene from the north (it was now the morning of June 1) was the artillery battalion in which Robert Stiles was serving as adjutant. The unit was brought to halt by some of Sheridan's marksmen who were shooting from the windows of a small house at the edge of a woods. The battalion commander said to Stiles, "Let's see how quickly you can drive those sharpshooters out of that house!"

Stiles relates: "Scarce sooner said than done. I sprang from my horse. [Lieutenant Morgan] Callaway's guns were in battery on the instant—I, by his permission, taking charge of his first piece as gunner. . . . A moment—and the gun was loaded, aimed, and fired; a moment more and the house burst into flame. The shells from the other three guns were exploded among the retiring skirmishers, who ran back toward the woods; while from the side of the house nearest to us two women came out, one very stout and walking with difficulty, the other bearing a baby in her arms and two little children following her. . . .

"I broke for these women, three or four of the men running with me. There was a fence between us . . . which I cleared 'hair and hough,' while the rest stopped to climb it. I took the baby and dragged the youngest child along with me, telling the other [child] to come on, and sent the younger woman back to help the elder. . . .

"By the time we reached the battery, more of the guns were in action, shelling the woods, and I became interested in the firing. . . . As they ran by me with ammunition, [the men of No. 5 gun] would stop a moment to pat the baby, who was quite satisfied and seemed to enjoy the racket, cooing and trying to pull my short hair and beard.

"This thing had been going on for several minutes . . . until one of the men ran up and, pulling me sharply around, pointed to the two women, who were standing . . . as far as possible out of the line of the bullets, which were still annoying us. There was a rousing laugh and cheer as I started back to deliver the little infant artilleryman to his mother.

"It turned out that the elder of the two women was the mother of the other, and had been bedridden for several years. We were exceedingly sorry to have burned their little house, but some of the boys suggested that if the cure of the mother proved permanent, the balance, after all, might be considered rather in our favor."

Narrator Stiles was in a good spot that morning, he says, to witness Phil Sheridan's "breaking of Col. Lawrence M. Keitt's big South Carolina regiment [of Kershaw's division, Anderson's corps]. . . . General Kershaw had put this and another of his brigades into action not far from where we had burned the house to dislodge the skirmishers. Keitt's men gave ground, and, in attempting to rally them, their colonel fell mortally wounded. Thereupon the regiment went to pieces in abject rout and threatened to overwhelm the rest of the brigade.

"I have never seen any body of troops in such a condition of utter demoralization. They actually groveled upon the ground and attempted to burrow under each other in holes and depressions. [It is said that one man, as a comrade struggled to get beneath him, growled, "Stop it. I'm too high already!"]

"Major [J. M.] Goggin, the stalwart adjutant-general of the division, was attempting to rally them, and I did what I could to help him. It was of no avail. We actually spurred our horses upon them, and seemed to hear their very bones crack; but it did no good. If compelled to wriggle out of one hole, they wriggled into another."

The Confederates soon suspended their offensive and began entrenching, for it was learned that advance units of Union General Wright's Sixth Corps had reached the field from the north. One of the bluecoats marching with the rearward elements of Wright's long column was Surgeon George Stevens, back with his regiment after his detached duty with the wounded in Fredericksburg.

"The march was a hard one. The day was sultry, and the dust, ankle-deep, raised in clouds by the column, was almost suffocating. It filled the air and hung upon the leaves of the trees like snow. . . . As we neared Cold Harbor . . . we fell in with the column of General Smith's command [from Richmond]. . . . They reached us tired and almost discouraged by their unusual march . . . their trains and baggage being left behind. . . .

"We had [also] fallen in with ambulances returning with wounded cavalrymen, and learned from them that Sheridan had engaged the rebel cavalry at Cold Harbor . . . and that he was now fighting both infantry and cavalry. Toward that point the troops pushed on rapidly, reaching the cavalry line at about four o'clock. [All of Wright's troops, and those of Baldy Smith, were now on the field, Smith's on the right and Wright's on the left.]

". . . Skirmishers, as usual, had advanced and prepared the way for the lines of infantry and the artillery. The shots of the skirmishers had become more and more frequent, till the sharp rattle of musketry told of the actual presence of the enemy. The artillery of the Sixth Corps was at once run out, and a brisk fire opened upon the rebels, who replied with their guns. . . . The commands of Wright and Smith were at once formed in line of battle. . . .

"In front of our line was an open space two-thirds of a mile in width, beyond which was a strip of pine woods. In these woods the enemy had intrenched. . . . The rebels [Anderson's corps from the north and Hoke's division from Beauregard's James River forces] occupied a strong position between our advance and Richmond. The order for the charge was given, and [our] two commands, weary and exhausted—the veterans of the Sixth Corps from many days and nights of most severe labor, and both corps by the tedious march of the day—dashed impetuously [forward] . . . with shouts and cheers, making for the rebel works. . . .

"Volleys rang out upon the evening air, crashing louder and still louder. The First and Third divisions of the Sixth Corp, in heavy columns . . . cleared the abatis and seized the rebel works, while the Second division, on the left, discovering a strong force of the enemy planting a battery on our flank, engaged them and forced them back. Smith's command . . . by a desperate charge [was also largely successful]. . . .

"The whole line thundered with the incessant volleys of musketry, and the shot and shell of the artillery shrieked and howled like spirits of evil. The sun was sinking red in the west, and the clouds of dust and smoke almost obscured the terrible scene. Hundreds of our brave fellows were falling on every side, and stretcher-bearers were actively engaged in removing the wounded from the field.

"The First division, after a stubborn resistance . . . was forced to give up the line of works it had captured. . . . Only the Third division held its ground. The others [Smith's command included] . . . in spite of most determined efforts . . . were forced to swing back. . . .

"The gallantry shown by our Third division in taking and holding

The first day at Cold Harbor

the enemy's works was acknowledged with true soldierly generosity by the other divisions of our corps. . . .

"As darkness came on, the conflict still raged, and sheets of flame rolled from one end of the line to the other. . . . As the sound of battle died away at nine o'clock, the advantages gained by us were still held, and our men set to work to strengthen the works they had captured from the enemy, and to throw up new ones. . . .

"The movement at Cold Harbor . . . had secured our communications with White House Landing, which now became, after two years, for the second time the base of supplies for the Army of the Potomac."

The sounds of the day's fighting had carried to Richmond. Most of the citizens, although naturally concerned, retained their faith in Lee's ability to keep Grant at bay. "The Northern mind," says the literary Sallie Putnam, "was buoyed up with the report of the certainty of the capture of the 'rebel capital' within the usual time—'ten days.' But it was altogether too fast. The circumstance of the close proximity to the city, the view of the spires of the churches and domes of prominent edifices in Richmond, did not mean that the army of the enemy were quite in occupation, as was proven by the defeat of General McClellan, who was so near that he might almost, with good glasses, have looked in upon our breakfast tables. And the 'retreat of Lee,' as usually understood by the Federals, was simply to counteract and check every movement attempted by General Grant from the time of his advance at the battle of the Wilderness up to the time that he . . . succeeded in establishing himself at Cold Harbor."

21

The Deadly Climax

The narrative is taken up by Union staff officer Horace Porter: "General Grant had maneuvered skilfully with a view to compelling Lee to stretch out his line and make it as thin and weak as possible. . . . A serious problem now presented itself to General Grant's mind—whether to attempt to crush Lee's army on the north side of the James, with the prospect, in case of success, of driving him into Richmond, capturing the city perhaps without a siege, and putting the Confederate government to flight; or to move the Union army south of the James without giving battle, and transfer the field of operations to the vicinity of Petersburg [south of Richmond, where measures could be taken to sever the capital city's railroad communications with essential parts of the Confederacy].

"It was a nice question of judgment. After discussing the matter thoroughly with his principal officers and weighing all the chances, he decided to attack Lee's army in its present position. . . . The general considered the question not only from a military standpoint, but he took a still broader view of the situation. The expenses of the war had reached nearly four million dollars a day. Many of the people in the North were becoming discouraged at the prolongation of the contest. If the army were transferred south of the James without fighting a battle on the north side, people would be impatient at the prospect of an apparently indefinite continuation of operations; and, as the sickly season of summer was approaching, the deaths from disease among the troops . . . would be greater than any possible loss encountered in the contemplated attack. . . . Besides, there were constant rumors that if the war continued much longer European powers would recognize the Confederacy, and perhaps give it material assistance. . . . There was at present too much at stake to admit of further loss of time in ending the war, if it could be avoided."

June 2 was a day of preparation on both sides. Lee notified the war department in Richmond: "This morning, the enemy's movement to our right continuing, corresponding changes were made in our lines." Significant among Lee's alterations was the transfer of two of A. P. Hill's divisions from the Totopotomoy to the army's extreme right. Grant had ordered Hancock's corps down to his extreme left. This extended the battle arena southward to the marshy lowlands of the Chickahominy River. (See "Cold Harbor" map for final dispositions.)

The day teemed with skirmishing, sharpshooting, and artillery exchanges, but there was also a great deal of digging and woodcutting. Says Confederate officer Jed Hotchkiss: "Lee's veterans had, by this time, all become skillful military engineers." They threw up "lines of defense abounding in salients whence heavy guns could send forth searching crossfires, at short range, against every portion of an attacking enemy. The infantry were well provided with loopholes and crevices between logs, from which to fire, also at short range, with deliberate aim. Hunger but made them fiercer combatants."

Southern artillery officer Robert Stiles, whose unit was attached to Kershaw's infantry division, tells of his personal part in the preparations: "With the aid of the division pioneer corps, I opened roads through the woods for the more rapid and convenient transmission of artillery ammunition, and put up two or three little bridges across ravines with the same view.

"While I was superintending this work, the fire at the time being lively, I heard someone calling in a most lugubrious voice, 'Mister, Mister, won't you please come here?' I glanced in the direction of the cry and saw a man standing behind a large tree in a very peculiar attitude, having the muzzle of his musket under his left [armpit] and leaning heavily upon it. Supposing he was wounded, I went to him. . . . He pointed to the butt of his gun, under which a . . . copperhead snake was writhing; and the wretched skulker actually had the face to whine to me, 'Won't you please, sir, kill that snake?' I knew not what to say to the creature, and fear what I did say was neither a very Christian nor a very soldierly response; but no one who has not seen a thoroughly demoralized man [this one, it seems, had fled the front and taken shelter behind a tree, only to encounter a new horror] can form

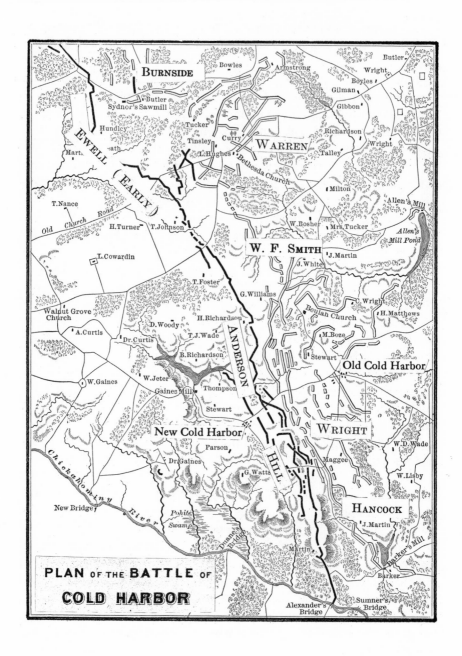

PLAN OF THE BATTLE OF

COLD HARBOR

the slightest conception of how repulsive a thing such a wretch is."

Stiles apparently left without relieving the "wretch" of his predicament. The artilleryman continues: "The headquarters of General Kershaw . . . was close up to the lines and just back of the position of some of our guns. . . . He might have found a safer place, but none nearer the point of peril and the working point of everything. The position, however, was so exposed that he found himself compelled to protect it [with earth and logs]. . . . Thus he had a place where he and his officers could safely confer, and a very short distance from their commands; but it was, after all, a ghastly place, and very difficult and dangerous of approach. All the roads or paths leading to it were not only swept by an almost continuous and heavy fire of musketry, but I had to keep a force of axe-men almost constantly at work cutting away trees felled across the ammunition roads by the artillery fire of the enemy. Col. Charles S. Venable, reputed to be one of the roughest and most daring riders on General Lee's staff . . . told me he believed this headquarters position of Kershaw's at Cold Harbor was the worst place he was ever sent to."

The day was uncomfortably warm, and the troops on both sides welcomed the rain that came in the afternoon. It not only cooled the terrain but also helped to settle the dust that hazed the roadways.

Twilight found the opposing lines still being changed in minor ways. Union artilleryman Frank Wilkeson's battery was a part of one of Hancock's movements. "There was considerable confusion as the infantry marched in the darkness. In our front we could see tongues of flame dart forth from Confederate rifles as their pickets fired in the direction of the noise they heard, and their bullets sang high above our heads.

"My battery went into position just back of a crest of a hill. Behind us was an alder swamp. . . . Before we slept we talked with some of the Seventh New York Heavy Artillery, and found that they were sad of heart. They knew that they were to go into the fight [as infantry] early in the morning, and they dreaded the work. The whole army seemed to be greatly depressed the night before the battle of Cold Harbor."

This fight would become known as Second Cold Harbor, since a good part of these woods, fields, and swamps had been fought over during McClellan's campaign. Some of the combatants were even utilizing sections of the original earthworks, now green with sod. Principally, the battle would involve the Union corps of Hancock, Wright, and newcomer Smith in opposition to Anderson, reinforced with the troops from Richmond, and Hill, reinforced by those from the Shenandoah

An incident of the skirmishing on June 2

Valley. As usual, Grant was far stronger numerically, while Lee had the considerable advantage of his cover.

Union narrator Frank Wilkeson continues: "Before daybreak of June 3d the light artillerymen were aroused. We ate our scanty breakfast and took our positions around the guns. All of us were loath to go into action. In front of us we could hear the murmurs of [our] infantry, but it was not sufficiently light to see them. We stood leaning against the cool guns, or resting easily on the ponderous wheels, and gazed intently into the darkness in the direction of the Confederate earthworks. How slowly dawn came!

"Indistinctly we saw moving [Union] figures. Some on foot, rearward bound—cowards hunting for safety; others on horseback riding to and fro near where we supposed the battle lines to be [forming]; then orderlies and servants came in from out [of] the darkness leading horses, and we knew that the regimental and brigade commanders were going into action on foot.

"The darkness faded slowly; one by one the stars went out; and the Confederate pickets opened fire briskly. Then we could see the Confederate earthworks, about six hundred yards ahead of us. . . . They were apparently deserted . . . but it was still faint gray light. . . . We filled our sponge buckets with water and waited, the Confederate pickets firing briskly at us the while, but doing no damage.

"Suddenly the Confederate works were manned. We could see a line of slouch hats above the parapet. Smoke in great puffs burst forth from their line, and shell began to howl by us. Their gunners were getting the range. We sprung in and out from the three-inch guns [in preparation to firing] and replied angrily. To our left, to our right, other batteries opened. . . .

"It was daylight. We, the light artillerymen, were heated with battle. The strain on our nerves was over. In our front were two lines of blue-coated infantry, one well in advance of the other, and both lying down. We were firing over them. The Confederate pickets sprang out of their [advanced] rifle pits and ran back to their main line of works. Then they turned and warmed the battery with long-range rifle practice, knocking a man over here, killing another there, breaking the leg of a horse yonder, and generally behaving in an exasperating manner. . . .

"The air began to grow hazy with powder smoke. . . . Out of the powder smoke came an officer [in blue] from the battle lines of infantry. He told us to stop firing, as the soldiers were about to charge. He

Outbreak of the fighting on June 3. Federals in foreground

disappeared to carry the message to other batteries. Our cannon became silent. The smoke drifted off of the field. I noticed that the sun was not yet up. Suddenly the foremost line of our troops, which were lying on the ground in front of us, sprang to their feet and dashed at the Confederate earthworks at a run."

This same thing was happening at many spots along a front extending for nearly three miles. Confederate officer D. Augustus Dickert (back with his regiment in Kershaw's division, Anderson's corps, after recuperating from his light Wilderness wound) assumes the narrative: "When near us, the first line came with a rush at charge bayonets, and our officers had great difficulty in restraining the men from opening fire too soon. But when close enough, the word 'fire' was given, and the men behind the works raised [themselves] deliberately, resting their guns upon the works, and fired volley after volley into the rushing but disorganized ranks of the enemy.

"The first line reeled and attempted to fly the field, but were met by the next column, which halted the retreating troops with the bayonet, butts of guns, and officers' sword, until the greater number were turned to the second assault. All this while our sharpshooters and men behind our works were pouring a galling fire into the tangled mass of advancing and retreating troops. The double column, like the first, came with a shout, a huzzah, and a charge. But our men had by this time reloaded their pieces, and were only too eagerly awaiting the command 'fire.' . . . When it [came] the result was telling—men falling on top of men, rear rank pushing forward the first rank, only to be swept away like chaff."

Confederate Colonel P. D. Bowles, commanding the Fourth Alabama, Anderson's corps, interjects: "Our artillery was not idle, but firing double-shotted canister, and at the distance of one hundred yards was cutting wide swaths through their lines at every fire, literally mowing them down by the dozen, while heads, arms, legs, and muskets were seen flying high in air."

Returning to Southern officer D. Augustus Dickert: "Smoke settling on the ground soon rendered objects in front scarcely visible, but the steady flashing of the enemy's guns and the hail of bullets over our heads and against our works told plainly enough that the enemy were standing to their work with desperate courage, or were held in hand with a powerful grasp of discipline. The third line of assault had now mingled with the first two, and all lying stretched upon the ground."

Not all of the men on the ground were firing. In some zones they were simply trying to stay alive and were waiting an opportunity to fall back. As explained by Union Private W. P. Derby, a member of the First Brigade, Second Division, Eighteenth Corps: "It was impossible for the brigade to retrace its steps without doubling the loss already sustained. . . . So fierce and unsparing was the musketry that the slightest movement was at the risk of life. The living clutched the ground, not knowing that many around them were dead. Some worked the soil from beneath them and settled their bodies into the ground, and not a few so arranged the bodies of the dead that the living could crouch their heads behind them for cover and defense. The surface of the field seemed instinct with life from the incessant plowing of shot and shell. The air was alive with all-mysterious sounds, and death in every one of them. . . . Above the din of battle came the wail of the wounded."

It was only a few minutes since the assault had begun. The Federals achieved a single temporary breakthrough, and the troops involved were those of Hancock's zone that had made their start in front of the artillery battery to which Frank Wilkeson belonged. Wilkeson says that as the attackers made their approach the enemy's cannon "belched forth a torrent of canister; the works glowed brightly with musketry; a storm of lead and iron struck the blue line, cutting gaps in it. Still they pushed on and on and on. But how many of them fell!

"They drew near the earthworks, firing as they went; and then, with a cheer, the first line of the Red Division of the Second Corps—Barlow's—swept over it. And there in our front lay, sat, and stood the second line, the supports. Why did they not go forward and make good the victory? They did not.

"Intensely excited, I watched the portion of the Confederate line which our men had captured. I was faintly conscious of terrific firing to our right and of heavy and continuous cheering on that portion of our line which was held by the Fifth and Sixth Corps. For once the several corps had delivered a simultaneous assault, and I knew that it was to be now or never.

"The powder smoke curled lowly in thin clouds above the captured works. Then the firing became more and more thunderous. The tops of many [Confederate] battle flags could be seen indistinctly, and then there was a heavy and fierce yell, and the thrilling battle cry of the Confederate infantry floated to us. 'Can our men withstand the charge?' I asked myself.

"Quickly I was answered. They came into sight clambering [back] over the parapet of the captured works. All organization was lost. They fled wildly for the protection of their second line and the Union guns, and they were shot by scores as they ran. The Confederate infantry appeared behind their works and nimbly climbed over, as though intent on following up their success, and their fire was as the fury of hell.

"We manned the guns and drove them to cover by bursting shell. How they yelled! How they swung their hats! And how quickly their pickets ran forward to their [previously abandoned] rifle pits and sank out of sight! The swift, brave assault had been bravely met and most bloodily repulsed."

In the zone to the north these moments found Confederate brigade commander E. M. Law leaving his headquarters in the rear for a visit to the front. "On my way I met a man . . . running to the rear through the storm of bullets that swept the hill. He had left his hat behind in his retreat, was crying like a big baby, and was the bloodiest man I ever saw. 'Oh, General,' he blubbered out, 'I am dead! I am killed! Look at this!' showing his wound. He was a broad, fat-faced fellow, and a minie ball had passed through his cheek and the fleshy part of his neck, letting a large amount of blood. Finding it was only a flesh wound, I told him to go on; he was not hurt. He looked at me doubtfully for a second as if questioning my veracity or my surgical knowledge, I don't know which; then, as if satisfied with my diagnosis, he broke into a broad laugh, and, the tears still running down his cheeks, trotted off, the happiest man I saw that day.

"On reaching the trenches, I found the men in fine spirits, laughing and talking as they fired. There, too, I could see more plainly the terrible havoc made in the ranks of the assaulting column. I had seen the dreadful carnage in front of Marye's Hill at Fredericksburg, and on the old railroad-cut which Jackson's men held at the Second Manassas; but I had seen nothing to exceed this. It was not war; it was murder."

While Law was at the front he was nicked by the fire of a still-surviving Yankee. The wound gave the general a dubious distinction: he was the highest-ranking Confederate to be hit that morning.

Turning to Southern officer James H. Franklin (another member of the Fourth Alabama): "Line after line came out of the opposite woods, only to melt away under our continuous fire, until with the last line, which went the way of all the others, came a tall color-bearer, a sergeant, who bore his charge high in the air, as with steady tread he confidently advanced, looking only to the front and oblivious to his isolation. Amazed at his persistence, our men withheld their fire and called to him to go back. But he did not hear, or if perchance he did, he did not take his orders from our side. However that may be, he gave no sign, and all alone, with not a comrade in sight, he came unfalteringly on. Not even desiring to capture so brave a fellow, our men in gray mounted the works, and waving their hats to attract his attention, fairly shrieked, in their intense admiration and excitement, 'Go back! Go back! We don't want to kill you! Go back!'

"Then this man of iron halted, looked carefully to his right hand as he surveyed the field, and then as carefully to his left—not a man of his regiment in sight! It would have been no disgrace to have dropped [to the ground] or hurried back as fast as he could. Admirable courage! He did neither, nor was there a show of any anxiety. He took his flagstaff from its socket, rolled up his color with provoking deliberateness in our faces—the dipping of it we thought an unconscious tribute to our forbearance—and when done, touched his cap to us in grateful appreciation. A right-shoulder shift, an about-face, and he then began his march back to his own lines with a step as steady as had been his advance. . . . Tremulous with excitement, we threw up our hats and yelled in admiration until his retiring figure was lost in the deep recesses of the faraway lines."

Within half an hour after it began, the massive Union effort had been wholly shattered. Grant had lost about 7,000 men, as compared with less than 1,500 by Lee. Later, under cooler circumstances, Grant would entertain deep regrets at having made this attack, but right now he could not accept its failure, sending orders to the corps commanders that it be renewed.

There was little response. Neither the commanders nor the troops had any heart to continue an effort they knew to be useless.

This disastrous day brought Grant's casualties for the campaign as a whole to about 60,000 in killed, wounded, captured, and missing. He had lost nearly as many men as Lee had in his army. Lee's casualties for the period are uncertain, but they probably came to about 25,000.

2 2

Toward a New Campaign

In neither the North nor the South was there anything like a consensus of opinion regarding the significance of Grant's efforts to date. There were Northerners who felt that the campaign was succeeding because the army had drawn ever closer to Richmond, but there were many others who faulted Grant for his losses and his inability to crush Lee. As for the Administration, it was subjected to a good deal more censure than praise. A few days after Cold Harbor, Lincoln was nominated by the Republican Party to run for a second term, but the President couldn't help but wonder at his chances for reelection. The Democrats, declaring the war a failure, were preparing to oppose him with a "peace candidate," as yet unnamed but expected to be General McClellan, replaced by Lincoln after performing so haltingly in 1862.

In the South some people saw Grant's persistence as dooming, but substantial numbers believed that the war was still winnable. Lee's performance in the campaign, climaxed by the shattering Cold Harbor repulse, had bolstered their hope. In the words of Richmond's Sallie Putnam: "The barefooted, ragged, ill-fed rebel army, which had been under fire for more than a month, had achieved a succession of victories unparalleled in the history of modern warfare. . . . We had witnessed the failure of the seventh expedition sent out for the capture of Richmond."

The truth about the series of battles was that matters had ended strongly in Grant's favor, his repulses and his losses notwithstanding. Lee's fine army had been battered to the point where it was no longer capable of offensive operations. Of course, this does not mean that its defensive skills were failing. Far from it.

Confederate staff officer John Esten Cooke takes up: "General Lee remained facing his adversary in his lines at Cold Harbor . . . confident of his ability to repulse any new attack, and completely barring the way to Richmond. [Lee was secure enough to be able to dispatch Jubal Early and 8,000 men toward the Shenandoah Valley, where a new Union threat was rising.] The Federal campaign, it was now seen, was at an end on that line, and it was obvious that General Grant must adopt some other plan, in spite of his determination expressed in the beginning of the campaign to 'fight it out on that line if it took all summer.' The summer was but begun, and further fighting on that line was hopeless."

Switching to the Union side and to Private Theodore Gerrish: "We now found ourselves, at a sickly season of the year, in the deadly swamps of the Chickahominy, where to remain with an army for any length of time was an impossibility. The sun glared down upon us like a globe of fire. . . . The air was filled with malaria and death. The water was very poor and unhealthy. Sickness, as well as battle, was doing fearful work in our ranks. We were now in the position from which General McClellan had been driven two years before.

"It was a fortunate thing for the destiny of this nation, in this dreary period, that we had at the head of our army a man who knew nothing of the word defeat—one who was equal to the emergency. Undoubtedly General Grant was disappointed that the fruits of the campaign had not been more decisive, but he well understood that General Lee had lost heavily in the campaign, and that it would be a difficult task for him to replenish his decimated ranks, and so he conceived the idea of throwing his army across the James River, if possible capture Petersburg, cut the lines of railway connecting Richmond with the South, and thus compel the surrender of the rebel capital."

Grant was still thinking in terms of ending the war quickly, and the maneuver he now began—one of the greatest in military history—offered another such opportunity. (His fifty-mile march from Cold Harbor to Petersburg is shown on the map in Chapter 6 labeled "Routes of Lee & Grant.")

Returning to Theodore Gerrish: "To deceive the enemy, our line of breastworks was strengthened as if we were to remain in them. . . . The various corps were to [withdraw rearward and] move in different directions, so that Lee would not know where the blow was to fall. Sheridan, with his gallant cavalry, was raiding upon the enemy's country and cutting Lee's communications. . . . Our corps [Warren's Fifth], preceded by the cavalry of General Wilson, forced a passage across the Chickahominy at Long Bridge, and marched in the direction of Richmond. This was to conceal from General Lee the movements of the remainder of the army. The rebel commander . . . stood in [Richmond's] defense."

According to Southerner Robert Stiles: "Thus far during the campaign, whenever the enemy was missing, we knew where—that is, in what direction and upon what line to look for him; he was certainly making for a point between us and Richmond. Not so now. Even Marse Robert, who knew everything knowable, did not appear to know what his old enemy proposed to do, or where he would be most likely to find him."

Union Surgeon George Stevens tells of Grant's march as it was made by Wright's Sixth Corps, which crossed the Chickahominy on the evening of June 13: "Two years before, we had crossed the same stream not far from this very spot. . . . The corps bivouacked on high grounds a mile from the river, glad to rest from the toiling march. We were astir early on the morning of the 14th, taking our line of march through a delightful section of country. . . . As we began to descend from the high lands toward the plain, on which stands the little cluster of houses called . . . Charles City, we beheld, in the distance, the James River . . . spreading widely between its banks.

"A magnificent prospect opened before us. The river . . . [was] bordered by green fields, . . . large fields of grain . . . [and] long rows of corn. . . . Fine groves . . . gave a charming diversity to the scene, and the old mansions, embosomed in vines and trees and surrounded by colonies of outhouses, reminded us of the ease and comfort which had reigned here before the ravages of war had desolated Virginia. . . .

"In the vicinity of Charles City we halted a little while before noon. The Second Corps, which was in the advance, had already reached the James at Wilcox's Landing, and was preparing to cross. The men of our corps were delighted with the opportunity of once more spreading their tents over clean grassy turf, and each quickly pitched his shelter tent preparatory to a refreshing rest.

"Within two miles of our camp was the residence of the late ex-president, John Tyler, which was visited by many of our officers. It was a charming spot. . . . The house was stripped of almost everything. . . . The large library had lost many of its choicest volumes, while the remainder, with heaps of letters, lay thrown in wild confusion about the floor. The pile of sheet music which had been left on the piano by the family had been culled over and nearly all taken away. . . .

"On the morning of the 15th the corps moved to the riverside, where it remained while other troops were crossing by ferry and on an immensely long pontoon bridge. The river was full of shipping, the forests of masts making strange contrasts with the native forests on the river banks.

"Near the crossing was a superb old mansion . . . surrounded by its little village of Negro cabins. Here many officers of the corps resorted to spend the time in walking among the grand old trees, or to stroll through the garden, admiring the elegant and rare exotics which adorned the grounds. . . . Within the mansion, we were met with the accustomed bitterness. . . .

"Among the slaves on the premises was a white-haired Negro who was one hundred and eight years old. . . . When asked his age by the boys, he was accustomed to answer, 'Well, massa, I'se going on *two hundred* now.' The old fellow manifested no sympathy for the cause of his master, and even he sighed for freedom. When asked of what value freedom could be to him now, he answered . . . 'Well, massa, isn't a hundred and eight years long enough to be a slave?' "

By this time, news dispatches concerning Grant's maneuver were being sent north. Charles Page informed the readers of the *New York Tribune:* "The movement to the James River and beyond it, now being made, is precisely what was intended when the campaign was first mapped out, in the event that the battles which it was known must be fought on the way should not destroy Lee's army. . . . Anchor your souls to one fact. . . . *This army cannot be beaten back from its purpose.* Its morale is high by continual reinforcements. It numbers today . . . larger than it did on the Rappahannock. The slightly wounded of the first battles are resuming their places by thousands. The conviction is universal, shared alike by Generals Grant and Meade and the humblest soldier, that this is the last grand campaign—the last because it will accomplish the practical destruction of the Confederacy."

Lee was still uncertain of Grant's intentions and kept the bulk of his army covering Richmond. Nevertheless, says Southerner John Esten Cooke, "the attempt of General Grant to seize upon Petersburg by a surprise failed. His forces were not able to reach the vicinity of the place until the 15th, when they were bravely opposed behind impromptu works by a body of local troops [along with some of Beauregard's regulars] who . . . succeeded in holding [most of] the works until night ended the contest. When morning came, long lines were seen defiling into the breastworks [this was Hoke's division, making its return to Beauregard after its temporary duty with Lee] . . . giving assurance that the possession of Petersburg would be obstinately disputed."

With more and more of Grant's troops reaching the scene, the fighting continued on June 16 and 17. Beauregard increased his defense force to about 14,000 men by divesting Bermuda Hundred of most of the units that had been containing Butler. Butler now became Lee's responsibility, and he sent two divisions to Bermuda Hundred. At Petersburg Beauregard managed to hold on against superior numbers, largely because of Union hesitancy.

The narrative is assumed by D. Augustus Dickert, of Lee's army: "Lee . . . was yet in doubt whether Grant had designs directly against the Capital, or was endeavoring to cut his communications by the capture of Petersburg. Beauregard had kept General Lee and the war department thoroughly advised of his peril and of the overwhelming numbers in his front, but it was not until midnight of the 17th that the Confederate commander determined to change his base . . . to the south side of the James. It was at that hour that Kershaw's brigade received its orders to move at once. For the last few days the army had been gradually working its way towards the James. . . . From the manner in which we were urged forward, it was evident that our troops somewhere were in imminent peril. The march started as a forced one, but before daylight it had gotten almost to a run. . . . We reached Petersburg about sunrise."

It was a nick-of-time arrival. The Federals were getting into position for a major attack. In the city itself, according to Robert Stiles, "the whole population . . . appeared to be in the streets and thoroughly alive to the narrow escape they had made. . . . They seemed to be overflowing with gratitude to us. Ladies, old and young, met us at their front gates with hearty welcome, cool water, and delicious viands, and did not at all shrink from grasping our rough and dirty hands. There is nothing more inspiring to a soldier than to pass through the streets of a city he is helping to defend, and to be greeted as a deliverer by its women and children."

Returning to Confederate narrator Dickert: "Before our division lines were properly adjusted . . . [the Federals] made a mad rush upon the works, now manned by a thin skirmish line, and seemed determined to drive us from our entrenchments by sheer weight of numbers. But Kershaw displayed no inclination to yield until the other portions of our corps came upon the field. After some hours of stubborn fighting,

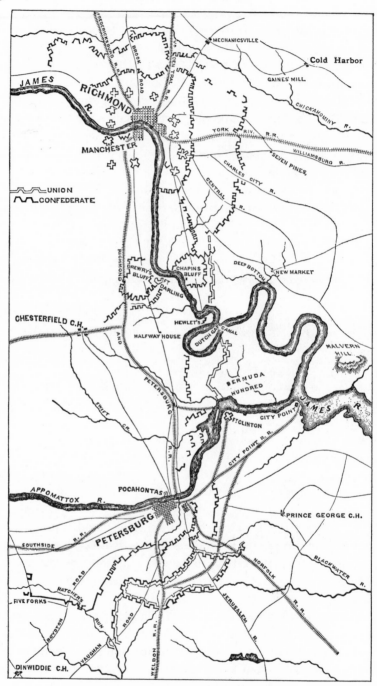

Defenses of Richmond and Petersburg

and failing to dislodge us, the enemy withdrew to strengthen and straighten their lines. . . .

"About four o'clock in the afternoon Meade organized a strong column of assault composed of the Second, Fifth, and Ninth Army Corps, and commanded in person. . . . A destructive fire was opened upon us by fifty pieces of the best field artillery. The infantry then commenced the storming of our works, but Field's Division had come up and was on the line.

"General Lee had given strength to our position by his presence . . . and gave personal direction to the movements of the troops. The battle raged furiously until nightfall, but with no better results on the enemy's side than had attended him for the last three days. . . . By noon the next day Lee's whole force south of the James was within the entrenched lines of the city, and all felt perfectly safe and secure."

But a few days later, according to Southerner John Esten Cooke, Lee was called upon to meet another threat, "this time more to his right, in the vicinity of the Weldon Railroad, which runs southward from Petersburg. A heavy line was advanced in that quarter by the enemy; but, observing that an interval had been left between two of their corps, General Lee threw forward a column under General Hill, cut the Federal lines, and repulsed their [movement], bearing off nearly three thousand prisoners [actually, about 1700]."

At this same time, Cooke goes on to explain, Grant and Meade sent "an important cavalry expedition . . . westward to cut the Weldon, Southside, and Danville Railroads, which connected the Southern army with the South and West. . . . The Federal cavalry tore up large portions of the tracks of all three railroads, burning the woodwork, and laying waste to the country around; but the further results of the expedition were unfavorable. They were pursued and harassed . . . leaving behind them twelve pieces of artillery and more than a thousand prisoners; and [it was] with foaming and exhausted horses [that they] regained the Federal lines. . . . The railroads were soon repaired and in working order again. . . .

"It was now the end of June, and every attempt made by General Grant to force Lee's lines had proved unsuccessful. It was apparent that surprise of the able commander of the Confederate army was hopeless. His works were growing stronger every day, and nothing was left to his great adversary but to lay regular siege to the long line of fortifications."

On July 1 the Union chaplain from Pennsylvania, A. M. Stewart, said in a letter home: "Here is the Potomac army at a seemingly dead stand.

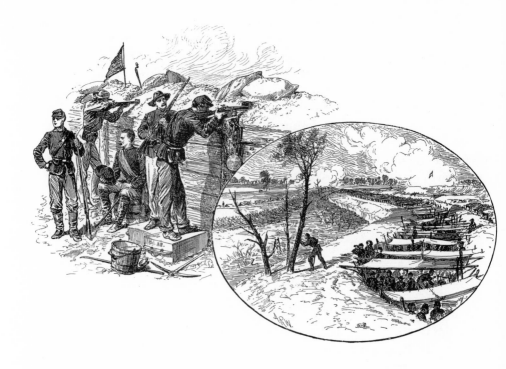

Union positions at Petersburg

. . . Richmond not yet captured, nor soon likely to be. Notwithstanding the fearful amount of blood, toil, and treasure, with frequent change of base and locality, during the past two months, yet has no apparent advantage been gained over Lee—scarcely an insignificant rifle-pit taken from the rebels and retained. General Grant finds it a far different matter pushing aside Western armies and capturing Vicksburg, to conquering Lee and entering Richmond. This, nevertheless, a dogged perseverance may yet accomplish; though before Petersburg, which is but an outpost of Richmond, we may be compelled to burrow for six months to come."

Even while the chaplain was writing, events were conspiring—in a totally unexpected way—to give Grant one more chance to bring the war to a speedy end.

23

The Battle of the Crater

Each side was hastening to perfect an elaborate trench system combined with a series of earth-and-log forts. At some places the opposing lines swung close to each other, and only 500 feet separated the advanced trenches of Union Fort Morton from Confederate Fort Elliott (see map on p. 273). The work here was accompanied by the steady crack of sniper fire, and the range made much of the fire deadly.

It was Union General Ambrose Burnside's Ninth Corps that held the lines that included Fort Morton, and one of Burnside's regiments was the 48th Pennsylvania Volunteers, about 400 troops under Colonel Henry Pleasants. The 48th had been recruited in Pennsylvania's Schuylkill County, a region rich with anthracite coal, and many of the men had come straight from jobs in the mines. Colonel Pleasants himself was a mining engineer. Mining was hard and dangerous work, and these men were of a strong and determined breed. Most were inveterate tobacco chewers, commonly seen with a greatly distended cheek, and possessing a fine talent for spewing brownish streams. Some of the hardiest claimed they could swallow the juice with no ill effects.

One day in late June Colonel Pleasants was inspecting his trenches when he heard a man say of Fort Morton's counterpart: "We could blow that damned fort out of existence if we could run a mine shaft under it." Pleasants was impressed with the idea. Destroying the fort would create a breach that could be exploited by an assault force. And there happened to be a hillock behind the fort, one holding an old church and a cemetery, that would be a good point to head for. Its occupation would make the breach unmendable.

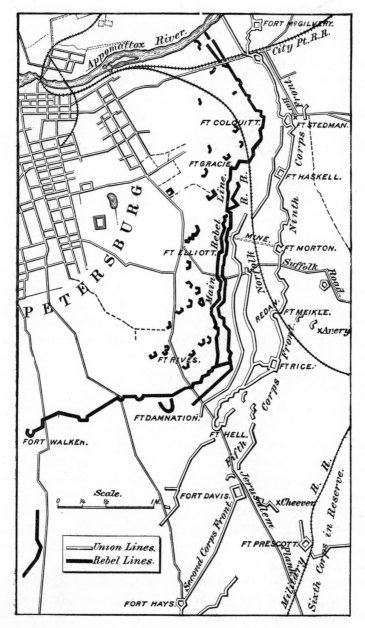

Petersburg lines showing location of mine between Fort Morton and Fort Elliott

Pleasants went to a bombproof that held a group of his regiment's officers. "That goddamned fort," he said, "is the only thing between us and Petersburg, and I have an idea we can blow it up." The proposal was sent up the chain of command to the division commander, Robert Potter, who carried it to Burnside. Both men were favorably impressed. Grant and Meade showed no great faith in the plan, but they felt it would at least give the men of the 48th something to do during a dismal period.

News of the project traveled about the camps, and its progress was followed by some of the more inquisitive officers, who acquainted themselves with the details. Regis de Trobriand, a French-born brigadier in Hancock's command, learned that the first thing that had to be done "was to get the exact distance from the mouth of the mine to the redoubt which it was intended to blow up. The instruments necessary were at headquarters, but the use of them could not be obtained. The chief engineers of the army and other authorities declared *ex cathedra* that the project was senseless and foolish; that a military mine as long as that had never been dug; that it could not be done; that the men would be stifled by the lack of air, or crushed by the falling-in of the earth, etc. . . . With *specialists,* the thing that has not been done cannot be done, and, if you propose to them any innovation not found in their books, nine times out of ten they will tell you that it is impossible or absurd.

"General Burnside, who persisted in [the] idea, sent to Washington for an old theodolite [a surveyor's device] which . . . enabled Colonel Pleasants to determine that the length of the direct gallery must be five hundred and ten feet, at the end of which lateral galleries, curving in an arc of a circle, must be dug to the right and left, each thirty-eight feet long.

"It follows, of course, that all assistance was refused by the engineer corps, which did not wish to take any part in an enterprise of which it had proclaimed the absurdity. Following suit, the superior officers of the army were greatly amused by the [foolishness].

"Colonel Pleasants, left to himself without other encouragement than that of Burnside and Potter, continued his work with an unshakable perseverance. He was refused timber; he sent for it to a sawmill out of the lines. They refused him mining picks; he had the common picks in the division fixed over. They refused him wheelbarrows; he had the earth carried out in cracker boxes bound with iron taken from old fish barrels. So that he was equal to every requirement without employing

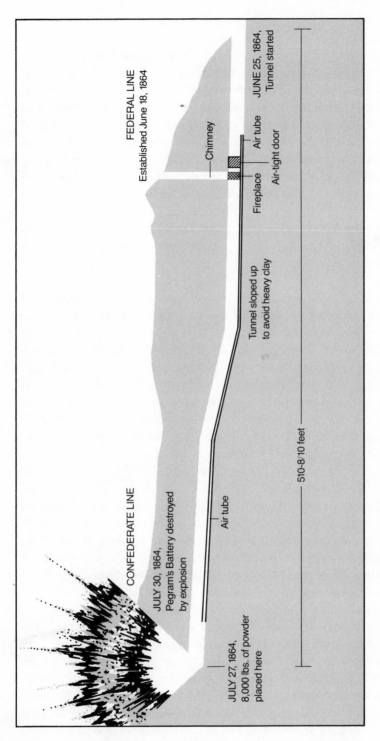

The mine in cross section. A particular problem of the digging was the matter of keeping the air fresh. It was not feasible to install a series of vertical air shafts as the work progressed, since these would have been spotted by the enemy. The solution was a single shaft made early, with a fire kept burning beneath it. As the hot air rose, fresh air was drawn into the mine through a square wooden pipe passing under an airtight door at the entrance. The smoke from the fire was visible to the enemy. This drawback was handled by keeping numerous other fires burning along adjacent parts of the line a person outside of his own regiment of four hundred men."

There was no concern about the enemy's spotting the mine entrance, for it was located in the side of a rise facing away from his view. (See diagram "The mine in cross section.") The tunnel, or gallery, was about five feet high; its base was about the same, but its sides tapered to about two feet at the ceiling. "Water was met with not far from the entrance," says an unidentified Union newsman, "and for a time gave no little trouble. The floor, however, was planked, and the sides and ceiling shored up. . . . The oozing of the water formed mud in several places, so that the regiment came from their daily labors bespattered and stained. In fact, it was easy . . . to recognize a 48th man by his muddy boots. . . . The lighting of the tunnel was effected simply by placing candles or lanterns along the walls at a distance of about twenty feet apart."

The Confederates across the way—Bushrod Johnson's division of Beauregard's command—were not long in complete darkness about the Federal project. As explained by W. Gordon McCabe, a captain who served in the area: "From mysterious paragraphs in the Northern papers, and from reports of deserters—though those last were vague and contradictory—Lee and Beauregard suspected that the enemy was mining in front of some one of the three salients on Beauregard's front, and the latter officer . . . directed counter-mines to be sunk from all three, meanwhile constructing gorge-lines in the rear upon which the troops might retire in case of surprise or disaster."

Captain George B. Lake, of the 22nd South Carolina, tells of activities at the threatened salient: "We sunk a shaft on each side of the four-gun battery [that of William J. Pegram], ten feet or more deep, and then extended the tunnel some distance to our front. We were on a high hill, however, and the enemy five hundred and ten feet in our front, where they began their work, consequently their mine was far under the shaft we sunk. At night when everything was still we could hear the enemy's miners at work. . . . The idea of being blown into eternity without any warning was anything but pleasant."

The first Southern narrator, Captain McCabe, says that "the counter-mining on the part of the Confederates was after a time discontinued, owing to the lack of proper tools, the inexperience of the troops in such work, and the arduous nature of their service in the trenches."

Conditions were particularly difficult for the Confederates around Fort Elliott (or Elliott's Salient), since Union General Burnside kept them under an almost continual fire as a part of his efforts to cover his miners. Even aside from this, life at the salient was a trial, as explained by one of its officers, Colonel F. W. McMaster: "The soldiers slept in the main trench. At times of heavy rains the lower part of the trench ran a foot deep in water. The officers slept in burrows dug in the sides of the rear ditches. There were traverses, narrow ditches, cross ditches, and a few mounds over officers' dens. An ordinary mortal would not select such a place [to reside]."

A visiting general who toured the salient asked McMaster where the men slept. "I pointed out the floor of the ditch. He said, 'But where do the officers sleep?' We happened to be in the narrow ditch in front of my quarters, and I pointed it out to him. He replied, in language not altogether suitable for a Sunday School teacher, that he would desert before he would submit to such hardships."

Regardless of all the discomforts and perils, however, the Confederates surely would have tried to do more against Burnside's mine if their information about it had been accurate. There was a wide range of thought about the project. Many Confederate engineers believed, along with most of their Union counterparts, that a tunnel of such a length could not be completed. By contrast, there were citizens in Petersburg who believed that their entire town was being undermined. This belief, actually, had more behind it than hysteria. It was common knowledge that, in some of the nation's coal regions, miners like these, in their relentless quest for their "black gold," *had* burrowed beneath residential areas. These mine systems, of course, had been years in developing. But the Petersburgers did not know that only four hundred men were digging toward them. It might have been many thousands.

Returning to the Union narration by Regis de Trobriand: "The work, begun June 25, was finished on July 23, without accident, in spite of all predictions and of all derision. It was then necessary to change the tone. The fact must be recognized that the thing was serious. That which had been declared impossible was done. The explosion, if it succeeded, and if we knew how to get the benefit of it, must deliver Petersburg to us."

By this time General Grant was a true believer in the mine's potential. He had been distracted from his siege duties for a time because of developments in other theaters of the war, chiefly by a crisis at Washington. Confederate General Jubal Early, detached from Lee's army after Cold Harbor, forced his way northward through the Shenandoah Valley and marched upon the capital from the northwest. Grant sped reinforcements to Washington's garrison, and the audacious Early was dissuaded from attacking, choosing retreat as the better part of valor.

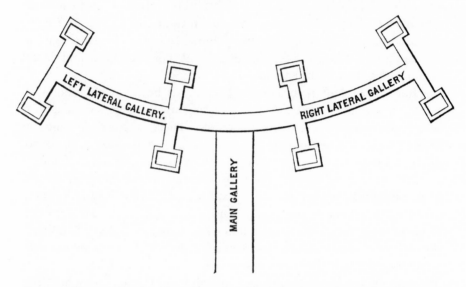

Section of mine that lay directly under Confederate works. Main gallery in center leads back to Union lines

Now, at Petersburg, Grant sent Hancock and Sheridan north of the James to make a raid toward Richmond, the chief purpose of the expedition being to force Lee to throw a good part of his strength northward and thus leave Petersburg open to easy assault. The scheme worked perfectly. Less than half of Lee's army was left in the Petersburg lines.

Regis de Trobriand continues: "Everything, then, seemed to promise success, provided that the assault should be made with vigor and in unison. That was the great point, and, unhappily, the one as to which the measures taken gave rise to serious apprehensions. The choice of the Ninth Corps to lead the attack was far from being the best that could have been made. That corps, which had rendered good service in North Carolina, in the Army of the Potomac, and in Tennessee, had been so reduced by these various campaigns that it had been necessary to renew it almost entirely. Troops of all sorts, mostly newly raised, had been incorporated in it. . . . It would have been much better to have trusted the assault to more hardy troops. . . . But Burnside, who had taken the lead in having the mine dug, held it as a point of honor to complete the work.

"However, it was not without taking account of the real condition of his command. So he had concluded to put at the head of the column of attack his fourth division, composed of colored troops [commanded by white officers], who, more numerous and less fatigued than the others, were, taking all things into consideration, the ones on whom he could best depend."

Immediately after the explosion of the mine, the black division was to charge through the breach, closely followed by Burnside's other three divisions. "After them," de Trobriand goes on to explain, "would advance the Eighteenth Corps, and our success was assured. For it must be remembered that Lee, having sent five divisions to the north of the James, had but three left at Petersburg. Once established on the hill [that held the church and cemetery], the city was ours."

The men of Burnside's black division, heretofore used only as support troops, were proud to have been chosen to spearhead the attack. One of the war's issues was the bondage of their race, and now they were to have a vital role in bringing the war to a head. They were taken to the fields behind the lines to practice their maneuver, and they became adept and confident. Both on the training field and around their campfires at night, they sang, in rich and resonant tones, sacred hymns and songs of war, some of the latter self-composed. "We looks like men a-marchin' on," they sang; "We looks like men o' war."

It was on July 26 that Burnside presented his plan of attack to General Meade. The response was that Burnside must make a change in his deployment: a white division must be substituted for the black one in the advance. Although Meade was prepared to believe that the black troops had the capacity to fight well, he was concerned that they had never been tested, and he felt that putting them in the advance at this time, when so much was at stake, was an unacceptable risk. Burnside appealed to Grant, who sided against him, saying later he was convinced that Meade was right when he made the added point "that if we put the only colored division we had in the advance, and the affair turned out badly, it would be said, and with a show of reason, that we killed off those troops because we cared nothing about them." The fact that Lincoln was beginning his campaign for a second term was also a consideration. Grant and Meade did not want to risk giving the opposition an issue to use against him. It must not appear that Lincoln the emancipator was careless with black lives.

"The final decision," says de Trobriand, "was announced to General Burnside on the 29th, twelve or fifteen hours before the time fixed for the explosion. It was a cause of great disappointment and embarrassment to him. Which of the three divisions should he choose to replace the fourth? Such was his hesitation that . . . he resorted to the strange expedient of putting the result to lot. The lot—which is of course blind, and sometimes is pleased to give us some severe lessons—fell upon the very division which, if it was not worse than the others, was certainly worse commanded. . . .

"The whole night was devoted to the last preparations, the attacking divisions forming at their posts as they were relieved in the trenches. Our division [one of the relieving units] . . . took the place of the Eighteenth and a part of the Tenth Corps. . . . My brigade was the nearest to the mine, from which it was separated by a curtain of woods. . . .

"The hour set for the mine explosion was half-past three in the morning. I have stated that the principal gallery of the mine ended in a traverse gallery in the shape of an arc. . . . In the walls of the latter [were] . . . eight chambers, each containing a thousand pounds of powder—in all, eight thousand pounds. That would make a fine explosion. So from three o'clock everyone was up, the officers [with] watch in hand, eyes fixed on the fated redan, or in that direction.

"There were [more than] two hundred men in that work, sleeping tranquilly a sleep from which they would awake in eternity. Perhaps they were dreaming of returning to their families . . . when, beneath them, Colonel Pleasants . . . was applying the fire to the match [i.e., the fuse]. . . . Silence reigned everywhere, but in our lines all eyes were open. . . .

"From half-after-three the minutes were counted. It was still too dark, it was said. At four o'clock it was daylight. Nothing stirred as yet. At quarter past four a murmur of impatience ran through the ranks. What has happened? Has there been a counter-order? Or an accident? Has the assault been deferred?

"It had happened that the match, which was ninety feet long, had gone out at a splice about halfway of its length. . . . Two intrepid men, Lieutenant Jacob Douty and Sergeant Harry Reese, volunteered to see what was the cause of the delay, and to relight the match. Both returned safe and sound. The redoubt had a respite of a quarter of an hour.

"Suddenly the earth trembled under our feet. An enormous mass sprang into the air. A mass without form or shape, full of red flames and carried on a bed of lightning flashes, mounted towards heaven with a detonation of thunder. It spread out like a sheaf, like an immense mushroom whose stem seemed to be of fire and its head of smoke. Then everything appeared to break up and fall back in a rain of earth mixed with rocks, with beams, timbers, and mangled human bodies, leaving floating in the air a cloud of white smoke which rose up to the heavens, and a cloud of gray dust which fell slowly towards the earth. The redan had disappeared. . . .

"All our batteries opened at once on the enemy's intrenchments. The projectiles whistled, roared, burst. [Some of them carried into Petersburg, where fires were started, compounding the consternation of people who had jumped from their beds at the sound of the blowup.] Through the deafening noise of the artillery firing was heard a cry, and the first division advanced to the assault. It had nothing in front of it. The Confederate troops occupying the lines to the right and the left in the immediate vicinity of the mine had fled precipitately through fright and fear of further explosions. . . . The way was completely open to the summit of the hill, which was protected by no other line of works."

The narrative is taken up by William H. Powell, a staff officer with the Federal advance: "As no part of the Union line of breastworks had been removed [to make the passage easy] . . . the troops clambered over them as best they could. This in itself broke the ranks, and they did not stop to re-form, but pushed ahead toward the crater, about 130 yards distant, the debris from the explosion having covered up the abatis and *chevaux-de-frise* in front of the enemy's works.

"Little did these men anticipate what they would see upon arriving there: an enormous hole in the ground about 30 feet deep, 60 feet wide, and 170 feet long, filled with dust, great blocks of clay, guns, broken carriages, projecting timbers, and men buried in various ways—some up to their necks, others to their waists, and some with only their feet and legs protruding from the earth. One of these near me was pulled out, and proved to be a second lieutenant of the battery which had been blown up. The fresh air revived him."

Another disinterred Confederate, although somewhat battered, made up a joke about his experience. He said that he and several of his comrades were blown high in the air, but that he himself commenced rising later than the rest, so that he was still going up while they were starting down, and that they shouted as they passed him: "Straggler!"

Now an incredible thing happened. Instead of shaping their efforts toward the hill that was their goal, the Federals broke their remaining formations and began milling about, marveling at the size of the crater, digging up more Confederates, poking about in the fascinating debris, and even gathering souvenirs. Only a relatively few men in the advance got as far as the maze of works beyond the crater, where they began exchanging fire with a handful of the enemy that hadn't fled the area. By and large, the unit leaders of the main body were ignored as they shouted and pointed their swords at the hill, and there was no one of superior authority at hand to save the situation. The division commander, James H. Ledlie, was back in the Union lines in a bombproof, his brain numbed by liquor. Burnside, Meade, and Grant, were at retired command posts. Burnside, at least, should have been at the front.

Observing the scene at the crater from a vantage point in the Union lines was Colonel Henry Pleasants and his high-mettled miners, who had been celebrating their prodigious success with whoops and back-slaps. At first the men could not believe that what they were now seeing was really happening. Thousands of additional Federals were moving toward the crater and its flanks, most to jam up with those who had gone before. A portion got through to join the fragments in the far trenches, but the critical hill remained bare of Union flags, which by this time should have been waving high and proclaiming success. The miners began to groan and swear, and the volume of their protest made a respectable second to that of the Union artillery fire.

The Confederates were given plenty of time to recover their nerve and begin a defense. As recounted by John Wise, an officer in Bushrod Johnson's command: "From our ten-inch and eight-inch mortars in the rear of the line, a most accurate fire was opened upon the troops in the breach; and our batteries to north and south began to pour a deadly storm of shell and canister upon their crowded masses. The situation looked desperate for us, nevertheless, for it was all our [rallying] infantry could do to hold their lines [against the Federals in the fore, who were now exerting pressure], and not a man could be spared to meet an advance upon Blandford Cemetery heights, which lay before the Union troops.

"At this juncture, heroic John Haskell, of South Carolina, came dashing up the plank road with two light batteries, and from a position near the cemetery began the most effective work of the day. Exposed to the batteries and sharpshooters of the enemy, he and his men gave little heed to danger. Haskell, in his impetuous and ubiquitous gallantry, dashed and flashed about. . . . Now he darted into the covered way to seek [Brigadier General Stephen] Elliott, and implore an infantry support for his exposed guns. Elliott, responding to his appeal, was severely wounded as he attempted, with a brave handful of his Carolinians, to cover Haskell's position."

Additional Confederates of Bushrod Johnson's command were rallying, but reinforcements were needed. Heavier numbers of Federals were filtering into the captured trench system. Chosen by General Lee to come to the scene was William ("Little Billy") Mahone, whose division was located about two miles along the line to the south. Mahone relates: "The first I knew of the crater, beyond the tremendous report of the explosion, came from a soldier who, from thereabouts, hatless and shoeless, passed me, still going, and only time to say, 'Hell has busted!'

"About this time, Colonel Venable, of General Lee's staff, rode up and said, 'General Lee requests that you send two of the brigades of your division to the support of Gen. Bushrod Johnson.' . . . I said to Colonel Venable, 'I can't *send* my brigades to General Johnson, I will go with them myself.' The Virginia and Georgia brigades . . . were ordered to drop back in such order to the ravine in the rear as to avoid possible disclosure [to the enemy] of this denuding of my front. They were so conducted by ravines in the general direction of the crater as to conceal the march. . . .

"The morning was warm and sultry. Before reaching the covered way which led up to the rear of General Johnson's line covering the crater, the brigades were halted and ordered to strip [for action]. Reaching the entrance of the covered way, the head of the column was turned into it, and I rode over to General Johnson's headquarters. . . . I asked . . . what frontage on his line the enemy occupied. . . . Calling to some lieutenant of his staff, he said to him, 'Show General Mahone the way to Elliott's Salient, or Pegram's Battery.'

". . . With the lieutenant, I proceeded hurriedly . . . in the direction of the disaster. . . . The lieutenant said to me, 'If you will go up that slope there, you can see the Yankees.' Moving quickly to the high ground next to the crater, I found myself suddenly in full view of General Johnson's [disrupted line], now crammed with Federal soldiers and thickly studded with Federal flags. For the moment I could scarcely take in the reality."

Mahone first dispatched a courier southward to order up another of his brigades, then deployed the two at hand for an assault toward the crater. General Lee breathed a sigh of relief.

Meanwhile, something momentous was happening on the Union side: Burnside's black division was being sent in. As the regiments began moving forward, according to Grant's aide Horace Porter, "a white sergeant, who was being carried to the rear with his leg shot off, cried out, 'Now go in with a will, boys. There's enough of you to eat 'em all up.' A colored sergeant replied, 'Dat may be all so, boss; but the fac' is, we habn't got jis de bes' kind ob an appetite for 'em dis mornin'.' "

Union observer Regis de Trobriand says that "the blacks advanced resolutely, passed over the passive mass of white troops, not a company of whom followed them, and, although their ranks were necessarily broken by the obstacle, they charged under a deadly fire of artillery and musketry which reached them from all sides at once. They even reached the enemy, took from him two hundred and fifty prisoners, captured a flag, and recovered one of ours taken by him."

This happened, of course, in the trenches on the Confederate side of the crater. The blacks were now supported by some of the whites who had been fighting there, but the attack was soon stopped by two of the regiments of Elliott's brigade that had rallied after the blow-up. Colonel McMaster, who had assumed command of the brigade at Elliott's wounding, says that the blacks in the advance were "welcomed . . . to hospitable graves at 9 o'clock A.M.

"At about 9:30 A.M., Old Virginia [i.e., Billy Mahone's Virginia brigade] . . . with eight hundred heroes rushed into the trench . . . and slaughtered hundreds of whites and blacks, with decided preference for the Ethiopians."

The narrator exaggerates the slaughter, but it was brutal enough. Some of the blacks were shot, clubbed, or bayoneted to death while cringing and pleading for mercy. The Federals, black and white, who were not cut down or captured fled toward the crater.

The blacks taken prisoner were relieved to have been spared, but, according to a Confederate observer, Major William Miller Owen: "They had been told we would hang them if we caught them, and they believed it. Their white officers had torn their shoulder-straps off, so we should not recognize them as officers; but the fresh marks showed plainly upon their sun-burned jackets, and they could not deceive Major Bob W., of A. P. Hill's staff, who nearly scared the life out of them by standing them apart from the Negroes and impressing the fact upon them that they were to swing *instanter*. How they begged, and, without exception, said they had been forced in; they could not avoid commanding the blacks, and all that."

By ten o'clock the Confederates had regained all but a fifty-foot section of trench, this near the crater, and Billy Mahone sent his Georgia brigade to tidy things up. But there were enough alert and belligerent Federals in this zone to repel the Georgians with severe losses. Now the Confederates intensified their bombardment of the crater, which was so thickly crowded with Federals, sweltering under a fiery sun, that many could barely move. No skilled sighting was needed. The barrage, which included mortars, was thrown over the heads of Confederates lying close to the rim.

"Our fellows," says Confederate officer John Wise, "seized the [bayoneted] muskets abandoned by the retreating enemy, and threw them like pitchforks into the huddled troops over the ramparts. Screams, groans, and explosions throwing up human limbs made it a scene of awful carnage. . . . About one o'clock, the Alabama brigade of Mahone's division . . . formed and charged, and the white flag went up from the crater. [By this time, however, the great majority of the surviving Federals were falling back, helter-skelter, upon their original lines.]

"Out of [the crater] . . . filed as prisoners eleven hundred and one Union troops, including two brigade commanders; and we captured twenty-one standards and several thousands of small arms. Over a thousand of the enemy's dead were in and about the breach, and his losses exceeded five thousand effective troops [actually, about 500 were left dead, and total losses were around 4,000], while our lines were reestablished just where they were when the battle began."

A Federal officer back from the combat zone was asked, by a man who had not participated, the result of the fight. The officer replied, "They have whipped us like hell!"

"The unfortunate affair," explains Union narrator Regis de Trobriand, "... closed the series of direct attacks against Petersburg. They had cost us more than twenty thousand men. It was full time to adopt a ... method ... exclusively directed against the communications remaining open between the city and the South."

The mine fiasco—entirely the product of bungled leadership—was especially painful to General Grant, who said in a wire to Washington: "Such opportunity to carry fortifications I have never seen, and do not expect again to have." The failure had the effect of prolonging the war for nearly nine months.

Before putting the Battle of the Crater behind him, Grant was obliged to attend to a sad and humiliating detail. Confederate officer William Miller Owen tells about it in a diary entry dated August 1:

"This morning Gen. Lee allowed Gen. Grant an armistice of three hours to bury his dead, left in front of our works [and now terribly offensive after being broiled in the sun]. . . . A long trench was dug equidistant between our works and the enemy's, and the Negro prisoners were made to [help] carry the dead bodies to the trench and throw them in.

"I went down to the flag of truce, and there met [a party of high-ranking Union commanders]. . . . These officers were very courteous and chatty, and brought out buckets of lemonade and other refreshments in profusion. They were desirous of getting a glimpse of some of our generals, and had pointed out to them Gen. Bushrod Johnson, clad in a linen duster and a straw hat; and A. P. Hill, in a gray flannel shirt, standing upon the edge of the crater. They were anxious to see Gen. Lee, but 'Uncle Robert' didn't gratify them.

"At the expiration of the three hours a signal-gun was fired, and the armistice ended. We lifted our hats to the Federal officers, bowed, and each retired to their respective lines, ready to renew hostilities."

Quotation Sources

Annals of the War. Philadelphia: The Times Publishing Co., 1879.

Battles and Leaders of the Civil War, vol. 4. Robert Underwood Johnson and Clarence Clough Buel, eds. New York: The Century Co., 1888.

Blake, Henry N. *Three Years in the Army of the Potomac.* Boston: Lee & Shepard, 1865.

Buell, Augustus. *The Cannoneer: Recollections of Service in the Army of the Potomac.* Washington, D.C.: The National Tribune, 1890.

Caldwell, J. F. J. *The History of a Brigade of South Carolinians.* Philadelphia: King & Baird, Printers, 1866. Facsimile edition by Morningside Bookshop, Dayton, Ohio, 1974.

Casler, John O. *Four Years in the Stonewall Brigade.* James I. Robertson, Jr., ed. Dayton, Ohio: Morningside Bookshop, 1971. Facsimile of 1906 edition.

Coffin, Charles Carleton. *Redeeming the Republic.* New York: Harper & Brothers, 1890.

————. *The Boys of '61.* Boston: Estes & Lauriat, 1884.

Cooke, John Esten. *Robert E. Lee.* New York: D. Appleton & Co., 1871.

Crotty, D. G. *Four Years Campaigning in the Army of the Potomac.* Grand Rapids, Mich.: Dygert Bros. & Co., 1874.

Dana, Charles A. *Recollections of the Civil War.* New York: D. Appleton & Co., 1898.

Davies, Henry E. *General Sheridan.* New York: D. Appleton & Co., 1895.

Davis, Varina Howell. *Jefferson Davis: A Memoir by His Wife,* vol. 2. New York: Belford Co. Publishers, 1890.

Derby, W. P. *Bearing Arms in the Twenty-Seventh Massachusetts Regiment of Volunteer Infantry.* Boston: Wright & Potter Printing Co., 1883.

De Trobriand, P. Regis. *Four Years with the Army of the Potomac.* Boston: Ticknor & Co., 1889.

Dickert, D. Augustus. *History of Kershaw's Brigade.* Dayton, Ohio: Morningside Bookshop, 1976. Facsimile of 1899 edition.

Evans, Clement A., ed. *Confederate Military History,* vol. 3. New York: Thomas Yoseloff, 1962. Reprint of edition by Confederate Publishing Co., 1899.

Gerrish, Theodore. *Army Life: A Private's Reminiscences of the Civil War.* Portland, Me.: Hoyt, Fogg & Donham, 1882.

Gordon, John B. *Reminiscences of the Civil War.* New York: Charles Scribner's Sons, 1904.

Goss, Warren Lee. *Recollections of a Private.* New York: Thomas Y. Crowell & Co., 1890.

Grant, U. S. *Personal Memoirs.* New York: Charles L. Webster & Co., 1894.

Hopkins, Luther W. *From Bull Run to Appomattox.* Baltimore: Fleet-McGinley Co., 1908.

Humphreys, Andrew A. *The Virginia Campaign of 1864 and 1865.* Campaigns of the Civil War, vol. 12. New York: Charles Scribner's Sons, 1883.

Johnson, Rossiter. *Campfires and Battlefields.* New York: The Civil War Press, 1967. First published in 1894.

Jones, John B. *A Rebel War Clerk's Diary at the Confederate States Capital,* vol. 2. Philadelphia: J. B. Lippincott, 1866.

King, W. C., and W. P. Derby. *Campfire Sketches and Battlefield Echoes.* Springfield, Mass.: W. C. King & Co., 1887.

Lee, Fitzhugh. *General Lee of the Confederate Army.* London: Chapman & Hall, Ltd., 1895.

Lee, Captain Robert E. *Recollections and Letters of General Robert E. Lee.* New York: Doubleday, Page & Co., 1904.

Longstreet, James. *From Manassas to Appomattox.* Philadelphia: J. B. Lippincott, 1896.

McCarthy, Carlton. *Detailed Minutiae of Soldier Life in the Army of Northern Virginia 1861–1865.* Richmond: Carlton McCarthy & Co., 1884.

McClellan, H. B. *The Life and Campaigns of Major General J. E. B. Stuart.* Boston: Houghton, Mifflin & Co., 1885.

[McGuire, Judith W.] *Diary of a Southern Refugee during the War.* New York: E. J. Hale & Son, 1867.

Nichols, G. W. *A Soldier's Story of His Regiment.* Kennesaw, Ga.: Continental Book Co., 1961. Facsimile of 1898 edition.

Oates, William C. *The War between the Union and the Confederacy.* New York: The Neale Publishing Co., 1905.

Owen, William Miller. *In Camp and Battle with the Washington Artillery.* Boston: Ticknor & Co., 1885. Second edition by Pelican Publishing Co., New Orleans, 1964.

Page, Charles A. *Letters of a War Correspondent.* Boston: L. C. Page & Co., 1899.

Pollard, Edward A. *The Early Life, Campaigns, and Public Services of Robert E. Lee; with a Record of the Campaigns and Heroic Deeds of His Companions in Arms.* New York: E. B. Treat & Co., 1871.

———. *The Lost Cause.* New York: E. B. Treat & Co., 1866.

Porter, Horace. *Campaigning with Grant.* New York: The Century Co., 1897.

[Putnam, Sarah A.] *Richmond during the War.* New York: G. W. Carleton & Co., 1867.

Richardson, Albert D. *A Personal History of Ulysses S. Grant.* Hartford, Conn.: American Publishing Co., 1868.

Sheridan, Philip H. *Personal Memoirs,* vol. 1. New York: Charles L. Webster & Co., 1888.

Stevens, George T. *Three Years in the Sixth Corps.* New York: D. Van Nostrand, 1870.

Stewart, A. M. *Camp, March and Battlefield; or Three Years and a Half with the Army of the Potomac.* Philadelphia: Jas. B. Rodgers, Printer, 1865.

Stiles, Robert. *Four Years under Marse Robert.* New York and Washington: The Neale Publishing Co., 1903.

Stine, J. H. *History of the Army of the Potomac.* Philadelphia: J. B. Rogers Printing Co., 1892.

Swinton, William. *Campaigns of the Army of the Potomac.* New York: Charles Scribner's Sons, 1882.

———. *The Twelve Decisive Battles of the War.* New York: Dick & Fitzgerald, 1867.

Taylor, Walter H. *Four Years with General Lee.* New York: D. Appleton & Co., 1878.

The War of the Rebellion: A Compilation of the Official Records of the Union and Confederate Armies. Series 1, vol. 26, part 1. Washington, D.C.: Government Printing Office, 1891.

Under Both Flags: A Panorama of the Great Civil War. Chicago: W. S. Reeve Publishing Co., 1896.

Urban, John. *Battlefield and Prison Pen.* Edgewood Publishing Company, 1882.

Walker, Francis A. *History of the Second Army Corps in the Army of the Potomac.* New York: Charles Scribner's Sons, 1886.

Wallace, Francis B. *Memorial of the Patriotism of Schuylkill County in the American Slaveholder's Rebellion.* Pottsville, Pa.: Benjamin Bannan, 1865.

Wilkeson, Frank. *Recollections of a Private Soldier in the Army of the Potomac.* New York and London: G. P. Putnam's Sons, 1887.

Worsham, John H. *One of Jackson's Foot Cavalry.* New York: The Neale Publishing Co., 1912.

Wright, Mrs. D. Giraud. *A Southern Girl in '61: The Wartime Memories of a Confederate Senator's Daughter.* New York: Doubleday, Page & Company, 1905.

Supplementary References

Angle, Paul M., and Earl Schenck Miers. *Tragic Years, 1860–1865,* vol. 2. New York: Simon & Schuster, 1960.

Bill, Alfred Hoyt. *The Beleaguered City: Richmond 1861–1865.* New York: Alfred A. Knopf, 1946.

Blackford, W. W. *War Years with Jeb Stuart.* New York: Charles Scribner's Sons, 1945.

Bloor, Alfred J. *Letters from the Army of the Potomac.* Washington, D.C.: McGill & Witherow, 1864.

Cadwallader, Sylvanus. *Three Years with Grant.* Edited by Benjamin P. Thomas. New York: Alfred A. Knopf, 1955.

Catton, Bruce. *Never Call Retreat: The Centennial History of the Civil War,* vol. 3. New York: Doubleday & Co., 1965.

———. *The Army of the Potomac: A Stillness at Appomattox.* Garden City, N.Y.: Doubleday & Co., 1953.

Commager, Henry Steele. *The Blue and the Gray.* Indianapolis and New York: The Bobbs-Merrill Co., 1950.

Cooke, John Esten. *Wearing of the Gray.* New York: Kraus Reprint Co., 1969. Reprint of 1867 edition.

Coppée, Henry. *Grant and His Campaigns.* New York: Charles B. Richardson, 1866.

Dana, Charles A., and J. H. Wilson. *The Life of Ulysses S. Grant.* Springfield, Mass.: Gurdon Bill & Co., 1868.

Davis, Jefferson. *The Rise and Fall of the Confederate Government,* vol. 2. South Brunswick, N.J.: Thomas Yoseloff, 1958. Reprint of edition by D. Appleton & Co., 1881.

Douglas, Henry Kyd. *I Rode with Stonewall.* Chapel Hill, N.C.: University of North Carolina Press, 1940.

Dowdey, Clifford. *Lee's Last Campaign.* Wilmington, N.C.: Broadfoot Publishing Co., 1988.

Early, Jubal Anderson. *War Memoirs.* Bloomington, Ind.: Indiana University Press, 1960. Reprint of 1912 edition.

Eggleston, George Cary. *A Rebel's Recollections.* New York: Kraus Reprint Co., 1969. Reprint of 1905 edition.

Frassanito, William A. *Grant and Lee: The Virginia Campaigns, 1864–1865.* New York: Charles Scribner's Sons, 1983.

Freeman, Douglas Southall. *Lee's Lieutenants,* vol. 3. New York: Charles Scribner's Sons, 1944.

Gerrish, Theodore, and John S. Hutchinson. *The Blue and the Gray.* Portland, Me.: Hoyt, Fogg & Donham, 1883,

Greeley, Horace. *The American Conflict,* vol. 2. Hartford: O. D. Case & Co., 1867.

Guernsey, Alfred H., and Henry M. Alden. *Harper's Pictorial History of the Great Rebellion,* vol. 2. Chicago: McDonnell Bros., 1868.

Hergesheimer, Joseph. *Sheridan: A Military Narrative.* Boston and New York: Houghton Mifflin Co., 1931.

Holland, J. G. *The Life of Abraham Lincoln.* Springfield, Mass.: Gurdon Bill, 1866.

Holstein, Anna M. *Three Years in Field Hospitals of the Army of the Potomac.* Philadelphia: J. B. Lippincott & Co., 1867.

Jones, Katharine M. *Ladies of Richmond.* Indianapolis and New York: The Bobbs-Merrill Co., 1962.

Long, E. B., with Barbara Long. *The Civil War Day by Day.* Garden City, N.Y.: Doubleday & Co., 1971.

Lossing, Benson J. *Pictorial Field Book of the Civil War,* vol 3. New York: T. Belknap & Co., 1868.

Lykes, Richard Wayne. *Campaign for Petersburg.* Washington, D.C.: Government Printing Office, 1970.

Pember, Phoebe Yates. *A Southern Woman's Story: Life in Confederate Richmond.* Edited by Bell Irvin Wiley. Jackson, Tenn.: McCowat-Mercer Press, 1959. First published in 1879.

Pennypacker, Isaac R. *General Meade.* New York: D. Appleton & Co., 1901.

Pryor, Mrs. Roger A. *Reminiscences of Peace and War.* New York: The Macmillan Co., 1904.

Smart, James G., ed. *A Radical View: The "Agate" Dispatches of Whitelaw Reid, 1861–1865,* vol. 2. Memphis: Memphis State University Press, 1976.

Steere, Edward. *The Wilderness Campaign.* Harrisburg, Pa.: The Stackpole Co., 1960.

Tenney, W. J. *The Military and Naval History of the Rebellion.* New York: D. Appleton & Co., 1865.

Thomas, Emory M. *Bold Dragoon: The Life of J. E. B. Stuart.* New York: Harper & Row, 1986.

The War of the Rebellion: A Compilation of the Official Records of the Union and Confederate Armies. Series 1, vol. 26, parts 2 and 3. Washington, D.C.: Government Printing Office, 1891.

Wheeler, Richard. *Voices of the Civil War.* New York: Thomas Y. Crowell Co., 1976.

Wheelock, Julia S. *The Boys in White: The Experience of a Hospital Agent in and around Washington.* New York: Lange & Hillman, 1870.

Wilkinson, Warren. *Mother, May You Never See the Sights I Have Seen.* New York: Harper & Row, 1990.

Williams, T. Harry. *Lincoln and His Generals.* New York: Alfred A. Knopf, 1952.

Index

Ambulance corps, 144–45
Angle. *See* Battle of the Angle
Armistice, following Battle of the Crater, 286
Army of Northern Virginia
  number in, 21
  size of, 72
Army of the Potomac
  general post office, 9
  Grant's arrival at, 46
  headquarters at, 45
  number in, 21
  reinforcement for, 51, 53
  reorganization of, 49
  size of, 69, 72
Army thieves, 211–12
Ashland Station, predawn raid at, 164

Banks, Nathaniel P., instructions to, 68
Bathing, in Confederate camps, 36–37
Battle of the Angle, 179
  brutal contest at, 212
  hand to hand at, 210
  losses at, 218
  uniqueness of, 219
Battle of Cold Harbor, 259–62
  incident of skirmishing, 256
  losses at, 262
  outbreak of, 257–59
  plan of, 254
  preparation for, 252–53, 255, 257
Battle of the Crater, 282–86
  armistice following, 286
Battle of the North Anna
  plan of, 234

Battle of the Wilderness, 88, 90–92
  end of, 145
  losses in, 145
  plan of, 89
Beaver Dam Station, events at, 159, 161–62
Blacks
  at Beaver Dam Station, 162
  in Confederate camps, 36
  leaving plantations, 228–31
  sighing for freedom, 266
  taken prisoner, 285
  in Union army, 279–80
  working in fields, 222
Blake, Henry N. (Union Captain)
  on great march, 66
  on life in Union winter camps, 8
  on treatment of wounded, 211–12
Bloody Angle, 208. *See also* Battle of the Angle
  hand to hand at, 210
Bowles, P. D. (Confederate Colonel), on Battle of Cold Harbor, 259
Breastworks, Confederate, at Spotsylvania, 187
Brockway, Charles B. (Union Captain), on encounter on Plank Road, 107–9
Brush fires, 102
  Federals trying to save wounded from, 103
  helpless wounded and, 117
  Union wounded and, 138
Buell, Augustus (Union Cannoneer)
  on Battle of the Wilderness, 145
  on Confederate prisoner, 131–32

Buell, Augustus (cont.)
  on Grant's increase in popularity, 47
  on renewal of fighting, 129, 131
Burnside, Ambrose E. (Union General),
    Ninth Corps under, 51, 53
Butler, B. F. (Union General)
  instructions to, 68
  operation intrusted to, 47, 49

Caldwell, J. F. J. (Confederate
    Lieutenant)
  on attack by Union cavalry, 28–29
  on encounter on Plank Road, 111–12
  on events at Bloody Angle, 209,
    217–18
  on Lee meeting Grant's challenge, 79
  on manual labor in Confederate
    camps, 28
  on reenlistment in Confederate armies,
    29
Carroll, Samuel S. (Union General),
    retaking line of intrenchments
    and, 141
Casler, John O. (Confederate Private)
  on burying the dead, 150
  on pets in Confederate camps, 30–31
  on plundering the dead, 194
  on scanty rations, 242
  on searching the dead, 150
  on situation at Spotsylvania, 196–97
  on snowball battles in Confederate
    camps, 31, 33
  on theatricals in Confederate camps,
    33, 35
Cavalry corps, Sheridan appointed as
    leader for, 49, 51. See also Union
    soldier(s)
Chancellorsville, march to, 80, 82–83
Chaplain(s)
  encounter on Plank Road and, 111
  at executions in Union camps, 20
  practical jokes on, 10–11
  worthlessness of, 11
Charles City, 265
Charlottesville, wounded Confederate
    soldiers at, 182–83
Chesapeake Bay, waterways of, 48
Coehorn mortars, Union, 216
Coffin, Charles Carleton (Union field
    correspondent)
  on arrival of Ninth Corps, in
    Washington, 51, 53
  on events after crossing Pamunkey
    River, 240, 242
  on the great movement of Union
    army, 66

on negroes leaving plantations, 228,
    230–31
  on reinforcement for Army of the
    Potomac, 51, 53
  on religious interest in Union camps,
    83, 85
  on situation at Spotsylvania, 188, 193
Cold Harbor
  arrival at, 248
  first day at, 250
  plan of battle of, 254
Confederacy, bounds of, 2
Confederate armies
  call for reenlistment in, 29
  Lee's concern about provisions for, 56
  military situation of
    on General Grant's arrival in East,
      45–46
Confederate breastworks, at Spotsylvania,
    187
Confederate camps
  bathing in, 36–37
  drilling in, 28
  executions in, 36
  Negroes in, 36
  pets in, 30–31
  religion in, 25
  snowball battles in, 31–33
  theatricals in, 33–35
Confederate front, of Turnpike and
    Plank Road, 117
Confederate salient at Spotsylvania, 198
  brutal contest at, 212
  events at, 202–5
  Hancock's troops breaking through,
    201
  map of, 199
Confederate soldier(s)
  assault on Hancock's burning
    breastworks by, 140
  awaiting orders during Wilderness
    fighting, 110
  captured, 170–71
  on events at Yellow Tavern, 168
  frontline troops urging Lee to go to
    rear, 126
  on morning of fight at Yellow Tavern,
    165
  prisoners, 131–32
  snowball fight, 31, 32
  straggler, 81
  surrendering at Bloody Angle, 215, 217
  theatricals, 33–35
  wounded, 182–83
Cooke, John Esten (Confederate staff
    officer)
  on defense of Petersburg, 266–67

Cooke, John Esten *(cont.)*
  on Lee at Cold Harbor, 264
  on Union attempt to cut railroads, 269
Corduroy road, Federals laying, 241
Crater
  battle of, 282–86
  following explosion of Fort Elliott, 282
Crotty, D. G. (Union Color Sergeant)
  on events following Battle of the
    Angle, 220
  on execution in Union camps, 19–20
  on life in Union winter camps, 8
  on renewal of fighting, 122
Culpeper Court House
  General Grant's headquarters at, 46
  Union camps around, 6
Custer, George A. (Union General)
  on events at Yellow Tavern, 166
  picture of, 160
Custis, Mary Randolph (Mrs. Robert E.
    Lee), 27

Dana, Charles A. (Assistant Secretary of
    War)
  on acting as emissary for President
    Lincoln, 146–47
  on news from Washington, 218
Davies, Henry (Union brigade
    commander), on results at Yellow
    Tavern, 169
Davis, Jefferson
  letters to, 56
  loss of child, 59
  picture of, 57
Davis, Joseph Emory (son of Jefferson),
    death of, 59
Davis, Varina (wife of Jefferson)
  on loss of her child, 59
  on Richmond Raid, 172
de Trobriand, Regis (Union Brigadier
    General)
  on black troops with Burnside, 279
  on blowing up Confederate Fort
    Elliott, 274, 276, 277
  on events following explosion of Fort
    Elliott, 284, 286
  on explosion of Confederate Fort
    Elliott, 280–81
Derby, W. P. (Union Private), on Battle
    of Cold Harbor, 260
Deserters from union camps, 19–20
Dickert, D. Augustus (Confederate
    officer)
  on Battle of Cold Harbor, 259
  on dead and wounded men, 138
  on death of General Wadsworth, 151
  on defense of Petersburg, 267, 269

on encounter on Plank Road, 118–19
on James Longstreet's Corps, 60, 63
on renewal of fighting, 125, 127
on surgeons, 150–51
on wounded and dead, 150–51
Discharge, from Union camps, 20
Discipline
  under General Grant, 47
  in winter camps, 18–20
Drilling
  in Confederate camps, 28
  in Union winter camps, 16

Entrenchments, Confederate, on North
    Anna River, 232
Ewell, Richard S. (Confederate General)
  description of; 60
  on morning of Battle of Wilderness, 88
  picture of, 62
  Second Corps under, 59
Executions
  in Confederate camps, 36
  in Union winter camps, 19–20

Federals. *See* Union soldier(s)
Field, Charles (Confederate General)
  on death of General Wadsworth, 129
  on death of Micah Jenkins, 136
  on Hancock's retreat from Longstreet,
    134, 136
Field hospitals. *See* Hospitals,
    Confederate; Hospitals, Union
Fifth Corps. *See* Union soldier(s)
Fifth New York Cavalry, injured man
    aided by Confederates, 114–15
Flank movement, Hancock's, 184
Franklin, James H. (Confederate officer),
    on Battle of Cold Harbor, 261–62
Fremantle, Arthur (Confederate
    Colonel), on General Lee, 21

Galloway, G. Norton (Union enlisted
    man), on events at Bloody Angle,
    206–8, 214–15, 217
General Post Office, Army of the
    Potomac, 9
Germanna Ford, Grant's headquarters at,
    83, 84
Germans, 16, 18
Gerrish, Theodore (Union Private)
  on events
    following Battle of Cold Harbor,
      264–65
    on Turnpike front, 93, 97–98, 101–2

Gerrish, Theodore (cont.)
  on practical jokes
    on chaplain, 10–11
    on picket lines, 11–14
    on recruits, 8, 10
  on preparations for campaign against
      Richmond, 54–55
  on situation following Battle of Cold
      Harbor, 264
  as victim of practical joke, 14–15
Gordon, John B. (Confederate General)
  on assault by Union army, 221
  on Battle of the Angle, 219
  on Confederate camps, 25–26
  on encounter on Plank Road, 119
  on events
    at Confederate salient, 202–5
    on Turnpike front, 98–99, 99–100
  on General Lee, 21, 23
  on General Lee's concern over
      northern wing, 142
  on Lee's preparations after Battle of
      the Wilderness, 149–50
  on military significance of northern
      rim of the salient, 208–9
  picture of, 24
  on Union armies advancing to
      Richmond, 78
Goss, Warren Lee (Union Private)
  on chaplains of the army, 11
  on discharge from army, 20
  on encounter on Plank Road, 116–17
  on making sketch of picturesque
      homestead, 226, 228
  on march toward Richmond, 223
  on region of Virginia untouched by
      war, 222
  on spirit of men, during great
      movement, 66
  on Union winter huts, 6
Graham, J. (Confederate Sergeant), letter
    to sweetheart, 243
Granger, Henry W. (Union Major), death
    of, 166
Grant, Julia Dent (Mrs. Ulysses S.)
  letters to, from General Grant, 69
  opinion of, 54
  picture of, 71
Grant, Ulysses S. (Union General)
  arrival in East, military situation at,
      44–46
  on attention paid him in Washington,
      44
  campaign adopted by, 47, 49
  after crossing Rapidan River, 74, 77
  dealing with disruption of northern
      plan, 143–44
  description of, 73

efforts of, opinions on, 263
encounter on Plank Road and, 115–16
on evening at White House, 42
events following Battle of the Angle,
    221–22
farm woman and, 213–14
in the field, 213
headquarters of, 45, 46
  at Germanna Ford, 83, 84
on how long to get to Richmond, 77
instructions from, for campaign against
    General Lee, 68–69
Lee meeting challenge of, 78–80,
    82–83, 85–86
letters to Mrs. Grant, 69
on loss of men, 193
on march to Spotsylvania, 154–55
military capacity of, enlisted men's
    discussion on, 46–47
night before Battle of Wilderness, 88
picture of, 39
popularity of, in camp, 47
preparations following Battle of the
    Wilderness, 147, 149
receiving commission from President
    Lincoln, 44
reorganization of Army of the Potomac
    by, 49
route of, 76
summoned to come East, 38
in Washington
  arrival of, 38
  attention paid to, 44
  final visit, 53
  meeting Mrs. Lincoln, 42
  meeting President Lincoln, 40, 42
  meeting Secretary of State Seward,
      42
  objection to attention paid him, 44

Hancock, Winfield Scott (Union Major
    General)
  assault on burning breastworks of, by
      Lee's men, 138, 140, 141
  on Battle of the Wilderness, 91
  description of, 128
  on events at Spotsylvania, 183, 185–86
  meeting with Confederate General
      Johnson, 201
  picture of, 50
  retreat by, 134
  Second Corps under, 49
Hancock's Flank Movement, 183
  map of, 184
Hand to hand fighting, at Bloody Angle,
    210

Hill, Ambrose Powell (Confederate
    General)
  description of, 60
  encounter on Plank Road and, 111
  Third Corps under, 59
Hopkins, Luther W. (Confederate
    prisoner)
  on captivity, 170
  on Sheridan's situation at Richmond,
    173–74
  on turn of events at Richmond, 174
Hospitals, Confederate, in Wilderness
    clearing, 139
Hospitals, Union
  behind the lines, 211–12
  in the field, 189
Hotchkiss, Jedediah (Confederate officer)
  on Grant's march toward Richmond,
    238
  on Lee's anticipation of Grant's march
    to Richmond, 231
  on lines of defense, 253
  map of Lee's march from North Anna
    drawn by, 239
  on situation at Spotsylvania, 198

Irishmen, 16

Jenkins, Micah (Confederate Brigadier
    General)
  death of, 136
  on Hancock's retreat, 136
Johnson, Edward (Confederate General)
  on events at Spotsylvania, 200
  meeting with Union General Hancock,
    201
  on situation at Spotsylvania, 198
Johnston, Joseph E. (Confederate
    General), army of, military
    situation of on Grant's arrival in
    East, 45
Jokes, practical. *See* Practical jokes
Jones, John B. (War Department clerk),
    on Richmond Raid, 172

Ladies, in Union winter camps, 8
Lake, George B. (Confederate Captain),
    on enemy plans to blow up Fort
    Elliott, 276
Law, E. M. (Confederate General)
  on Battle of Cold Harbor, 261
  on events at Spotsylvania, 188, 191
  on Lee meeting Grant's challenge,
    78
  on Longstreet's Corps, 63–64

Lee, Fitzhugh (Confederate General), at
    Yellow Tavern, 168
Lee, Mary Randolph Custis (Mrs. Robert
    E.), 27
Lee, Robert E. (Confederate General)
  army of, 45
  concern over northern wing, 141–42
  description of, 21, 125
  on developments north of Rapidan
    River, 56
  events following Battle of the Angle,
    222
  incapacitated by illness, 233, 235
  interrogating Federals captured in
    Wilderness, 135
  letter to wife, 231
  march from North Anna, 239
  meeting General Grant's challenge,
    78–80, 82–83, 85–86
  notice to war department in
    Richmond, 253
  picture of, 22
  preparations of
    for campaign across Rapidan River,
      59–60, 63–64
    following Battle of the Wilderness,
      149–50
  on provisions for his army, 56
  reinforcements for, 231
  route of, 76
  salient at Spotsylvania and, 201–2
  solicitude of, for his men, 28
  survey of Union camps by, 21, 23
Les Miserables incident, 214
Lieutenant general, reinstatement of
    rank of, 3–4
Lincoln, Abraham
  General Grant receiving commission
    from, 44
  meeting with General Grant, 40, 42
  nominated for second term, 263
  pen and ink sketch of, 41
Lincoln, Mary Todd
  meeting with General Grant, 42
  picture of, 43
Log breastworks (Union)
  after Battle of the Wilderness, 148
  Lee's assault on, 138, 140, 141
Lomax, Lunsford (Confederate General),
    at Yellow Tavern, 165–66
Long, Armistead L. (Confederate
    Brigadier General), on General
    Lee, 87
Longstreet, James (Confederate General)
  on being wounded, 136
  character of, 136–37
  description of, 59–60
  First Corps under, 59, 60, 63–64

Longstreet, James *(cont.)*
  on General Grant, 60
  picture of, 61
  on renewal of fighting, 124, 124–25
  wounded in shoulder, 183

Mahone, William (Confederate General),
    on events following explosion of
    Fort Elliott, 283–84
Mattapony River, fording of, 225
McCabe, W. Gordon (Confederate
    Captain), on enemy plans to blow
    up Fort Elliott, 276
McClellan, Henry B. (Confederate Staff
    Officer)
  description of, 157
  on Jeb Stuart, 164–65
  on Jeb Stuart's plans, 163
  on Richmond Raid, 157, 159
McGuire, Judith (diarist)
  on death of Jeb Stuart, 176, 178
  on events in Richmond, 164
  on Richmond Raid, 172–73
  on situation in Richmond, 58–59
  on Southern soldiers, 26, 28
McMaster, F. W. (Confederate Colonel)
  on conditions around Fort Elliott, 277
  on events following explosion of Fort
    Elliott, 284–85
Meade, George G. (Union General)
  argument between General Sheridan
    and, 156
  command of army under, 49
  picture of, 70
Milk, from plantation, 14–15
Mine between Union Fort Morton and
    Confederate Fort Elliott
  in cross section, 275
  explosion of, 280–82
  map showing location of, 273
  preparations for blowing up of, 274,
    276–77, 279–80
  results of explosion, 282
  section of, directly under Confederate
    works, 278
Mitchell, W. G. (Union Major), on events
    at Spotsylvania, 198, 200, 200–201
"Mule Shoe," at Spotsylvania, 179

Navy, aid from, 222
Negroes. *See* Blacks
Nichols, G. W. (Confederate Private)
  on captured generals Shaler and
    Seymour, 144

on events
    following Battle of the Angle,
      220–21
  on Turnpike front, 99
  on winter weather, 29–30
Ninth Corps, as reinforcement, 51, 53
North, effort of, poor management of, 1,
    3
North Anna River
  Confederate entrenchments on,
    232
  Grant's arrival at, 233
  plan of battle of, 234

Oates, William C. (Confederate Colonel)
  on General Lee, 125
  on indecisive fighting near
    Totopotomoy Creek, 243, 245
Owen, William Miller (Confederate
    officer), on events following Battle
    of the Crater, 286

Page, Charles A. (Union newsman)
  on conditions after Battle of the
    Wilderness, 151–52
  on encounter on Plank Road, 116
  on events during march to Richmond,
    242–43
  on Grant's maneuver following Battle
    of Cold Harbor, 266
  on renewal of fighting, 133–34
  on retaking Hancock's line of
    intrenchments, 141
  on sunset and silence, 142–43
Pamunkey River, crossed by Union army,
    238, 240
Pegram, John (Confederate Brigadier),
    meeting with Union troopers, 23
Pegram, William Johnson (Confederate
    Colonel), encounter on Plank Road
    and, 109
Perry, W. F. (Confederate Colonel), on
    renewal of fighting, 124, 129
Petersburg
  defenses of, 268
  location of mine between Fort Morton
    and Fort Elliott, 273
  Union positions at, 270
Pets, in Confederate camps, 30–31
Picket lines, 17
  in Confederate camps, 28
  practical jokes on, 11–14
Plank Road, encounter on, 107–9,
    111–12, 114–19

Pleasants, Henry (Union Colonel)
  on blowing up Confederate Fort
    Elliott, 274
  description of, 272
Pollard, Edward (*Richmond Examiner*
    editor), on General Lee, 23, 25, 28
Pontoon bridges
  construction of, 66
  crossing Rapidan River on, 74, 75
Porter, Horace (Union Captain)
  on Battle of the Wilderness, 92
  on encounter on Plank Road, 115–16
  on events at Cold Harbor, 252–53
  on events following explosion of Fort
    Elliott, 284
  on Grant
    after crossing Rapidan River, 74, 77
    dealing with disruption of plan,
      143–44
    during fighting at Confederate
      salient, 212–13
    final visit to Washington, 53
    meeting President Lincoln, 38, 40, 42
    preparations after Battle of the
      Wilderness, 147, 149
    receiving commission from President
      Lincoln, 44
    in Washington, 44
  on Hancock
    in battle, 128
    and continuance of offensive, 128
  on incident involving Union officer and
    Southern woman, 214
  on morning of campaign, 73
  on night before campaign, 68–69, 72
  on parley at Grant's Chancellorsville
    headquarters, 85
  on renewal of fighting, 120
  on Sheridan's arrival in Washington, 51
  on situation at Spotsylvania
    May 10th, 195–96
    May 11th, 197–98
  on Union plan and its disruption, 138,
    141
Powell, William H. (Union staff officer),
    on explosion of Confederate Fort
    Elliott, 281–82
Practical jokes
  on chaplain, 10–11
  on picket lines, 11–14
  on recruit, 8, 10
  when securing milk from plantation,
    14–15
Prayer
  encounter on Plank Road and, 111
  Richmond Raid and, 172–73
  wounded soldiers and, 191–92

Punishments, in Union winter camps,
    18–19
Putnam, Sarah A. (Sallie)
  on events at Cold Harbor, 251
  on unease and apprehension in
    Richmond, 58
  on winning the war, 263

Rapidan River
  ice breaking up on, 29
  pontoon bridges for across, 66
    crossing on, 74, 75, 80
  regions of, 5
Recruits
  increase of, 47
  practical jokes on, 8, 10
Reenlistment, in Confederate armies,
    29
Reinforcements, for General Lee, 231
Religion
  in Confederate camps, 25
  at death of Jeb Stuart, 176
  encounter on Plank Road and, 111
  in Union camps, 83, 85
Richardson, Albert D. (war
    correspondent)
  on General Grant coming East, 38
  on Mrs. Grant's opinion, 54
Richmond, Virginia
  campaign against, preparations for,
    54–55
  defenses of, 268
  events in, 171
  march to, 171–72
  Sheridan's raid, 158
  situation in, 58–59
  unease and apprehension in, 58
Richmond newspaper, on death of Jeb
    Stuart, 176
Richmond Raid, 156–57, 159, 161–66,
    168–69
  map of, 158
Rodenbough, Theophilus F. (Union
    Junior Officer), on Richmond Raid,
    156–57
Runaway slaves, 229

Salient, Confederate, at Spotsylvania, 198
  brutal contest at, 212
  events at, 202–5
  Hancock's troops breaking through,
    201
  map of, 199
Second Cold Harbor. *See* Battle of Cold
    Harbor

Seward, William H. (Secretary of State),
    General Grant meeting with, 42
Seymour (captured Union General),
    Confederate private's description
    of, 144
Shaler (captured Union General),
    Confederate private's description
    of, 144
Sheridan, Philip H. (Union General)
    advantage over Jeb Stuart, 156
    argument between General Meade
        and, 156
    arrival of, in Washington, D.C., 51
    cavalry corps intrusted to, 49, 51
    on events at Richmond, 171, 175–76,
        178
    picture of, 52
    on situation at Richmond, 173
    on treatment of prisoners, 170–71
Sheridan's Richmond raid, 158
Sherman, William T. (Union General)
    command of Union armies committed
        to, 45
    instructions to, 68
Sigel, Franz (Union General)
    instructions to, 68
    operation intrusted to, 49
Sixth Corps
    review of, 54
    under Sedgwick, 49
Slaves, runaway, 229
Snowball battles, in Confederate camps,
    31–33
Soldiers. See Confederate soldier(s);
    Union soldier(s)
Southern women, 25–26
Spotsylvania
    "angle" at, 179
    breastworks at, 187
    events at
        May 10th, 179, 181–83, 185–86, 188,
            190–94
        May 11th, 195–98, 200–205
    losses at, 192
    "mule shoe" at, 179
    positions of opposing forces at, 180
    salient at, 198
        map of, 199
    situation at, May 10, 183
    Union field hospital at, 189
Steuart, George H. (Confederate
    General)
    capture of, 200–201
Stevens, George T. (Union Surgeon)
    on events on Turnpike front, 105–6
    on ladies in winter camps, 8
    on march to Cold Harbor, 248–49, 251
    on march to Petersburg, 265–66

on preparations for campaign against
    Richmond, 54
on transporting wounded, 181–82
Stewart, A. M. (Union chaplain)
    on encounter on Plank Road, 112
    on marches from Spotsylvania to
        Pamunkey River, 238, 240
    on situation at Petersburg, 269, 271
    on wounded, 145
Stewart, Joseph R. (Union Corporal),
    personal experience of, 127–28
Stiles, Robert (Confederate Artillery
    Officer)
    on defense of Petersburg, 267
    on driving sharpshooters from small
        house, 247–48
    on events
        following Battle of Cold Harbor, 265
        at Spotsylvania, 186, 188, 191–92
    on Lee meeting Grant's challenge,
        78–79
    on Longstreet's character, 136–37
    on moment of pleasure, 223, 226
    on mood of troops, 79–80
    on morning of Battle of Wilderness, 88
    on observations of Federal camps, 23
    on preparations for Battle of Cold
        Harbor, 253, 255
    on Sheridan's breaking of Col. Keitt's
        South Carolina regiment, 248
Stragglers, Confederate, 81
Stuart, Flora (daughter of Jeb), death of,
    163
Stuart, James Ewell Brown ("Jeb";
    Confederate General)
    burial of, 178
    cavalry under, 59
    concern of
        over damage at Beaver Dam Station,
            163
        over family, 163
    death of, 176, 178
    on gunfire in Richmond, 173
    missed by Lee, 233
    picture of, 177
    Sheridan's advantage over, 156
    wounded
        taken to Richmond, 173
        at Yellow Tavern, 168–69
Supply wagons, Union, 67
Surgeons, 150–51
Surgery, behind the lines, 118
Surrendering, by Confederate soldiers,
    215, 217
Swinton, William (Union newsman)
    on Battle of the Wilderness, 88, 90–91,
        91–92

Swinton, William *(cont.)*
  on campaign adopted by Grant, 47, 49, 51
  on events on Turnpike front, 106
  on Grant's preparations after Battle of the Wilderness, 149
  on great march, 68
  on Hancock's retreat, 134
  on military situation at Grant's arrival in East, 44–46
  on poor management of Northern effort, 1, 3
  on situation at Spotsylvania, 179
  on Union army crossing Rapidan River, 80

Taylor, Walter H. (Confederate Colonel)
  on march toward Richmond, 231, 233
  on race for Spotsylvania, 155
Theatricals, in Confederate camps, 33–35
Totopotomoy-Cold Harbor line, map of, 239
Turnpike front, events on, 93–94, 96–102, 104–6

Union Army
  advances to Richmond by, 78
  crossing Rapidan River, 75, 80
  defeats for, 221
  fighting in Wilderness, 95
  movement of
    orders for, 65–66
    spirit of the men during, 66
  supply wagons, 67
Union camps
  around Culpeper Court House, 6
  chaplains in
    at executions, 20
    practical jokes on, 10–11
  deserters from, 19–20
  discharge from, 20
  discipline in, 18
  drilling in, 16
  execution in, 19–20
  under General Grant, 47, 49
  Germans in, 16, 18
  Irishmen in, 16
  ladies in, 8
  life in, 6–8, 10–16, 18–21
  picket lines in, 17
  post office in, 9
  practical jokes in, 8, 10–15
  punishments in, 18–19
  survey of, by Lee, 21, 23
  winter huts in, 6, 7
Union Coehorn mortars, 216

Union front
  of Turnpike and Plank Road, 117
  Wilderness viewed from, 123
Union lines, entered by runaway slaves, 229
Union soldier(s)
  on blowing up Confederate Fort Elliott, 272
  break in a march, 244
  captured, 159, 161–62
    in Wilderness, 135
  crossing Rapidan River on pontoons, 75
  on events following Battle of the Angle, 220
  on events on Turnpike front, 102, 104–5
  field hospital at Spotsylvania, 189
  fighting
    at Battle of Cold Harbor, 258
    in Wilderness, 95
  fording Mattapony River, 225
  on Hancock meeting with Johnson, 201
  injured Fifth Cavalry man, 114–15
  injured man aided by Confederates, 114–15
  invasion of a Virginia home, 224
  laying a corduroy road, 241
  on march to Richmond, 171–72
  positions at Petersburg, 270
  surrendering at Bloody Angle, 217
  throwing up breastworks at Wilderness front, 113
  trying to save their wounded from flames, 103
  under Warren, 49
  and Virginia woman, 227
  wounded, 179, 181–82
    at Spotsylvania, 191–92
Upton, Emory (Union Colonel), on events at Spotsylvania, 190–91, 192
Urban, John (Union soldier)
  on being taken prisoner, 245–46
  on encounter on Plank Road, 117
  on events at Beaver Dam Station, 159, 161–62
  on events at Richmond, 174–75
  on Sheridan's situation at Richmond, 174

Virginia
  campaign in
    criticism by press, 72
    discussion on, 68–69
    familiarity with area and, 72
    Federals crossing Rapidan River on pontoons, 75

Virginia: campaign in *(cont.)*
  march to, 73–74, 77
  morning of, 73, 73–74
  night before, 66, 68
  press and, 72
  routes of Lee and Grant, 76
  task of Union forces in, 72
  Union supply wagons, 67
  Yankee invasion of home, 224
Virginia Peninsula, federals on, 238, 240

Waddill, J. M. (Confederate Junior
    Officer), on encounter on Plank
    Road, 112, 114–15
Wadsworth, James S. (Union General)
  death of, 129, 151
  picture of, 130
Walker, Francis A. (aide to Union
    General Hancock)
  on encounter on Plank Road, 107, 117
  on events at Bloody Angle, 209, 211
Washington, D.C.
  Grant in
    arrival of, 38
    meeting Mrs. Lincoln, 42
    meeting President Lincoln, 40, 42
    meeting Secretary of State Seward,
      42
  Sheridan's arrival in, 51
White, William P. (Confederate Colonel),
    encounter on Plank Road and, 114
White House, presidential reception at,
    38, 40, 42
Wilcox, Cadmus (Confederate General),
    on renewal of fighting, 122, 124
Wilderness
  Confederate hospital in clearing, 139
  fighting in, 95
    awaiting orders during, 110
  Lee interrogating Federals captured
    in, 135
  plan of battle of, 89
  second day in, viewed from Union
    side, 123
Wilderness front, Federals throwing up
    breastworks at, 113
Wilkeson, Frank (Union Private)
  on Battle of Cold Harbor, 257, 259,
    260–61

on confrontation at North Anna River,
    235–37
on discipline in winter camps, 18
on drilling the soldiers, 16
on events on Turnpike front, 94,
    96–97
on executions in winter camps, 19–20
on fighting in winter camps, 16
on Grant's military capacity, 46–47
on Hancock's retreat, 134
on march to Chancellorsville, 80,
    82–83
on march to Spotsylvania, 153–54
on march toward Richmond, 222–23
on orders for general movement of the
    army, 65–66
on preparations for Battle of Cold
    Harbor, 255
punishment for, 152–53
on punishments in winter camps,
    18–19
on quiet on the battlefield, 144
on renewal of fighting, 120, 122, 124,
    127
on talk among soldiers at
    Chancellorsville, 85–86
on wounded men, 128
Willard's Hotel, General Grant's arrival
    at, 38
Winter huts, union, 6, 7
Wise, John (Confederate Officer), on
    events following explosion of Fort
    Elliott, 283, 285–86
Wives, in union winter camps, 8
Women, Southern, 25–26
Worsham, John H. (Confederate soldier)
  on encounter on Plank Road, 118
  on events on Turnpike front, 100–101
  on life in Confederate camps, 35–37
Wounded, 138, 144–45
  brush fires and, 117, 138
  care of, 211–12

Yellow Tavern
  arrival at, 165
  cavalry fight at, 167
Young, John D. (Confederate Captain),
    on encounter on Plank Road, 109,
    111